WITH SCOTT
IN THE
ANTARCTIC

WITH SCOTT IN THE ANTARCTIC

HERBERT PONTING

AMBERLEY

To the memory of my late chief and comrades who, after reaching the South Pole, perished on their homeward way, bequeathing to the race a priceless heritage in the story of their heroism and self-sacrifice, and devotion to purpose, ideals and duty.

First published 1922, this edition 2014

Amberley Publishing
The Hill, Stroud
Gloucestershire, GL5 4EP

www.amberley-books.com

British Library Cataloguing in Publication Data.
A catalogue record for this book is available from the British Library.

ISBN 978 1 4456 3584 2 (print)
ISBN 978 1 4456 3600 9 (ebook)

Typeset in 9.5pt on 12pt Minion.
Typesetting and Origination by Amberley Publishing.
Printed in the UK.

Contents

Foreword

This book is written by one who had the honour to take part in that great adventure, The British Antarctic Expedition, 1910–13. Its object is to present, in simple language and pictures, some fresh aspects of the setting of that epic Polar drama which must ever stand out in the annals of exploration for the beauty of character revealed in those who took the leading parts, and perished in the final scene.

Whilst in the Great White South, during the winter of 1911, Captain Scott expressed to the author the sentiment that it was much to be desired that the youth of the Nation should become conversant with such adventure as Polar expeditions, as this would help to stimulate 'a fine and manly spirit in the rising generation.' The great explorer's words inspired the writing of this book.

If, therefore, this volume should help to foster in some of our boys that love of adventure which has animated all our great Empire Builders; and in the hearts of some of our girls that approval of chivalrous qualities and gallant deeds which has been the inspiration of the sterner sex throughout the ages, the writer will feel that his reward, for the years spent in securing and preparing the material for this book, will have been richer than he would have dared to hope for when he sailed into the South.

The author records, herewith, his gratitude to Lady Scott for graciously contributing the Introduction to this volume; his thanks to Messrs John Murray of London, and Messrs Dodd, Mead and Company of New York, for their kind permission to make many quotations herein from 'Scott's Last Expedition'; and his warm sense of obligation to his comrades of the adventure for the assistance they rendered him in the South whenever opportunity permitted.

– H. G. P.

Introduction by Lady Scott

The author has given me the manuscript of his book to look over, and what good reading it is! That Mr Ponting is a great artist with the camera is very widely known, but to find him also writing with so much lucidity and beauty is surprising and delightful.

In his book, which teems with appreciation of his leader, there seems no word of his leader's appreciation of him. This will never do! So let my form of introduction be to quote my husband.

Here, then, is what Captain Scott wrote in his diary soon after arriving in the South:

> Ponting is the most delighted of men; he declares this is the most beautiful spot he has ever seen, and spends all day and most of the night in what he calls 'gathering it in' with camera and cinematograph ... He is enraptured and uses expressions which in anyone else and alluding to any other subject might be deemed extravagant.
>
> Of the many admirable points in his work perhaps the most notable are his eye for a picture and the mastery he has acquired of ice subjects. The composition of his pictures is extraordinarily good; he seems to know by instinct the exact value of foreground and middle distance and of the introduction of 'life', whilst with more technical skill he emphasises the subtle shadows of the snow and reproduces its wonderfully transparent texture. He is an artist in love with his work, and it was good to hear his enthusiasm for results of the past and plans for the future.

Personally, I know Mr Ponting's work only by results. Over and over, and yet over again have I seen his cinematograph pictures of the Expedition, and I am still looking for further occasions of seeing them, for the beauty and wonder of them never varies. My husband, however, was marvelling at the dexterity of the artist, when he wrote on April 13th, 1911:

Next is the dark-room in which Ponting spends the greater part of his life. Such a palatial chamber for the development of negatives and prints can only be justified by the quality of the work produced in it, and is only justified in our case by the possession of such an artist as Ponting. My eye took in the neat shelves with their array of cameras, etc., the lead-lined sink and automatic water tap, the two acetylene gas burners with their shading screens, and the general obviousness of all conveniences of the photographic art.

Here, indeed, was encouragement for the best results, and to the photographer be all praise, for it is mainly his hand which has executed the designs which his brain conceived. In this may be seen the results of a traveller's experience. Ponting has had to fend for himself under primitive conditions in a new land; the result is a 'handy man' with every form of tool, and in any circumstances. Thus, when building operations were to the fore and mechanical labour scarce, Ponting returned to the shell of his apartment with only the raw material for completing it. In the shortest possible space of time shelves and tanks were erected, doors hung and windows framed, and all in a workmanlike manner commanding the admiration of all beholders.

It was well that speed could be commanded for such work, since the fleeting hours of the summer season had been all too few to be spared from the immediate service of photography. Ponting's nervous temperament allowed no waste of time. For him fine weather meant no sleep; he decided that lost opportunities should be as rare as circumstances would permit.

To Mr Ponting (in common, I like to believe, with all true artists), it is more important that good work should be done, than that he, himself, should do it; and the following quotation shows how freely he gave of his own knowledge so that others should 'train on' to replace him – eager that his pupils should get the best out of material that might come their way, and not his. That good work should at all costs be done, no matter who was the man to do it, seems, from the following, to have been Mr Ponting's aim:

The photography craze is in full swing. Ponting's mastery is ever more impressive, and his pupils improve day by day; nearly all of us have produced good negatives ... My incursion into photography has brought me in close touch with him, and I realise what a very good fellow he is; no pains are too great for him to take to help others, whilst his enthusiasm for his own work is unlimited. ... I would describe him as sustained by artistic enthusiasm. This world of ours is a different one to him than it is to the rest of us. He gauges it by its picturesqueness. His joy is to reproduce its pictures artistically, his grief to fail to do so. No attitude could be happier for the work he has undertaken, and one cannot doubt its productiveness. His results are wonderfully good, and if he is able to carry out the whole of his programme we shall have a photographic record which will be absolutely new in expeditionary work.

Mr Ponting had been a voracious traveller, and had sought out beauty in many strange and unfamiliar quarters of the world, taking splendid pictures as he went. Imagine, then, what a delight to the Antarctic travellers were the lantern-slides which he had the imagination and forethought to take South with him. These final quotations from my husband's diary speak for themselves:

May 29th, 1911. – To-night Ponting gave us a charming lecture on Japan with wonderful illustrations of his own. He is happiest in his descriptions of the artistic side of the people, with whom he is in fullest sympathy. So he took us to see the flower pageants, the joyful festivals of the cherry-blossom, the wistaria, the iris and chrysanthemum – and the paths about the lotus gardens where mankind meditated in solemn mood. We had pictures, too, of Nikko and its beauties, of temples and great Buddhas. Then, in more touristy strain, of volcanoes and their craters, waterfalls and river-gorges, tiny tree-clad islets – that feature of Japan – baths and their bathers, Ainos and so on. His descriptions were well given and we all of us thoroughly enjoyed our evening.

August 22nd, 1911. – Yesterday Ponting gave us a lecture on his Indian travels. He tells his story well, and his pictures are wonderful. In personal reminiscence he is distinctly dramatic – he thrilled us a good deal last night with a vivid description of a sunrise in the sacred city of Benares. In the first dim light the waiting, praying multitude of bathers, the wonderful ritual and its incessant performance; then, as the sun approaches, the hush – the effect of thousands of worshippers waiting in silence – a silence to be felt. Finally, as the first rays appear, the swelling roar of a single word from tens of thousands of throats: 'Awm.' It was artistic to follow this picture of life with the gruesome horrors of the ghat. This impressionist style of lecturing is very attractive and must essentially cover a great deal of ground. So we saw Jeypore, Udaipore, Darjeeling, and a confusing number of places – temples, monuments, and tombs in profusion, with remarkable pictures of the Taj Mahal – horses, elephants, alligators, wild boars, and flamingoes – warriors, fakirs, and nautch girls – an impression here and an impression there.

It is worth remembering how attractive this style can be. In lecturing one is inclined to give too much attention to connecting links which join one episode to the other. A lecture need not be a connected story; perhaps it is better it should not be.

September 10th, 1911. – The second weekly lecture was given by Ponting. His store of pictures seems unending and has been an immense source of entertainment to us during the winter. His lectures appeal to all, and are fully attended. This time we had pictures of the Great Wall and other stupendous monuments in North China. Ponting always manages to work in details concerning the manners and customs of the people in the countries of his travels; on Friday he told us of Chinese farms and industries, of hawking and other sports, and, most curious of all, of the pretty amusement of flying pigeons with aeolian whistling-pipes attached to their tail feathers.

June 22nd, 1911. – Midwinter Day. By the end of dinner a very cheerful spirit prevailed, and the room was cleared for Ponting and his lantern. He had cleverly chosen this opportunity to display a series of slides made from his own local negatives. I have never so fully realised the value of his work as on seeing these beautiful pictures. They so easily outclass anything of their kind previously taken in these regions. The audience cheered vociferously.

Ponting would have been a great asset to our party if only on account of his lectures, but his value as pictorial recorder of events becomes daily more apparent. No expedition has ever been illustrated so extensively, and the only difficulty will be to select from the countless subjects that have been recorded by his camera.

Surely Mr Ponting has it in his power greatly to delight!
– Kathleen Scott.

British Antarctic Expedition, 1910–13

Shore Party Officers:

Robert Falcon Scott Captain, C.V.O., R.N.
E. R. G. R. Evans Lieutenant, R.N.
Victor L. A. Campbell Lieutenant, R.N.
Henry R. Bowers Lieutenant, R.I.M.
Lawrence E. G. Oates Captain, 6th Inniskilling.

Dragoons:

G. Murray Levick Surgeon, R.N.
Edward L. Atkinson Surgeon, R.N., Parasitologist.

Scientific Staff:

Edward Adrian Wilson B.A., M.B., Chief of Scientific Staff, and Zoologist.
George C. Simpson D.Sc, Meteorologist.
T. Griffith Taylor B.A., B.Sc, Geologist.
Edward W. Nelson Biologist.
Frank Debenham B.A., B.Sc, Geologist.
Charles S. Wright B.A., Physicist.
Raymond E. Priestley, Geologist.
Herbert G. Ponting, Camera Artist.
Cecil H. Meares, in charge of dogs.
Bernard C. Day, Motor Engineer.
Apsley Cherry-Garrard B.A., Assistant Zoologist.
Tryggve Gran Sub. Lieut, Norwegian N.R., Ski Expert.

Men:

W. Lashly, Chief Stoker, R.N.
Thomas Clissold, Cook, late R.N.
W. W. Archer, Cook, late R.N. (2nd year).
Edgar Evans Petty Officer, R.N.
Thomas Crean Petty Officer, R.N.
Robert Forde Petty Officer, R.N.
Thomas S. Williamson Petty Officer, R.N. (2nd year).
Patrick Keohane Petty Officer, R.N.
George P. Abbot Petty Officer, R.N.
Frank V. Browning Petty Officer, R.N.
Harry Dickason Able Seaman, R.N.
F. J. Hooper Steward, late R.N.
Anton Omelchenko, Groom, Russian.
Dimitri Geroff, Dog Driver, Russian.

Above left: Captain Scott photographed by Ponting on his skis.

Above right: Herbert Ponting and his camera.

CHAPTER I

The Expedition Leaves England

Let us probe the silent places, let us seek what luck betide us;
Let us journey to a lonely land I know.

There's a whisper on the night-wind, there's a star agleam to guide us,
And the wild is calling, calling ... let us go.

Robert W. Service.

Before going to the Far South with Captain Scott's South Pole Expedition, my life – save for six years' ranching and mining in Western America; a couple of voyages round the world; three years of travel in Japan; some months as war correspondent with the First Japanese Army during the war with Russia; and in the Philippines during the American war with Spain; and save, too, for several years of travel in a score of other lands – had been comparatively uneventful.

I might almost say that I first met Captain Scott in Siberia. I may at least state that it was there that I first got to know him, for I occupied myself during a journey over the Trans-Siberian railway in January, 1907, by reading his recently published work *The Voyage of the Discovery*. I had bought the two volumes in Tokyo, thinking that they might furnish appropriate reading for a journey in the frigid conditions of climate which prevail in Siberia at that time of the year; and during my two weeks' incarceration in the train, as it meandered over a third of the circumference of the globe, from Vladivostok to Moscow, I found that virile story of adventure of absorbing interest. Little then did I imagine that I should one day meet the great explorer in the flesh; much less that before four years had elapsed I should be accompanying him on his second voyage to the Antarctic regions. Wonderful, indeed, are the ways of Fate in the framing of our destinies!

I was engaged in writing a book about my travels in Japan, at the time I met Captain Scott in real life in London, in November 1909. Up to that date nothing could possibly have been further from my thoughts than a voyage to such latitudes. Indeed, I was contemplating, and had almost entered into, arrangements for a project of a very different nature – a two years' tour of the British Empire.

But I was drawn strongly to the famous explorer on my first meeting with him. His trim, athletic figure; the determined face; the clear blue eyes, with their sincere, searching gaze; the simple, direct speech, and earnest manner; the quiet force of the man – all drew me to him irresistibly. During this, our first interview, he talked with such fervour of his forth-coming journey; of the lure of the southernmost seas; of the mystery of the Great Ice Barrier; of the grandeur of Erebus and the Western Mountains, and of the marvels of the animal life around the Pole, that I warmed to his enthusiasm. He told me of his plans for scientific research – for geology, zoology, biology, meteorology, physiography, and for photography. For more than twenty years I had been a keen enthusiast with the camera, and mine have been my inseparable companions in my wanderings over the earth, so when Scott finally stated that he considered photography was of such importance in exploration that it was his intention to make a special department of the art, and he asked if I would like to take charge of that part of the enterprise, though I asked for a day to think the matter over, I had already made up my mind that I would go if equitable arrangements could be made.

The next day I told Captain Scott of the alternative plan which I had had under consideration. Just, and willing to look at all sides, as later I always found him to be, he expressed the opinion that, with such an interesting prospect before me, it might be foolish to abandon it in order to embark upon an adventure fraught with such risks as a Polar expedition. I explained that all my previous travels had been made in the interests of Geography; that I felt that this was a chance, such as never would come to me again, to turn the experience that I had gained to some permanent benefit to Science, and that I was convinced that if I went, and were given a free hand to utilise my experience as I thought best, the photographic results might prove not only of great educational value, but a valuable asset to the enterprise. He thanked me for taking this view; and then and there it was decided that I should throw in my lot with the Expedition.

It seemed there were nearly ten thousand applications from adventurous spirits anxious to join the Expedition, the majority being from Army and Navy officers, many of whom were willing to sign on in any capacity – as stewards, grooms, or deck hands, rather than be left behind. Some of these enthusiasts were prepared to contribute sums as much as one thousand pounds, if accepted. But not one per cent of the total applications could be considered; I believe it gave Captain Scott real distress to be compelled to refuse so many of these fine fellows.

As I met my future shipmates of the scientific staff, I found each to be keenly enthusiastic about his own particular part of the great work. It seemed that the corners of the Empire had been searched to find the right pegs to fit the proper holes. Thus, Dr G. C. Simpson, of the Indian Weather Bureau, Simla, would have charge of the meteorological and magnetic work; Mr C. S. Wright, a young Canadian physicist, had come from Toronto; Mr Griffith Taylor, an Australian, was to be our chief geologist; and he and two other young geologists, Mr F. Debenham and Mr Raymond Priestley – the latter had been South before with Sir Ernest Shackleton – were to join us later in New Zealand.

Dr E. A. Wilson, the zoologist of the Expedition and Chief of the Scientific Staff, who was living in London, had been with Captain Scott in the *Discovery*. He reassured me, on my inquiring as to the difficulties of working with a camera in such low temperatures as he spoke of, by expressing the opinion that, with proper precautions and barring accidents, there is no reason why any ordinarily hardy man should not enjoy and benefit in health by a voyage to the Polar regions, though the mercury in the Antarctic sometimes falls one hundred degrees below what we should consider bitterly cold weather in England.

I found that the Expedition was to have two biologists. Mr D. G. Lillie, though quite a young man, was already a well-known authority on marine mammalia; and Mr E. W. Nelson had been for some years at the Plymouth Laboratory. Surgeon E. L. Atkinson, R.N., was to specialise in parasitology.

These completed the scientific staff of the Expedition; but Mr Cherry-Garrard, a young friend of Dr Wilson's – who, since leaving college, had been on a globe-trotting tour – was to assist the chief scientist in his zoological work.

Mr C. H. Meares, who was to have charge of the dogs, was already well-known to me. We had met in November, 1905, on a North German Lloyd steamer going from Yokohama to Shanghai, when I was on my way to India. Meares had already been there and, in addition to several other languages, could speak Hindustani. As he had been having a roughish time during the Russo-Japanese war, and needed a holiday, we had come to an arrangement by which he came along with me to act as interpreter, and for the following six months we had travelled together in Burma, India, and Ceylon. Meares had had a remarkably varied and adventurous life; and after parting with me in China he had added to his experiences by joining an expedition to the Tibetan frontier, on which the leader, Lieut. J. W. Brooke, lost his life.

Early in January, 1910, Meares left London for Siberia, to secure the dogs and ponies for transport purposes. His intimate knowledge of the Russian language and of eastern Siberia was a great asset to Scott at that time. Meares knew exactly where to go, and how to set about things when he got there. He took the entire responsibility of securing all the transport animals upon his own shoulders, thus solving for Scott what otherwise would have been a serious problem to find so well-qualified a substitute. Meares personally found, tried out and purchased the animals that were required – thirty dogs and nineteen ponies – and he shipped, accompanied and looked after them from Vladivostok to New Zealand, delivering all his charges safely at Lyttelton after what must have been to them a critical experience in passing through the Tropics. On the sea part of the journey he received the assistance of Lieut. Wilfred M. Bruce, R.N.R., the brother-in-law of Captain Scott, an officer of the Expedition ship *Terra Nova*.

In January I began my preparations, and the following eight months were a busy and interesting time for me. I was determined that nothing should be left to chance, and that success should certainly not be jeopardised by any lack of foresight. It was largely due to the complete manner in which every possible need was provided for at the outset, that we were able to do our photographic work with comparative comfort in the South.

Time, indeed, sped on all too quickly for me. The day for the sailing of the *Terra Nova* for New Zealand arrived at length; but weeks earlier it had been obvious that my preparations would not be completed in time for me to join the ship. I should have to follow by mail-steamer later.

June 1st, the date of the departure of the Expedition from London, was also a memorable day in another respect for me. It was the day on which my book, *In Lotus-Land* – a record of my travels in Japan, on which I had been working for the last six months – was published. Before leaving for the docks, I eagerly opened the parcel that had just arrived, and with no small pleasure contemplated the dozen volumes; the handsome embossed covers of red and gold; the large, clear print and margins wide, and the hundred or more full-page plates, each a triumph of the printer's art, that nestled among the neat, clean pages of the text. The publishers had sumptuously produced the work, and they could not have chosen a more auspicious day on which to offer it to the world.

The *Terra Nova* left the London Dock at noon, and, amidst the cheers of thousands on both sides of the river, steamed slowly down the Thames to the screaming of steamers' whistles and the wailing of ocean liners' sirens. Every craft on the river was 'dressed' for the occasion, and each dipped her flag and gave loud blasts in salute as we glided by. The progress of the rugged whaler down the Thames was like a triumphal procession.

I remarked to Captain Scott, as I stood near him on the poop: 'If this be your send-off, what will your home-coming be after discovering the South Pole?' He replied that he cared nothing for this sort of thing; that he would willingly forego all acclamation both now and later; that all he desired was to complete the work begun seven years ago, reach the goal of his hopes, and get back to his work in the Navy again. This reply was characteristic of the man. Ambitious, yet modest and unassuming, he was disdainful of the plaudits of the crowd, and show and ostentation were foreign to his nature.

At Greenhithe the *Terra Nova* was welcomed by salvos of cheers from the *Worcester* boys, who manned the yards of the old Training-ship which had been alma mater to two of our officers – Lieut. E. R. Evans, the Second in Command, and Lieut. H. R. Bowers, the Commissariat Officer. Here Captain Scott, his wife and several friends and I disembarked and returned to London, the ship going on to Cardiff to fill her bunkers with some hundreds of tons of coal which had been generously presented to the Expedition.

Captain Scott, and his wife – who would accompany him as far as New Zealand – left England in August, sailing by the Castle Line to Capetown.

Officers of the *Terra Nova*.

But it was mid-September before my preparations had been completed. I sailed by P&O liner to Australia, and thence to New Zealand, reaching Lyttelton three days before the rest of the Expedition – a month before we all finally sailed for the South. As soon as the *Terra Nova* arrived, unloading began without a day's delay, for numerous final additions had to be made to our equipment and stores; and it was necessary that the ship should go into dry-dock for a complete overhaul. She was then reloaded, every inch of space being tightly stowed, with due care that such gear and stores as would be needed first should be most readily accessible. It was as interesting as it was delightful to note that our Leader's wife spent many days checking packages as they were unloaded and then re-stowed.

This work took more than three weeks to complete, and during that time hospitality of the most warm-hearted kind was extended to the members of the Expedition by the kind people of Christchurch and Lyttelton, and many lasting friendships were formed. Not all of us, however, were able to grasp as freely as we would have liked the hand of good fellowship that was so warmly offered. For my own part I had arranged to spend some time visiting and illustrating some of the famous sights of that lovely land – the volcanic geysers, the Tasman Glacier, Mount Cook, and the Maori region. But alas! all social festivities and pleasure travels were, for me, completely debarred when I found that some intricate apparatus which I had sent out by the *Terra Nova* had been badly damaged by sea-water leaking into the cases. Consequently, almost every hour of my stay in New Zealand was fully occupied, with the help of a clever mechanic, in putting these things right. Had we not been able to repair the damage my hopes would have been well nigh crushed at the outset, for I should not have been able to accomplish more than a small part of the work that I had planned.

To Mr J. J. Kinsey[1] the genial agent of the Expedition, and Mrs Kinsey, I owe a debt of gratitude for some delightful hours spent at their beautiful country home, at Clifton; and for the assistance in my work which they so kindly gave me in placing their fine photographic laboratory at my disposal.

Captain Scott often spoke to me of the great value that Mr Kinsey's assistance had been to the Expedition, and of the vast amount of work that his friend had so generously taken off his own hands. To others of the kind people of warm-hearted New Zealand I feel none the less cordially because unable to avail myself of the hospitality they so freely offered. It is my earnest hope that some day I may return to accept it.

CHAPTER II

Into the 'Fifties'

All preparations having been at last completed, and every nook and corner of her hold and deck space tightly packed with equipment, stores and coal, the *Terra Nova* left Lyttelton for Port Chalmers. That was the last point at which we should touch ere finally leaving for the Antarctic, and we had a chance to get things ship-shape for the rough seas that we might expect to encounter in the South Pacific. Everyone has read of the 'Roaring Forties.' It is a term used by the skippers of the old 'wind jammers' to designate the strong, steady winds that blow in the region that lies between 40° and 50° S. lat. New Zealand is in the 'Forties': the fortieth parallel of latitude dissects the middle of the islands. Beyond the 'Roaring Forties' there are the 'Furious Fifties' and the 'Shrieking Sixties' for the storms become worse as one draws nearer to the South Pole. I do not know if the 'Seventies' have received any qualifying adjective; but the coldest word in the dictionary would certainly be appropriate – the 'Frigid Seventies,' if, indeed, the term be not used already.

Save for the ships that round Cape Horn, there is no navigation – except by the whalers and explorers who venture into these stormy seas – south of 47°; and no vessel has ever penetrated further south than the proximity of the seventy-eighth parallel of latitude. Beyond, is nothing but eternal ice and ice-clad mountains.

The *Terra Nova*, which was to convey us into this boisterous region, was a three-masted, barque-rigged vessel of about seven hundred tons register, with auxiliary steam and screw. She was an old Dundee whaler, whose keel had been laid some thirty years earlier, and had seen more Polar service than any other ship that ever sailed the seas. She had the right to fly the burgee of the Royal Yacht Squadron, of which Captain Scott had been elected a member; and she had the distinction of sailing under the white ensign, a privilege which, apart from the Navy, is enjoyed only by the units of the R.Y.S.

She was a picturesque sight as she lay alongside the quay at Port Chalmers. Confidence in her staunchness and ability for the tremendous task that lay ahead was bred in the knowledge of her years of fighting with the Polar ice, recorded in the log-books that formed the history of her gallant and honourable past; and imagination conjured up many a brave and thrilling fight with tempestuous seas of which her figure-head might tell, could those parted lips but speak.

On the 29th of November, 1910, the *Terra Nova* steamed out of the harbour of Port Chalmers, New Zealand. The sun was shining brilliantly, and everything seemed to promise well for the success of our enterprise. Some thousands of friends came to the wharf to see us off, and to the waving of handkerchiefs, cheers, and shouts of 'Good-bye!' and 'Good luck!' we slipped out quietly into the bay. Two gaily-decorated excursion tugs, crowded with passengers, accompanied us to The Heads, where we received the final farewells of our friends. Then our sturdy vessel proceeded on her lonely way, with her Plimsoll mark nearly a foot submerged.

The deck of the *Terra Nova* amidships was completely covered with three great cases, each containing a motor-sledge, and a quantity of timber for building the headquarters hut, in which we should have to live during the winter season. Two of the motor-sledge cases and a baulk of timber and scantling were arranged so as to form a 'corrall,' of which the ice-house made the fourth side. Except when heavy seas came aboard, this corrall constituted a sheltered home for a number of the dogs who were fortunate enough to be allotted to this desirable berth. In addition to this bulky material, which was securely lashed to the deck with ropes and chains, there were many tons of coal in bags, and numerous cases of petrol and paraffin oil. On top of this deck-hamper more dogs were berthed. There were thirty-three dogs in all – thirty of them Eastern Siberians, all males; two Eskimo dogs, given to the Expedition by Commander Robert Peary, the Arctic explorer (we christened them Peary and Cook); and a New Zealand collie bitch. Someone in England had presented Captain Scott with three English-bred Samoyedes; but these pretty exotics were quite unfitted for such arduous work as lay ahead – as Captain Scott knew from his experience of such dogs on the Discovery Expedition, and knew better still when he saw the rugged types that Meares had brought from Siberia. One of the Samoyedes died on the voyage to New Zealand; the two others, and several puppies they had produced, were given away to friends in Christchurch.

Just for'ard of the motor-sledges was the ice-house, in which a hundred carcasses of frozen mutton and several carcasses of beef were stored. The top of this ice-house formed a platform to which two invaluable instruments were fixed – the standard compass and the range-finder. This platform was surrounded by a brass rail, to which ten dogs were chained. Adjoining the ice-house and for'ard of it, were stalls for four of the ponies; fifteen additional ponies were berthed in the forecastle. The ponies were sturdy, picturesque creatures. White, shaggy and unkempt of coat and mane, these rugged little fellows seemed veritable symbols of the wild regions from which they had come, and of the eternal snows at the antipodes of the earth to which they were now going – whence they were predestined never to return. The ponies had been handed over by Mr Meares – whose time was now fully occupied in caring for the dogs – to Captain Oates, in New Zealand; and, like the dogs, they were doomed to have a miserable time of it during the next few days. As soon as we cleared The Heads a fresh breeze sprang up, causing the spray, from the waves which broke against the weather side of the ship, to drench the dogs, who curled up and lay shivering and dejected, each chained to his allotted berth. It was impossible to find for them any protection from the wet, which it was obvious they disliked exceedingly, however disdainful they might be of cold. But their hardy nature fitted them to endure this discomfort without any ill effect; and, knowing what frigid conditions of weather these robust animals could stand, we realised that this experience on the ship, though unpleasant enough, was to them no great hardship.

I found that life on a whaler was a very different matter to travelling on comfortable ocean liners. The *Terra Nova* seemed to me not only to know and practise every movement known to every ship in which I had previously sailed; but frequently to vary these with movements of her own, which I felt convinced that no other respectable ship knew anything whatever about. I found it almost impossible to sleep below deck in the narrow, stuffy cabins, crowded with our personal belongings. Moreover, for the first few days I was very seasick, in common with others of my landsman shipmates who had joined the ship at New Zealand. I therefore removed my bedding to the floor of my photographic laboratory on the poop.

This laboratory was a place to which I had given a great deal of thought and care, and had personally planned and supervised the building of it when the *Terra Nova* lay at the London docks. It formed one of three compartments in a substantial deck-house that had been erected on the port side of the forward part of the poop. It was 6 feet long, 4½ feet wide, and eight feet high. A lead-covered bench, eighteen inches wide, ran the length of the apartment, in the middle of which was a deep lead-lined sink; on each side of the sink there were cupboards under the bench. Water was laid on from an iron tank fixed under the roof, which was filled periodically until all such arrangements were finally rendered ineffective by the frost.

There was a ruby-glass scuttle, or port-hole, over the sink; and a window – protected by shutters and iron bars – which could easily be darkened, looked out astern. Three tiers of shelves ran round three sides of the room, with guard-rails to prevent anything from falling off, and on these and in the cupboards I was able to store an incredible quantity of gear; all plates, films, etc., being in hermetically-sealed tin cases. It was the three feet of free floor space of this apartment that I now used as a bunk.

Cape pigeons, mollymawks, petrels and other seafowl circled about the ship. The proud, majestic albatrosses, some of which must have measured ten feet from tip to tip, soared like aeroplanes about our wake, scarcely ever troubling to flap their wings, but simply setting them against the breeze. When, however, any scraps were thrown overboard from the galley, elegance went to the winds, and there ensued a noisy and undignified squabble for the prizes.

'Uncle Bill' – as our zoologist, Dr Wilson, was called by all – seemed to know the name of every bird that winged the waves. I never sought from him the name of any creature in vain. Thus, at the outset of our voyage I found how exhaustive was his knowledge of Antarctic fauna. It gave me no small satisfaction to know that, whilst my own ambition was to produce a pictorial record of our adventure – which might enlighten those who do not read expensive volumes on exploration, as to the objects, results and value of such an enterprise as ours – Dr Wilson was a man who was capable of investing any zoological photographs with such information as would render them of maximum value to Science. The estimate that I then formed of him strengthened as time went on, and each day added to my regard for this splendid man. Interrogating Uncle Bill as to the names of birds reminded me of the following incident, which I related to him.

A few years before, when I was travelling on a Pacific Ocean liner, and the ship was about half-way between Honolulu and Japan – many hundreds of miles from land – I observed a number of birds, such as I had not previously seen, flying over the surface of the sea. Just then the quartermaster of the ship came along, and I asked him: 'Quartermaster, can you tell me the name of those birds?' The old Irishman shaded his shaggy brows with his palm for a few seconds, closely scrutinising the birds; then he replied: 'Why, yess, sorr. Them's what we call 'seaburrds' sorr!' and he went about his work, with the air of one possessing superior knowledge, leaving me wondering if he thought that I had taken them for a covey of partridges, or barnyard fowls.

On the third day out from New Zealand I had the ill-luck, whilst endeavouring to make my way for'ard in a rather wobbly and unseamanlike manner, to stagger as the ship rolled, nearly precipitating my finest hand-camera overboard. I saved it by a hair's breadth; but, in the effort, I slipped and fell amongst the heavy timbers amidships, nearly breaking my left leg. I made my way back to my laboratory in a good deal of pain, and found that, though fortunately my sea-boots and thick corduroy breeches had saved the skin from breaking, there was a bruise five inches in length on my shin, just beside a permanent scar that I bear from an encounter with a skidding London motor-'bus, in which the honours were with my adversary – the 'bus sustaining no damage. I anointed the injured part with vaseline, and bound it up with a handkerchief.

That evening, as I was again trying to discipline my unruly underpinning on the poop, which was now rising and falling in a most dizzy and disconcerting manner – in the desire to photograph a beautiful scene of the sun setting behind the clouds, through openings in which shafts of light radiated to gild the leaden waves – the Bo'sun came along to 'pass the time o' day.' A happy genial son of the sea was Mr Cheetham – known to his shipmates of the forecastle when off duty by his Christian name of 'Alf' – a hale and hearty soul, whose contented spirit was indexed in the smile that almost perpetually illumined his rubicund features. The wind was rising rapidly, and he did not tarry long. As he parted from me, he cocked his eye up into the westward heavens, and, murmuring something, which was lost in the breeze, about 'in for dirty weather', went off to give some orders to the deck-hands.

A true prophet was our Bo'sun. He had read the signs aright. The high sea at present running was already giving some of us, and the animals, trouble enough; but it was a peaceful mill-pond in comparison with what we were to experience in the ensuing forty-eight hours. Soon after the red sun sank into the heaving waters it was blowing great guns from the west; and ere night fell on the sea, a full gale was howling and shrieking through the rigging, and tearing and roaring over the now mountainous waves. The ship rolled and plunged and squirmed as she wallowed in the tremendous seas which boomed and crashed all that night against the weather side, sending tons of water aboard every moment. Screaming gusts would strike her with hurricane force, and sometimes she would lay over to an angle of 40° – nearly half a right angle from an even keel – as I could tell from the arc described by a thermometer hanging on my laboratory wall, which was normally perpendicular. Yet so stoutly was the grand old vessel built that her massive timbers never uttered a squeak. Often the waves swept over the stern, almost carrying the helmsman off his feet, and he was frequently knee-high, and sometimes waist deep in water. This was the only part of the ship to which I could occasionally venture during the storm; for though I had looked forward with some anticipation to experiencing a gale in these seas, yet when the chance occurred I was quite unable to get on to the bridge to witness the grandeur of the storm, as I could not risk further injury to my leg.

Moreover, I had my work cut out to save my photographic gear from ruin. Each time a heavy sea came aboard, a stream of water spurted through the chinks of the door, which fitted badly; and this was added to by the water that periodically dribbled through the mushroom ventilator in the roof, so that the floor quickly became awash. All my valuable and indispensable apparatus was kept either on the shelves, or hung by hooks to the roof; but the cupboards were crammed with various stores, which I had hurriedly to re-stow as soon as the ship began to heel over, leaving the lower compartments empty. The sill of the door was a foot high, and my lab' was on the lee side. As the list became heavier, but for almost ceaseless baling from the floor to the sink, day and night, the water would have been nearly a yard deep in the cupboards. I had taken all possible care to make things fast and shipshape before leaving port; thanks to this precaution, and to the fact that all perishable supplies had been stored in hermetically-sealed cases, little damage was sustained.

During the storm I was so hard put to it to save my own belongings, that not until the danger was past did I learn the full tale of all that had happened during the two days the ship had been hove-to. The tons of water that broke inboard amidships could not, owing to the crowded state of the decks, find the scuppers quickly enough – the scuppers in any case being quite incapable of dealing with such volumes of it – and for a great part of the time the lee rail had been submerged. As the ship rolled and the water rushed from side to side, it carried with it cases of petrol and bags of coal which, battering into the bulwarks, loosened up the planks; and one tremendous sea, coming inboard on the port side, carried the whole of these planks away from the forecastle to the poop – so that there was now nothing to keep the seas from washing the waist of the ship from the lee side. There was then the grave danger of the deck opening up if the motor-sledges got loose as well, in which case we must inevitably have foundered. The seamen risked life and limb to get hold of the loose sacks and petrol cases – which bombarded them as they worked – to throw them overboard before a worse thing happened.

In the height of all this trouble, confusion became worse confounded by the choking of the pumps by the coal dust that had found its way into the suction-pipe in the bilge – which was now several feet deep with water. The pumps refused to work, and the water gradually rose until the stoke-hold was awash. Imminent danger now threatening the boilers, the engine room staff, assisted by the deck hands, the officers and several of the scientific staff, worked in two-hour shifts of ten men, night and day, 'baling out' in a hand-to-hand bucket-chain up the engine-room ladder. During this time mechanic Lashly worked up to his neck in the filthy rushing water, trying to clear the suction-pipe of the pump; but as the rising water now came in contact with the bottom of the big Scotch boiler, it became too hot for him to work there longer, and he had to abandon the effort. The fires had previously been drawn to enable the boiler to cool; for should the rising water reach the hot plates above the fire-box, there was the danger of their cracking and destroying the boiler, thus permanently putting the engine – on which we were dependent for forcing our way through the pack-ice – out of action.

In Lashly and Chief Engineer Williams, we had two splendid, efficient men, of whom no praise could be too great for the resource they displayed in these hours of peril.

From the way the ship was making water, which was now dripping through several loosened planks in the deck, everything depended on the freeing of the suction-pipe of the pump. As a last expedient, they set to work, in the sweltering heat, to cut through the steel bulkhead between the boiler and the hand-pump shaft, so as to gain access to the bottom of the pipe. Before midnight they had accomplished this difficult task, and Lieut. Evans crept through the opening, reached the pump shaft, and, working up to his neck in water, managed to clear away the coal debris that had choked the pipe. Providentially, too, the gale began to abate about this time; and when, regardless of the incoming seas, sixteen pairs of willing arms manned the long cranks amidships, and a thick stream of inky fluid at last gushed from the spout and found the scuppers, loud shouts of joy arose above the tumult of the storm, proclaiming to all aboard that the hand-pump was once more free.

As the water in the engine-room slowly fell to the efforts of these Spartans working in frequent shifts, the fires were re-lighted, and ere morning the steam-pump relieved them of this arduous labour.

By sheer resource, competence and superb seamanship the peril had been met, fought and averted; but the storm had levied a heavy tribute on our assets. We lost ten tons of precious coal, and scores of cases of petrol. Two ponies had died, and a third never really recovered from the weakened condition in which the severe buffeting had left him. Two dogs had been lost – one drowned and the other strangled by his chain. Another dog, Osman, who was washed overboard, was miraculously washed back on to the ship again on the crest of the next wave. He was grabbed by one of the sailors as he was again about to be carried into the sea, and saved. Though in a state of collapse for several days, he completely recovered, and lived to be the best dog of all, and the leader of the pack. Osman served with honours throughout the Expedition, and was comfortably pensioned and quartered for the rest of his life with friends in New Zealand.

During the storm no one on board had experienced a harder or more dangerous time than Meares and his kennel-man, Dimitri; repeatedly they had to risk the breaking seas that came aboard, in order to rescue their charges from drowning or strangulation. Captain Oates and Surgeon Atkinson had had an equally arduous task in caring for the ponies.

The storm was described in the log of the *Terra Nova* as of 'Force 10', which is within two units of the maximum, a hurricane. I do not suppose that any of my shipmates would care to repeat their experience of weathering a gale in a heavily overladen ship in the Fifties. Certainly I should not. It was rather too close a call for all of us, as our tortured barque wallowed amongst the hills and valleys of that wildest of all the wildernesses of the deep, and the worst two days that any of our number had ever spent at sea.

CHAPTER III

The *Terra Nova* Enters the Pack-Ice

Though the gale had now blown itself out, the ship was still rolling a great deal in a heavy swell that followed in the wake of the storm. The Fifties had done themselves proudly, so far, and had nobly maintained their furious reputation. Having shown us what they could do, I hoped they would rest content at that, and give us a sporting chance to get on with our work.

These gales are known as the 'Westerlies', and we could not expect to be out of the region of their prevalence until well over the sixtieth parallel of latitude. We were now about 55° S. The map of the world – Mercator's Projection is best for the purpose – shows that in the Eastern Hemisphere, below the southernmost point of New Zealand, there is no other land until the Antarctic continent is reached, about 65° to 70° S. Barring the extreme south part of South America, the narrow peninsula of Graham's Land, and a number of small islands – only two or three of which off Cape Horn and New Zealand are inhabited – there is open ocean all round the world for some twenty degrees of latitude, a swath of the globe's surface about twelve hundred geographical miles in width. Thus, there is nothing to break the force of the tremendous seas heaped up by the fierce tempests that ravage this region, which sweep round the world, gathering in violence as they go. That is why the waves encountered in these latitudes are more mountainous than are met with in any other ocean.

It is part of the work of scientific enterprises such as Polar expeditions to obtain data about storms; hence in Dr Geo. C. Simpson we had a meteorological expert who was equipped with every needful appliance for research into atmospheric disturbances. The results of his observations will not only be of great value to science, but to navigation, and thus indirectly to agriculture and industry; and to everyone who is affected by navigation. This means everyone in the British Isles, and in most other lands as well, for it is by navigation that we receive the greater part of our food supplies and the raw materials for our industries from overseas. A great part of the world is affected, in some way or other, by the tempests that are born in the region surrounding the South Pole

– the stormiest zone on earth. The nearer to their source these storms can be examined, the more valuable are the results attained; and as this was but one of the scientific objects of our enterprise, a Polar expedition, planned and led for such purposes as this, was not a mere 'dash' to locate a point on the earth's surface on which the foot of man had never trodden, but was a great scientific undertaking, from the results of which mankind might derive direct and permanent benefits. If this were better and more widely understood, we should less often hear the question asked 'What is the good of it all?' and those who give their lives to such a cause would not only be immortalised by Science, but in the hearts of all their countrymen.

On looking at my injured leg, which had not been undressed for several days and was still quite painful, I discovered that there was now a black contusion under the skin from the knee to the ankle. Not liking the look of this, I called Dr Levick, the ship's surgeon, who brought along Dr Wilson, and the two medicos decided that I must go below immediately for complete rest. For the next few days, therefore, I was compelled to lie low, and give the blood-clot a chance to be absorbed.

This enforced idleness was very galling, as I could hear the seabirds, that hovered and circled about the ship's wake, squealing as they fought for the refuse thrown overboard from the galley, and I imagined all sorts of camera-subjects that I might be missing. A friend in New Zealand had given me Marcus Clarke's *For the Term of His Natural Life* – a most blood-curdling tale of the days of transportation to Botany Bay for comparatively trivial offences, and often on account of the most deplorable miscarriage of justice – which I read through, but was glad to reach the end of so depressing though enthralling a story. I then commenced to read F. T. Bullen's *Cruise of the Cachalot*; one of the most stirring books of adventure ever written, every chapter of which was filled with information concerning the very creatures that the old ship, in which I now found myself, had been engaged in hunting during a great part of her career – whales. The Cachalot is better known by its English name, Sperm whale, and although we were now south of the haunts of these great sea mammals – which frequent warmer waters – we were soon to meet with other members of the numerous whale family, concerning which there is a mine of information in that fascinating volume.

Now that I was perforce an unwilling prisoner, I may as well give a few details of the ship's arrangements below decks. The 'ward-room' was a fairly spacious apartment, with walls painted white, on which hung signed portraits of King Edward VII and Queen Alexandra. This room was lit by a skylight from above, and it had a fireplace at one end.

It had a long table down the centre with benches at each side, at which the afterguard (the officers and staff) messed. On three sides of the ward-room were cabins containing sleeping bunks. Below the ward-room were the chronometer-room and the ship's lazarette.

All idea of the comfortable cabins of ocean liners must be dispelled in conjuring up a vision of our sleeping-quarters. They were narrow, sepulchral chambers, into each of which a feeble glimmer of light penetrated by way of a tunnel, about fourteen inches long, pierced in the massive timbers of which the ship's hull was built, at the outer end of which was a scuttle, six inches in diameter, of thick glass. Into these cabins as many bunks and as much luggage as possible had been crammed. Each bunk had a high outer side to keep its occupant from falling out in rough weather. In my cabin there were four bunks and the kit of the four occupants. Each tenant's kit was in a canvas bag; and his sea-boots, felt-boots, overcoats and wraps hung in the meagre corner space, or lay about the floor; so that one had to struggle amongst a pile of other people's belongings to find one's own. In the dungeon-like gloom this was anything but an easy matter, and usually the searcher came in for a good deal of banter from the onlookers; though the humorous aspect of the situation was not always so obvious to the seeker, especially when the ship was balanced on her beam ends. Over the ward-room a large deckhouse had been built, which replaced what had formerly been a skylight-hatch in the deck, and the present skylight was in the roof of the new addition. This deck-house was two feet wider than the original deck opening, the difference in width now forming a balcony where wet oilskins could be removed and hung up before descending to the ward-room – which, with its cheery fire, was a snug and welcome retreat in bad weather.

Into this room each morning, at 7.30, would come the steward, calling out 'Rise and shine, gentlemen! Rise and shine, gentlemen! Rise and shine!' This invocation to turn out of our bunks and wash, for such it was – an importation from the midshipmen's quarters of the Navy – usually caused never so much as a stir. It was received with unbroken silence, or perhaps a snore or two. The steward would then reappear ten minutes later, with 'Show a leg, gentlemen! Show a leg, gentlemen! Show a leg!' This would draw a few yawns and grunts, and again – silence. The steward's third visit was from cabin to cabin, and in stentorian tones he would exclaim, 'Show a leg, gentlemen! Show a leg, gentlemen!! SHOW A LEG!!!' and we knew that the three calls of grace were up. Etiquette demanded that we should tax the steward's patience no longer, and out we turned. But for a few days my leg wasn't fit to show anyone but the doctor, so the steward passed me by in peace.

After a sea-water sponge-down on the poop deck, by the more stoical, or a hand-basin wash below by the less hardened, a hearty breakfast of unlimited porridge, bacon, bread, butter and marmalade and jam served to fortify our tissues until lunch time.

In one cabin – much larger than any of the others, and containing six bunks, which was called the 'nursery' – there was a player-piano. Musical talent was not, however, the forte of the afterguard; but two or three could vamp and play the banjo and the mandolin a bit, and Lieut. Rennick was handy with the flute. Still, the piano was a boon to all, as beside it stood a cabinet containing an excellent assortment of rolls of music. There was also, of course, a gramophone.

After three days' rest, there was such a remarkable improvement in my leg that I was able to go on deck once more. I was glad to be out in the sweet, fresh air again, and to get some exercise. The weather was dull and the sea very rough and lumpy still; but I was now able to get about and take some interest in the working of the ship. It was fine to see the sailors furling the sails out on the yard-arms, the ends of which at times seemed almost to dip into the sea, as the ship heeled over in the great rolling waves. It was fine, too, to listen to the chanties that they sang – rough as most of their voices were. The words were set to simple, harmonious airs, and the chorus of each chanty had a stirring rhythm; one just had to join in the irresistible swing of the thing.

When hoisting the mainsail or the topsail, which is hard work, as the yards are very heavy, it is usual to haul during the chorus only, so the leader stood on the poop and sang the verses; then all pulled together with all the weight and strength they could muster. The chorus of one of these chanties, following on verses of a fine rolling old song of the sea, ran as follows:

> So we'll rant and we'll roar, like true British sailors.
> We'll rant and we'll roar across the blue sea;
> Until we strike soundings in the channel of old England,
> From Ushant to Scilly is forty-nine leagues.

And they did rant and roar too – as they straightened out their knees and their backs, putting all their weight and sinew into the work, making the tackle rattle through the blocks as they bellowed out each accented word – these true British sailors.

Another chanty, with a shorter metre and a chorus to every line, concerned the adventures of an American youth who was known to his shipmates by the name of 'Ranzo.' It went like this:

> **Solo.** Oh, Ranzo was no sailor.
> **Chorus.** Ranzo, boys, Ranzo.
> **Solo.** The son of a New York tailor.
> **Chorus.** Ranzo, boys, Ranzo.

And so on for twenty stanzas, or more: 'sailor' and 'tailor' and the end of every line of the lead being sustained for two or three bars. As the ballad progressed the story told how the hero grew more and more efficient until finally he became the captain of the ship. When hoisting the topgallant sail to this chanty, the hauling was done only as the name of the hero was pronounced. It had a good snappy tune, and always went with gusto.

Another fine song, with a beautiful swinging air, was 'A-Roving.' Here is the first verse:

> **Solo.** Her eyes are like two stars so bright,
> Mark you well what I do say!
> Her eyes are like two stars so bright,
> Her face is fair, her step is light,
> I'll go no more a-roving from you, fair maid.
> **Chorus.** A-roving, a-roving, since roving's been my ruin,
> I'll go no more a-roving from you, fair maid.

A favourite chanty, when manning the pumps, was 'Sally Brown,' which was a song of praise of the charms of a young lady of that name who supplanted her own mother in the affections of the singer; it is to be hoped that she merited the sums that would appear to have been lavished upon her. This is probably the most popular of all the songs which sailors sing, and here are a few of its verses:

> **Solo.** So I courted Sal, her only daughter,
> **Chorus.** Aye, aye, roll and go.
> **Solo.** For her I sail upon the water,
> **Chorus.** Spend my money on Sally Brown.
> **Solo.** Sally's teeth are white and pearly,

Chorus. Aye, aye, roll and go.
Solo. Her eyes are blue, her hair is curly,
Chorus. Spend my money on Sally Brown.
Solo. The sweetest flower in the valley,
Chorus. Aye, aye, roll and go.
Solo. Is my dear girl, my pretty Sally,
Chorus. Spend my money on Sally Brown.
Solo. Oh! Sally Brown, I had to leave you,
Chorus. Aye, aye, roll and go.
Solo. But trust me that I'll not deceive you,
Chorus. Spend my money on Sally Brown.

Sailors dearly love these old songs of the sea, as well they might, for, when sung under such circumstances as the present, there was a simple grandeur of melody about them that was really stirring. They are only known by the seamen of merchant sailing-vessels, as there is no occasion for their use in steamships. (The *Terra Nova* had auxiliary steam.) The chanties were usually led by Mr Cheetham, the Bo'sun, but Lieut. Bruce sometimes would take the lead; there seemed to be no song ever written that this genial sailor did not know.

One day Captain Scott came to my lab' to have a yarn about plans for the summer's work. He told me that as soon as we had landed all the stores and equipment, and had built the winter-quarters hut, a main party would proceed southwards to lay depôts of supplies for the use of the Polar Party on their journey next year. A party of six would proceed to King Edward VII Land; another party of five would explore South Victoria Land for a few weeks. It was his wish that as I was 'the oldest and most experienced traveller,' and had done a good deal of Alpine work, I should accompany, and have charge of this party. I was much pleased at this expression of confidence, and thanked him warmly; but, as will be seen later, these plans were changed. Other and more important work lay ahead of me, and I did not accompany the party.

On going to the forepart of the ship, to which I had not ventured since injuring my leg, I realised what a dreadful experience the gale must have been to the ponies berthed in the forecastle. It was there, of course, that the motion of the ship was felt more than anywhere else; and there two of the unhappy creatures had ended their earthly sorrows, whilst a third who had nearly joined them was a pitiful-looking object.

The sailors, too, hardened seamen as they were, had suffered great discomfort, and were endeavouring to dry their personal belongings, which had been drenched by the water that invaded their quarters from the waves coming aboard. These fine fellows were meeting their troubles now, as always, with jokes and songs.

In the vocabulary of the forecastle (usually clipped short in nautical parlance to 'fo'c'sle') I detected a strong affinity to the vernacular of the American gold-miners and cowboys, with which, in my 'Out West' days, my ears had not been unfamiliar. It was like the voice of an old friend. The fluency with which one of our Petty Officers addressed his ship-mates in times of stress commanded admiration; for though he seldom repeated himself, and his diatribes were full of biting satire, there was not a trace of venom in a word of them.

I noticed that some carcasses of mutton had been removed from the ice-house, and were now, wrapped in cheesecloth, hanging for airing in the mizzen shrouds – 'shrouds' being the nautical name for the hemp-covered wire ropes extending from the sides of the ship to the masthead, to stay the mast. It was reported that one of the 'tenderfoot' scientists had enquired of Petty Officer Evans as to why these ropes were called 'shrouds.' Evans, always quick-witted, and never at a loss to get a 'rise' out of anyone, replied 'Why, because we keep them wrapped-up carcasses hangin' to them, sir!' It was also reported that the tenderfoot had appeared quite satisfied with this explanation!

Dr Wilson, who was always on the watch for 'specimens', now began to set snares from the mizzen rigging, consisting of a hundred feet or so of strong, but very fine fishing-line, at the end of which there was a loop. These lines streamed out astern, pennant-like in the wind. Soon, one of the pretty, unsuspecting Antarctic petrels that circled over our wake became entangled, and was hauled aboard to be skinned for our zoological collection. Our voyage was not, however, at any time remarkable for the numbers of the seabirds that we met with. I had expected to see ten times as many.

We were now in waters where various members of the great cetacean family, both large and small, might at any time be met with, from the gigantic Sibbald's Rorqual, or Blue whale – mightiest of all mammals – to some of the smallest dolphins. Dennis Lillie, the ship's biologist, who was very clever with his pencil, therefore pinned up in the chart-room a card on which he had drawn diagrams of a number of whales, porpoises and dolphins; and under each of these sketches he had written their Latin names, so that all, who felt so disposed, might learn to identify any individuals they might see. I had started to study these, and had just mastered the first diagram of a creature described as *Lagynorynchus obscurus*, when I noticed some porpoises or dolphins alongside the ship. Without thinking of the diagrams, or of trying to identify them, and full of my newly-acquired knowledge, I shouted to Lillie, who was below, that there were some *Lagynorynchus obscurus* alongside. He dashed excitedly on deck, and jotted down some notes about the creatures as he watched them. Then he turned to me, and asked how I had identified them. Descrying from his manner that I had made a lucky shot, I resolved to dissemble, and replied that they had been easily recognisable from his excellent portraits. This greatly pleased Lillie; he told me I had missed my proper metier and ought to have been a biologist. I never confessed to him that it was a mere guess, and though I did not make much more progress with the Latin names, I shall never forget *Lagynorynchus obscurus*.

Ten days after leaving New Zealand, we felt the breath of frozen seas. There had been several false alarms the previous day, but there was no doubt about it this time. Early in the morning the cry came from the lookout in the 'crow's nest' that there was 'A large iceberg ahead, sir!' No one taxed the steward's patience that morning. He had no sooner added to his usual exhortation to us to 'Rise and shine!' the information that there was an iceberg and 'pack' ahead, than we all turned out of our blankets quickly enough for once – eager to make our first acquaintance with the ice. Hastily dressing, I went on deck, and saw a gleaming white, floating island near the horizon. The sun, already high in the heavens, for we were in latitude 65° S., bathed it with light, causing it to stand out in vivid contrast to the cobalt ocean and the sombre gloom of the distance. As I gazed at the wonderful and, to me, novel sight, I felt that we were at last really at the threshold of that Great White South – whence Providence alone knew how many of our number would return.

But there was little time for reveries or soliloquising, for we were rapidly approaching the berg; so, after a hasty breakfast, I hurried to get my cameras ready for a subject such as only those who venture into these southern latitudes ever behold – Arctic icebergs seldom being more than a fraction of the size of the colossal masses which every season break away and float northward from the Ross and other ice barriers, until the heavy seas and warmer water that they encounter break them up and reduce them to the element from which they sprang.

In all my travels I had seen nothing so magnificent as this stupendous work of Nature. The grandest and most beautiful monuments raised by human hands had not inspired me with such a feeling of awe as I experienced on meeting with this first Antarctic iceberg. It was flat as a table; about eighty feet in height, and a mile or more long. Its vertical cliffs were seamed with fissures, and near the water line the great mass was pitted with caverns into which the waves rushed and foamed, or, dashing against the cliffs, rose with a roar, far up the perpendicular precipices.

When we steamed as close as safety permitted, to enable me to take some photographs, from our maintop we could discern a long ice-foot that projected like a warship's ram from the submarine part of the berg. It is estimated that only about a sixth or eighth part of these great tabular bergs appears above water, so there was probably five or six hundred feet of ice below the surface. I thought it curious that it should have a ram below the water. One would naturally suppose that the action of the ocean currents would erode the ice more quickly under water than the wind and sun would weather it above; and that bergs would be more likely to exhibit an overhang above water, rather than any projection below. But this was by no means usually the case, even in bergs that bore evidence of having but recently parted from their source of origin. (Yet, when later we arrived off the Great Ice Barrier itself, we found, not that a submarine icefoot projected there-from, but that it was deeply undercut by the action of the waves.)

Icebergs were an almost hourly sight henceforward, and the next to follow this vanguard of the fleet was shaped like the hull of a battleship, with a ram above water; but it had a greater ram submerged as well.

A line of ice now loomed on the surface of the sea, near the horizon, and soon after passing these first bergs we were in the 'pack.' It was hard luck to encounter the pack-ice thus early in the voyage; Captain Scott had anticipated reaching a full degree further south before entering the ice.

We hoped this might be only some outlying fringe of floes, and that the main body of the pack might be some distance ahead. Such hopes were doomed to disappointment, however, for during the next three weeks the *Terra Nova* had to fight her way yard by yard through the heaviest ice-floes ever encountered by any exploring vessel in these regions. The pack extended, as it proved, with occasional breaks, for some six degrees of latitude, or about four hundred statute miles. The weather had become dull and the heavens lifeless soon after the ship entered the ice; but the skies cleared in the evening, and when the sun burst forth the scene became of almost indescribable beauty. Innumerable ice-floes, with edges upturned from constant contact with each other, lay upon the now unruffled surface of the sea, looking like huge *Victoria Regia* lily-pads on the placid surface of some tropical lake. When at midnight the great red orb dipped almost to the southern horizon, the blazing heavens turned the sea to molten gold; the lily-pads took on autumn tints of orange with russet shadows, and their upturned rims were topaz; whilst the distant icebergs slowly changed into blocks of mother-o'-pearl and jasper. It was amidst such never-to-be-forgotten scenes that I made my first acquaintance with the midnight sun.

CHAPTER IV

Battling with the Ice-Floes

On December 10th, 1910 – twelve days after leaving New Zealand – the *Terra Nova* crossed the geographical threshold of the South, the Antarctic Circle. She was now surrounded with ice-floes to the horizon.

To watch her battling with the ice was one of the most exhilarating experiences I have ever known. It was simply entrancing to lean over the fo'c'sle rail, and see the ship's iron-shod prow shearing through, or rending asunder the floes, turning them under her forefoot conversely as the coulter of a plough turns over the smooth furrows on to the land – whilst ever the graven figure at our bow gazed fixedly, as though in silent resolution, into the South. I know not in whose image her features had been moulded – whether of some vision of the carver's dreams, or of Psyche, Helen or Penelope; but that fixed and intent southward gaze seemed symbolic of our Argonauts, in search of the golden fleece.

Four years before, I had steamed into the harbour of Vladivostok in January, when the bay for some twenty miles was covered with six or eight inches of ice. The beautiful clipper-bowed Russian packet, that plied between the Siberian seaport and Japan, took the ice with a roar at eighteen knots, of which fifteen were immediately subtracted from her speed. But she crept along at about three miles an hour, cutting the ice with a rending sound, and leaving a watery wake astern not an inch wider than her breadth of beam. Those had been very different conditions from the present; for here the ice was not to be measured by inches, but too often by yards.

From the 'crow's-nest' – a barrel lashed to the main-topmast, with a rail and canvas windshield extending two feet above its upper rim – the officer of the watch would 'con' the ship, shouting his directions to the helmsman on the poop, fifty yards below. Warmly clothed and snugly sheltered from the wind – for when standing in the barrel his eyes were just above the rail – from this exalted perch he would gaze far and wide across the ice-fields, and select favourable openings in the floes, invisible to those on deck. These openings are known as 'leads', and if no lead appeared immediately ahead, the ship would try to make one; which she often could, provided the floes were not too large, and there were other leads to break to. Charging a mass of ice of the superficies of an acre or two, the shock would make her tremble from truck to keelson and from stem to stern; then, as her forefoot rose to the obstacle, she pressed with all her weight, and a crack, which rapidly widened into a black lane of water, would shoot across the white, cleaving the floe in twain, and into the breach her bow was slowly pushed.

The hull of the *Terra Nova* was specially built for battling with the ice. It was constructed from massive baulks of oak, fourteen inches thick; and the bow, which had to bear the brunt of all this buffeting, was a solid bulkhead of timber, nine feet thick, and sheathed with inch iron-plates.

Occasionally sodden 'brash' ice would be met with. This she would slip through rapidly, to a rustling, soughing sound – like waves receding on a shingled beach. Again, the floes would be small, and well-broken by some swell they had encountered; these she would scatter aside with a muffled roar. Often I saw her open floes well over one hundred yards across and two feet thick, but frequently they proved too large or too thick to break; then they had to be pushed aside, or a way found around them. When there was a reasonable chance to split a floe which had withstood the first onslaught, the engine was reversed and the ship was backed far enough to gather way for a fresh charge; then, with all the speed she could make, she would ram again, often with success. But there were times when the ice closed in too heavily upon us, and we were powerless to do aught but wait. Sometimes for days we had to possess our souls in patience, and go on waiting until the action of the ocean currents and the swell broke up and scattered our enemy – as we always knew these friendly allies would do sooner or later. Thus, yard by yard, for weeks we battered through the heaviest pack-ice ever encountered by any Antarctic expedition.

Coming abreast of a thick and hummocky floe the day after entering the pack, the ship was stopped so that we might get ice aboard to replenish our water supply. The condenser could not produce sufficient fresh-water for all our needs, and the process made extravagant inroads on our coal reserves: moreover, condensed water is not so palatable as fresh.

No ship need suffer for want of fresh-water in these seas, if heavy ice-floes can be found. When the sea freezes to the thickness of several feet, the brine is pressed or frozen out of the ice that floats above water, leaving it almost saltless. But many floes are hummocked with old pressure-ridges, or with fragments fallen from bergs; these hummocks we always found to be perfectly fresh, and it was alongside of such a floe that we now drew abreast.

The Bo'sun then took charge of operations. This genial soul hailed from the port of Hull, and he had seen more Antarctic service than any other man. The smell of the ice was as the breath of life to Alf Cheetham's nostrils; it seemed he could not keep away from it. Not content with having been on the *Discovery* and *Nimrod* expeditions, he now must needs venture once more into the rigours of the Antarctic, where his particular duties brought him into contact with the most inclement of the elements.[1]

Our Bo'sun's face since entering the pack had worn 'the smile that won't come off.' He now appeared with an implement known as an 'ice-anchor' – a ponderous, hook-shaped bar of iron, with a few barbs cut near its point – to which he 'bent on' a cable. One of these devices was put out at each end of the ship, and firmly planted into a hole that had been quickly excavated, with the help of crowbars, in the ice; and we soon warped in and made fast to the floe. Then all set-to with a will, taking turns with the picks and shovels, and in a few hours we had shipped ten tons of ice, which, as fast as it came aboard, was cast into iron tanks, and speedily converted into water by a jet of steam from the boiler. Thus we replenished our depleted fresh-water supply, and provided an animated scene for the kinematograph.

During this operation, Dr Wilson had seized the opportunity to shoot a few seabirds; those that fell into the water being picked up by Lieut. Bowers in the 'pram' – a light Norwegian dinghy that we carried for such purposes. It seemed strange that the noise of the gun did not frighten away the other birds that circled about us, fearing nothing because knowing nothing of the ways of man.

The most beautiful birds we met with were the Snow petrels which began to appear soon after we entered the pack; they are never found north of the ice. As their name implies, they are – save for their beaks and feet, which are black – white as the driven snows amidst which they live, and are about the size of a dove, with the flight of a swallow. As they darted from floe to floe, silently as bats in the night, they became alternately visible and invisible. Their lack of any colouring camouflaged them completely when alighted on or flying over the ice; but when they flew across a lead their presence was immediately betrayed by a dazzling flash against the deep blue of the sea. It seemed a heartless thing to take the life of such exquisite creatures; but the demands of Science were inexorable, and several of these dainty beauties of the snows paid the penalty of their trust and curiosity. Then, having replenished the water-tanks, we cast off from our friendly floe and sidled on our way.

We bumped along merrily enough for a time, the floes being now easy and then formidable to deal with, until some seals were sighted ahead, basking on the ice. We drew nearer until they were not a hundred yards away; when, as the pack was heavy hereabouts and stopping would incur no delay, our zoologist cast longing eyes in their direction. A Winchester repeater was produced by one of the afterguard, and fire was opened from the foc'sle. The whole lot, four, were bagged. These were the first and only seals shot whilst we were in the South; when we landed we found that we could approach and slay the unsuspecting creatures with impunity.

The getting of these seals aboard provided another interesting subject for the kinematograph, which was duly gathered in. They were 'Crab-eater' seals – so-called, so far as I could learn, because they have never been known to eat crabs. The Crab-eater seal has bifurcated, or forked, teeth for the purpose of straining its food, which chiefly consists of the *Crustacea* known as *Euphausia*, and other small creatures that swarm in these waters. Their coats – which are of short coarse hair, not fur – were of a russet-brown colour, streaked with darker and lighter patches. When the carcasses were stripped, the skins were salted down and packed in barrels, as also were the skeletons. A liberal ration of the meat was greatly appreciated by the dogs, and the whole ship's company dined off seal-liver curry the same night. It made a delicious meal.

The first Adélie penguins 'popped up' the same day. I use this expression because it is the only one I can think of that correctly expresses the manner of the first appearance of these comedians of the Antarctic. I was standing on the poop at the time, when suddenly there shot out of the water – quick as a Jack-in-the-box – several midget figures, seemingly dressed in swallowtail coats with an excessive expanse of shirt front; and they stood looking at the ship, first cocking their heads on one side, then on the other, quite obviously wondering what in the world the extraordinary object could be. Their amazement was extremely comical, as they regarded us with white-ringed eyes. Finding they could make nothing of the ship, they plopped back into the water as quickly as they had popped out of it, leaving us all greatly amused over this, our introduction to the real inhabitants of the Southland, and hoping that we should soon see more of them. We were not disappointed. A touring party next appeared. I assume they must have been a tourist band on pleasure bent, because at this time of the year all serious-minded Adelies should be attending to their young ones. These, I took it, were care-free individuals, unhampered by such responsibilities, and out to see the world. This contingent popped up several floes away, just as the ship was brought to a stop by heavy pack. They advanced in double file, extended formation; some sliding along on their bellies, whilst others waddled on their hind legs, which are at the extremity of their bodies. By this I do not mean to suggest that they possess more than the orthodox biped equipment; but it comes naturally to use the expression 'hind legs' when referring to penguins, because when they toboggan, or slide along on their bellies, they use their flippers as well as their legs as a means of propulsion, and appear to be going on all-fours. Having arrived close to the ship's quarter, they closed up their ranks, and entered upon a pow-wow of a serious nature, of which it was evident that the ship was the subject.

Someone tossed a potato on to the ice, an act which was productive of much excitement among our visitors, and the confab at once became of a more animated tone. The vegetable was at first regarded with suspicion, until one individual, bolder than the rest, decided to investigate; whereupon the whole company followed suit, each in turn closely scrutinising the strange object, with much expression of opinion in the nature of raucous, crow-like squawks. One after the other they eyed it critically and tested it with their beaks, lifting it and letting it drop, and then repeating the process, as though estimating its weight. Whilst each in turn examined it, the others solemnly looked on, passing remarks at appropriate intervals. Then one would try to make off with it, but the others followed and made him drop it. Finally, apparently finding the presence of such a strange object in such a place inexplicable, they camped around it and went to sleep. When they

Adélie Penguins at Cape Royds.

woke up, they regarded the potato with the same surprise and curiosity as before, and began their examination of it all over again.

Thus, at the outset of our meeting with these most interesting and amusing birds – for birds they are – we found that curiosity was one of their main characteristics; it is one of the traits that make these queer, amphibious creatures seem so human. Later, as we became more intimately associated with Adélie penguins, we learnt to regard them with respect and affection. I shall have more to say about these remarkable creatures in a subsequent chapter.

We now had a period of bad luck. We encountered floes so large and thick that the ship was brought to another complete halt. Admirably fitted as the *Terra Nova* was for battling with the ice-floes, economy in coal had not proved to be a virtue of her engine; so the fires were drawn until such time as the prison walls that hemmed us in should open, as we knew they must do sooner or later. For three days we were held fast in the heavy pack that had closed in upon us, and not until five days later did we recover the lee-way that the ship made during this time, owing to the northward drift of the ice.

Time was of vital importance to the main object of our enterprise. It was Captain Scott's hope to lay depôts of supplies, before the winter set in, for some two or three hundred miles south on the Great Ice Barrier – the highway to his goal. These depôts of fodder and food would provide sustenance for the Polar Party on their journey to the Pole next year. As every day, and indeed every hour was of such value, it was exasperating to be lying thus idly in the ice; and more exasperating still to know that we were drifting northwards every minute.

The *Terra Nova* imprisoned in the ice, with her canvas hanging idly, or clewed-up into picturesque folds, formed a striking picture. Close by her jibboom, where pressure had forced the thick floes upward, there stood a pillar of ice, perhaps fallen from some monster berg as it charged with irresistible force through everything it met with on its dying journey northward. This pillar had been sculpted by the elements into the likeness of almost human features, with a sardonic grin, as though in mockery of our present unhappy predicament. The leads were cobalt mirrors, which reflected the fleece-strewn heavens between gleaming ice-walls a yard in height, forming welcome foregrounds for pictures on which Wilson and I busied ourselves with pencil and camera.

The delay gave us a welcome chance to stretch our legs; so Lieut. Gran produced from the hold great bundles of the Scandinavian snowshoes, called ski. Tryggver Gran is a Norwegian, and one of the most expert ski-runners in the world. Amongst other notabilities, he informed us he had numbered the Queen of Norway as one of his pupils. He now took in hand a score or so of less exalted individuals. Ski have of recent years become very popular among winter-sporters in Switzerland. They are narrow strips of wood, about seven or eight feet long, which are strapped to the boots. The ideal surface for ski-ing is soft, smooth snow; but as Polar ice-floes have usually anything but a soft and even surface, and are liberally besprinkled with lumps and scarred with cracks and ridges, they do not form an ideal place to acquire the art. When ski-ing, one must slide each foot forward in turn; to attempt to lift the feet, as when skating, is to invite disastrous results. As most beginners naturally make this error, the scenes on the ice-floes in the region of the ship that day gave plenty of entertainment to the onlookers – limbs and ski being at times badly mixed, as the learner encountered an unexpected mound or pitfall. Everyone was anxious to learn, however, and Gran put us through some strenuous hours of exercise.

The dogs became wildly excited when they saw so much animation on the ice; so Meares and his kennel-man, Dimitri, harnessed some of them to a sledge, to give them a run. But the team catching sight of some penguins leaping out of the water in a near-by lead, got out of hand, and yelping with anticipation, bolted for the birds. For a minute it looked as though the team would end up in the sea, but Dimitri proved equal to the occasion and skilfully got the dogs under control again. In our progress through the pack-ice we had occasionally seen whales spouting in the open-water channels. Whilst I was photographing out on the ice-floes this day, I heard what must have been a huge one blow in a near-by lead. A loud, hollow-sounding blast made me look round, just in time to catch a glimpse of the head of a whale receding from view, and a cloud of vapour condensing in the air. It was probably one of the great Blue whales, or Sibbald's Rorqual. When these huge creatures breathe through such narrow openings in the ice as in this instance, they must stand on their tails and 'tread-water,' so to speak, in order to get their nostrils above water. I noticed that the whale's head disappeared perpendicularly.

After holding the ship in its grip for three days, the ice opened up under the influence of the currents; so the fires were relighted, and once more we proceeded on our way. Soon after starting, from the fo'c'sle I espied with my glass a strange object on the ice and, after carefully scrutinising it, reported the first Emperor penguin – thereby, I trust, attaining a little merit. He was a beautiful fellow, about forty inches in height, standing motionless, in an attitude of silent meditation. The ship was manoeuvred into range; but when the lethal gaze of our zoologist rested yearningly upon him along a rifle-barrel, his majesty seemed to scent the sacrificial altar; so, waddling to the ice-edge, with a graceful header he subsided from our view – thereby avoiding post mortem association with the earthly remains of his more diminutive, Adélie compatriots in the lab' adjoining mine.

Immense bergs had been in the offing during the time we had been icebound, and one of them, which had been slowly working nearer, was watched with some apprehension. Had it approached too close to windward, and the wind had risen, it might have borne down upon us with unpleasant results. Bergs, such as these, present a great area to the elements, and when they start to travel they demand undisputed right of way. There was always the danger, when icebergs were to windward in the pack, that they might bear down upon the ship and make a summary ending of the enterprise.

This berg was a remarkably picturesque and interesting sight for it was midway on its journey to decay. The process of erosion affects no two bergs alike. As, in course of time, the submarine portion becomes worn away by the currents, the centre of gravity changes; the berg tilts and finally turns over. Then the wildest efforts of imagination would fail to conceive the fantastic shapes that sometimes emerge to view as the formerly submerged portion of the ice-island rises to the surface. This berg had obviously tilted,

Terra Nova icebound.

exposing a large water-worn section at one end, whilst the list had caused the whole upper strata to slide off, leaving several large masses behind, ready at any moment to gravitate into the sea. It had likely enough spent more than one season drifting amidst the floes since starting on its northward way; but the next swell it encountered would send it thundering into a thousand fragments.

Like many others, this berg was the subject of much interesting discussion by our scientists; some maintaining that it was not a Barrier berg, but had parted from some pressure-tortured land glacier. From such differences of opinion amongst our experts – some of whom had not previously visited these regions – one gathered that their hypotheses were frequently founded on speculation, the most plausible theory being that accepted. Sound as their arguments always were, and advanced with a sincerity that no one could question, yet there often remained a doubt; thus one learned to form one's own theories about such things. I had formed my own idea about this berg before hearing the controversy which it excited, and I felt that I was progressing in Polar lore when both Captain Scott and Dr Wilson corroborated it, and pronounced it to be a Barrier berg. The picturesque ruin crept up to within half-a-mile of us, and provided material for some striking photographs and sketches.

I was anxious to secure a moving-picture film showing the bow of the *Terra Nova* cleaving the ice-floes; this ambition was now realised, thanks to the help of our worthy Bo'sun and Petty Officer Williamson, who rigged some planks extending ten feet from the starboard side of the fo'c'sle, to the end of which I fixed the kinematograph with its tilting-table. Spread-eagling myself on the end of these planks, I had a field of view clear under the overhanging prow. As the ship bumped into the floes, I hung on as best I could, and with one arm clung tightly to my precious camera lest it should break loose and fall into the sea, whilst with the other hand I turned the handle. But frequently I had to stop and grip the planks hard to avoid taking an unpremeditated header. Fortunately, however, no mishap occurred; and the result – showing the iron-shod stem of the ship splitting and rending the broken ice into the foaming sea – proved to be one of the most thrilling of all the moving-picture records of the Expedition.

One of the most remarkable bergs sighted during the voyage was almost conical in form, the apex of its low cone being in the centre of the berg, and the summit bearing every similitude to land. This berg was the cause of more discussion than any other that we saw, on account of its extraordinary resemblance to an island; the consensus of opinion, however, was that it was an iceberg. I had it under observation for an hour through a Zeiss 12 X prismatic binocular, presented to me by a friend just before leaving London. With the aid of this fine glass I carefully scrutinised the dark summit and the low ice-cliffs that were so unlike any other berg we saw. No one could explain its form, and, as all the arguments that I heard against its being land were unconvincing, I still wonder, when I look at the photograph of this berg, if some day an island will be discovered there.

One afternoon the ship entered a narrow lane of water, a mile or more in length, with low tabular bergs, of great area and from ten to twenty feet in height, on either side of us. It was a most ominous-looking place, as from the deck we could not see the end of the lead. The officer aloft in the crow's-nest must have seen it, however, or he would not have placed the ship in what appeared to us below as such a perilous situation. Had we found ourselves in a cul de sac and the bergs had drifted together, the ship must inevitably have been crushed to splinters. I think all on board experienced a sensation of relief when we finally steamed clear of this ill-omened-looking place.

Tedious as was our progress, we yet advanced slowly Pole-wards. The evening before Christmas again found the road closed to us by heavy pack, after having worked our way some sixty miles southward during the preceding five days. At night the sun was warm and bright, and there was not a breath of wind astir. It may seem strange that I should write of the sun shining at night, but we had now been fourteen days in the regions of constant summer daylight, day and night. I stayed up until long after midnight, busy with my cameras on the lovely effects of light and shadow created by the sun-beams as they played amongst the ice-floes.

It had been a source of great disappointment to me that the skies had been dull and overcast during the greater part of our progress through the pack – rendering photography of much of the finest ice scenery futile. In cloudy weather the ice-fields appeared blank and featureless, no matter how broken up they were; but a shaft of sunlight falling on the uneven surfaces instantly transformed desolation into entrancing beauty. No precious hour of sunshine could therefore be wasted – whichever of the twenty-four it might be.

Not a breath of wind ruffled the surface of the sea, on this most wonderful of all Christmas Eves. In its limpid mirror every cumulus or loafing cirrus in the heavens was faithfully imaged. A lone Adélie penguin jumped out of the looking-glass and stood on the floe for an hour, blinking at the ship in wonder, until, warmed by the grateful rays of the midnight sun and lulled by the silence that prevailed, it tucked its head under its flipper, and roosted where it stood.

Christmas Day found us still in these seasonable surroundings —in 69° 5' S., 178° 30' E. In spite of our long, vexatious delay, everything had gone merrily since we entered the pack-ice, and the spirit of camaraderie exhibited by all aboard was good promise for the future. Though the weather had become dull and cloudy, merging the ice-covered sea and the sky into shroud-like, shadowless white, the whole ship's company were in the sunniest of spirits. It was to be a day of rest and recreation. During the morning Captain Scott read the Church Service, and after lunch each of the afterguard went about his affairs, or read or snoozed in his bunk until it was time for dinner. The ward-room was gaily dressed with banners that many had brought along as sledging-flags, appliqued and embroidered with heraldic devices by soft, beloved hands at home. Our cooks had stretched their skill and drawn upon their resources to the utmost to do honour to the occasion, and ample justice was done by all to their noble efforts. An enormous sirloin of roast beef was preceded by a great tureen of turtle-soup, and an entree of stewed penguin's breasts and red currant jelly – a dish fit for an epicure and not unlike jugged hare. Then, amidst yells and cheers, came Christmas pudding, all afire, and mince pies, preserved fruits, sweets and crackers galore. We toasted our Leader and success to the enterprise in champagne, to which he replied in a short and characteristically appropriate speech; and we drank to each other. Then, after the 'Christmas parcels,' which many had brought, had been opened and their contents generously handed round, our musical talent, such as it was, was called upon.

The daylight night above was thick with falling snow; and long into the small hours sounds of revelry from the ward-room and the fo'c'sle broke the vast stillness of the icefields of the South.

CHAPTER V

The Great Ice Barrier

Interesting operations had intermittently been carried on aboard; I have alluded but once to the manning of the pumps. Our ship made a certain quantity of water; there was nothing unusual about that – all other ships do likewise. But the *Terra Nova* made an unusual quantity of water, a failing which added greatly to the labour of working her. She had sprung a leak on the voyage to New Zealand; but it was thought that when she had been drydocked and overhauled and caulked at Lyttelton, no more would be heard of the trouble. When, however, she was refloated and reloaded the leak was found to be almost as bad as ever. Not until the ship returned to New Zealand – six months later, after landing the Expedition in the South – was the cause discovered. It was then found to be due to a badly-fitting bolt in her timbers, underneath the upper part of the iron sheathing of her forefoot, and through this hole a miniature cataract gushed unceasingly.

As the steam-pump ate heavily into our precious coal reserves, it was necessary to make frequent use of the hand-pump to get rid of the water thus made. When we were running under canvas only, or were lying ice-bound with fires banked, the latter only could be used. This hand-pump was at the foot of the main-mast, and was operated by means of a heavy, cranked iron bar, extending therefrom on either side athwart the ship to bearings on the bulwarks. The radius of this handle was from about a man's forehead to his knees.

I had cause to remember this crank, about sixteen months later. On the homeward voyage, I had gone for'ard one day when the seas were sweeping through the ship's waist, and after watching my chance to get back, I made a dash for it, just after a sea had found the scuppers. As I was wearing a sou'wester hat, I did not see the pump-handle, and, running into it, I got a knock-out blow. I managed to crawl to the poop ladder before the next wave came, which might have washed me overboard, and Lieut. Bruce, who was on the bridge, helped me up. I received 'two lovely black eyes,' but was thankful to have got off without a broken nose.

Twice, daily, and once in the night watches, sixteen of the ship's company, officers and men together, would man this crank, and to the lively chanty 'Ranzo, boys, Ranzo,' a flood of water poured from the lip of the pump, until the soloist reached the stanza reciting the hero's promotion to the command of the ship, about which time chuckling and gurgling sounds emerging from the well, and the easy swing of the great cranks, indicated that the valves were sucking air and that the bilge was once more normal.

There was nothing particularly inspiring about this work, other than its effect on arms and abdomens. When we were held up in the pack-ice a more entertaining operation was 'sounding.'

This was always carried out by Lieut. H. de P. Rennick, one of the best-natured and kindest-hearted sailors that ever trod a quarter-deck or entered up a log. It is with a sad heart that I pen his name, for many a time and oft have I kept watch with 'Parney' on the *Terra Nova*'s bridge. When homeward bound through those stormy southern seas, we would 'swap yarns' and sing through our repertoires in the night hours, to the accompaniment of the wind that howled and whistled through the rigging, and of the waves that went hissing and soughing by. The gallant young officer, for whom I formed a life-long friendship, now lies in a sailor's grave in the North Sea, sent there by his country's enemies when H.M.S. *Hogue* went down. He left a young bride to mourn his loss.

For plumbing the ocean depths a Lucas Sounding Machine – a small hand-winch fastened to a heavy steel tripod, which was bolted to the port side of the fo'c'sle – was used. The reel of this winch held five miles of piano wire, to the end of which a lead weight would be attached. This was then dropped over the side to the bottom of the sea, carrying with it an instrument for ascertaining the temperature. When the plummet touched bottom, the jerk released a reversing registering thermometer, which recorded the temperature, whilst a pocket in the base of the weight entrapped a sample of the ocean bed. Other reversing thermometers were fixed to the line at various intervals. Thus, in addition to ascertaining the depth, several other important results were secured at a single operation.

The samples brought up by the weight from time to time showed that the ocean floor was either blue mud, *globigerena* ooze, or diatom ooze. These oozes are of great biological interest. *Globigerena* ooze is a calcareous deposit of unknown thickness, formed of the shells of tiny *Crustacea* which fall to the bottom of the sea when the microscopic organisms that inhabit them die. Diatom ooze is a siliceous deposit formed of the skeletons of minute sea plants, which, like the dead *globigerenes*, are continually falling like rain to the bed of the ocean. *Globigerena* ooze is not found at a greater depth than 2,000 fathoms, as beyond that depth the shells dissolve; but the siliceous skeletons of diatoms are indissoluble in sea-water, and may be found at any depth. When dry, *globigerena* ooze is a white powder; and it is of such deposits that the chalk beds, now on land, were originally formed in the bed of the sea.

The greatest depth recorded in the pack-ice was 2,108 fathoms (over two miles), at which depth the temperature was about two degrees higher than the surface water. In subsequent soundings the depth gradually decreased until the shelf of the Antarctic continent was reached. The weighing, or winding in, of all this wire with the instruments attached to it, by means of a small winch operated by hand, was a gruelling task for a number of hands working in ten-minute shifts for several hours. But when the ship returned South a year later, she carried a small petrol engine for this purpose; this saved the afterguard – who had hitherto taken spells at weighing the wire – some hours of real back-breaking, shoulder-racking punishment, each time we sounded. During this and the subsequent voyages made by the *Terra Nova* after landing us on Ross Island, the numerous soundings taken have greatly added to knowledge of the southern seas. On one occasion a whale ran into the wire and parted it, and the apparatus was lost. On another occasion the weight dropped on to a whale's back, it was supposed, as it seemed to touch bottom, and immediately afterwards the wire began to pay out again for many hundreds of fathoms.

Important experiments were also carried out by our two biologists, D. G. Lillie and E. W. Nelson, with tow-nets of various kinds. One was a long tapering affair, made of strong but loosely woven fabric attached to a rim some sixteen inches in diameter, from which it was reduced by a truncated, cone-shaped, additional piece of the same fabric to a smaller rim of about six inches diameter, which formed the opening. A lead weight was fixed to the end of the device, and it was dropped overboard and towed astern for a while – the weight being sufficient to keep the net a few feet below the surface of the water. Through the opening in this trap, obliging diatoms, and minute forms of organic life with which these Polar seas swarm, and perhaps a few tiny *Crustacea* would enter; and having entered must perforce abandon hope. The net would then be hauled aboard, the contents carefully sorted, and selected specimens subjected to microscopical examination.

In the biological laboratory there were rows of glass jars, in which these low forms of life were hermetically sealed in spirit and preserved for examination in after years at our home laboratories – for it takes years to examine and report on the biological results of an expedition such as this.

To peep through the eye of our biologist's microscope at the details of their catch, was to enter such a world as quite bewilders description. Seen through this magic medium, organisms so diminutive as to be almost invisible to the unaided sight assumed a girth of inches; less minute organic forms became ferocious beasts; and tiny crustaceans, a millimetre long, became such monsters as one almost shrank from, with evil eyes and voracious-looking jaws.

Diatoms are so numerous in these waters as to stain yellow the bottom of the ice-floes to which they cling. On these the smallest of organic creatures feed; and these again are preyed upon by the lower forms of *Crustacea*; which, in turn, provide a cannibalistic menu for their bigger relatives. The largest of these surface crustaceans, *Euphausia* – a sort of shrimp an inch or more in length – form the diet of fish and penguins, from which a ferocious seal, called a Sea-leopard, makes a two-course dinner of fish and fowl; and then the Killer whales devour the seals. (How another, and human link was nearly added to the chain a week later – when the writer narrowly escaped providing a personal repast for a party of these wolves of the sea – you shall hear in time.)

Thus the struggle for existence wages; life in the sea being, as indeed it is on land, a never-ending warfare of creatures preying on some other. One has but to learn that the immense Baleen whales that swarm in these seas – monsters running to one hundred feet in length, or more – subsist largely on the little *Euphausia*, to realise how prodigious must be their numbers.

Sometimes our biologists would lower into the ocean depths an instrument called an Insulated Water Bottle – an intricate piece of apparatus which would imprison and bring up a sample of the sea-water from any desired depth, for analytical purposes. Why anyone should want to know the salinity of the water in the depths of the Antarctic Ocean may not be obvious to the layman; but Science demanded such information, and, as time went on, some hundreds of bottles of these samples were accumulated and carefully stored away for examination on our return to England.

Another interesting instrument was the Current Meter, which recorded the direction and velocity of the ocean currents – for volumes of water are always moving in some direction in the sea. This device, which resembled a great gadfly, or a miniature aeroplane with folded wings – the wings or blades being for the purpose of keeping its head to the stream – was only used at such times as the ship was icebound. It was lowered through a hole cut in a floe, the operation being carried out by our two biologists.

Occasionally Lieut. H. L. Pennell would take a large compass out on to the ice, and check its readings with those of the standard instrument aboard; or he would take observations with a sextant used in conjunction with a box containing a tiny lake of quicksilver, called an Artificial Horizon.

Harry Pennell, our Navigating Officer, was the most energetic man I have ever known. The end of a day's work that might well have wearied the hardiest, would find him fit and fresh as the beginning; and during the entire voyage, no matter how inclement the weather, he never slept elsewhere than wrapped up in blankets on the chart-table on the *Terra Nova*'s bridge. He seldom came below except for meals. When Pennell was not occupied with navigating problems, he was either on watch, or conning from the crow's-nest, or else out on the yard-arms helping the seamen set or shorten sail, or otherwise assisting in the handling of the ship. He was a 'whale for work.'

The services of this brilliant officer were of inestimable value to the Expedition; for, after the exploring parties had been landed in the South, he was in command of the *Terra Nova* during her subsequent voyages. His quiet, modest, unassuming manner only accentuated his obvious intellectual talents; and all his friends marked him out for a distinguished career. But, like so many others of Britain's best and bravest, he gave his life for his country five years later – in the North Sea, not far from where his friend Lieut. Rennick died. He went down in H.M.S. *Queen Mary*, of which he was Navigating Commander, in the Battle of Jutland. Harry Pennell also left a young bride to mourn him.

Every morning before breakfast the spartan Bowers would undergo a stoical ordeal on the poop. A small hand-pump, with which he and others had been wont regularly to raise water for their matutinal shower, was now frozen and a mass of icicles. Not to be done, however, out of his daily mortifying of the flesh, Bowers would cast a bucket over astern, and hauling it aboard full of icy water and slush, would upset it, or persuade a comrade to upset it, over his nude anatomy, and then repeat the process. After these acts of self-affliction, Bowers – who normally differed from the rest of his shipmates by the remarkable pinkness of his skin – would exhibit a fiery glow from head to foot.

No wonder Scott wrote of him: 'He is the hardiest man that ever went into the Polar regions.'

With the exception of Wilson, Atkinson and Nelson, who had also kept up occasional fresh-air ablutions after entering the pack-ice, such methods now lacked attraction for the rest of us. We contented ourselves with a hand-basin wash below each day, and a weekly tub by means of a bucket of warm water in the engine-room.

Three days after Christmas, whilst we were again held up in heavy pack, the ship's poop presented for several hours the appearance of a pleasure-steamer in mid-Pacific; as all the afterguard lay about the deck asleep, basking in the rays of the sun. This anomalous condition of affairs for such latitudes was due to the fact that there was not so much as a zephyr astir, and the 'mercury' had risen within a couple of degrees of the freezing-point. So free from moisture is the air in these regions, that when the temperature rose to anywhere near 32° Fahrenheit, and there was no breeze, the warmth became almost oppressive.

Later in the day, the look-out in the crow's-nest reported that the ice appeared to be thinner and more broken up ahead; so the banked fires were stoked once more, and we started off on what proved to be our last lap in the pack-ice.

As we progressed, the floes were more easily navigable than they had been for many days. They were small and well-broken, proving that they had recently been subjected to a swell, and had not become re-cemented by the frost. They were heaped up in places by pressure and by over-riding one another; and presently the shapes that the piled-up fragments had assumed became weirdly beautiful and fantastic. Some of the forms were almost like huge flowers, whilst but little effort of imagination turned others into the very similitude of animals – for fancy easily runs riot in these regions. The sunbeams played amongst this zoological ice-garden bewitchingly, and I ran to fetch my kinematograph to record the extraordinary scene. But before I could get it ready we had passed out of the region of these wonders – one of the strangest and most beautiful appearances we saw whilst in the ice-floes.

Soon after midnight we passed through the last of the out-lying belts of mushy, broken ice, and steamed at our full speed of seven knots into the open water of the Ross Sea. We had entered the ice on the morning of December 9th, 1910, in latitude 65½°; and we passed out of it about midnight on December 29th, in latitude 71½° S. We had been but a few hours short of three weeks among the floes, and during that time had steadily worked our way south for over four hundred statute miles.

It was with a feeling almost of regret that I saw the last of the pack-ice; we had been in it so long, and it had been so ever-changing in its aspects, and had seldom failed to have some daily novelty and surprises. Unearthing from the pigeon-holes of memory episodes of my wanderings o'er the earth, those three weeks among the ice-floes stand out in luminous relief; and as I write these lines I can almost hear the swish and roar and grinding of the ice, and can almost feel the shocks that set us staggering as the *Terra Nova*'s ironshod prow forced aside the floes, or split them silently asunder. The good old ship had become to me an object of affection, an almost human thing – a token of all that is steadfast, sound and true. She was like some great and forceful personality, scorning difficulties, and, resolute and undaunted, wearing down all opposition and overcoming every obstacle, pressing ever forward to success.

Though we sighted other streams of pack-ice, we did not become involved in them; but a strong wind now rising, Captain Scott decided to lay-to in the smooth water in the lee of the belt, so as to secure easier conditions for the ponies, which were in no fit condition to stand a repetition of the buffeting they had been submitted to a month ago.

The New Year saw us clear of all our troubles. Bright sunny weather, an ice-free sea and a fair wind were all that we could desire, and we bowled merrily along with all our canvas pulling and bellying to the breeze. Great swelling billows of cumulus – glorious contrasts of light and shadow – floated in the heavens, or detached themselves into woolly clusters. Such weather made the very drawing of the breath of life a joy. It filled one with a sensation of delight to throw back the arms, expand the chest, and, opening wide the lungs, inhale great stimulating draughts of the sweet exhilarating air. It made one thrill and tingle with very gladness to be alive, and to have health and strength and feel the marvel of it all.

On January 3rd, 1911, after two days of uneventful sailing, a curious illusion appeared in the lowering clouds – a brilliant glare of light reflected from some ice which lay ahead of us. This was the phenomenon known to Polar explorers as 'Ice Blink.' From the masthead we could see that this strange effect was produced by a wall of ice which loomed up on the southern horizon. It was the Great Ice Barrier at last!

Forty miles away on the starboard bow, Mt Terror, the great dormant volcano on Ross Island, was a magnificent sight as it reared its lava slopes far up into the clouds that shrouded its waist; but Erebus, its active mate, had not as yet appeared – being behind Terror, and hidden amongst the mists. It was thrilling and inspiring to gaze on this Antarctic land which that great adventurer, Sir James Ross, had been the first to see – seventy years before.

Shortly after noon we hove-to off the Barrier to reconnoitre. Away to the east the interminable rampart meandered into the distance; ahead of us it barred all further progress, a bulwark sixty feet in height. But we seemed to have been wandering for years amongst icebergs, and, after our long association with 'chips of the old block,' our meeting with the parent body itself excited little surprise or comment. To us, icebergs, either free or fast, no longer held the spell of the unusual.

The face of the cliff was pitted and caverned by the waves, and in and out and round about those grottoes joyous penguins disported themselves, doing the most astonishing aquatic tricks and gambols. Some leapt along over the water like dolphins; or as a flat stone cast into a pond ricochets over the surface again and again, a dozen times or more. Others sprang out of the water on to, or nose-dived from the ice-blocks. That they were performing thus for our entertainment, I am not prepared to affirm; that they even found the ship an object of much diversion I had some doubts, though some of them made excursions alongside of us, and, jumping on to ice-rafts, eyed our craft with curiosity unmingled with any trace of fear. For all the interest the penguin population exhibited in our arrival, ships might have been coming here daily for years, instead of twice previously during the present generation.

The Great Ice Barrier, discovered by Sir James Ross in 1840, is the greatest known ice-sheet on earth. Extending from South Victoria Land in the west, to King Edward VII Land in the east, a distance of over 400 miles; and southwards to the mountains that border the Polar Plateau, 400 miles or more from its edge – it is estimated to be at least 160,000 square miles in area, or nearly the size of the total area of France.

Authorities differ as to whether the Barrier rests on land, or floats. Captain Amundsen, who spent a winter on it, three miles from its edge, states positively that it rests on land. Captain Scott was equally positive that it is afloat.

Amundsen based his opinion on the lack of any perceptible movement during his stay, and to the constant level maintained by his theodolite. Scott's conviction was founded on barometric and other observations made during three years at a number of points; and on soundings taken along the Barrier edge from end to end. These soundings showed that the sea exceeded 1,800 feet in depth along the greater part of the distance. At this was frequently more than ten or twenty times the height of the exposed ice, there could be no question that the front, at least, was afloat. Our scientists were also unanimously of the opinion that the Barrier is a floating ice-shelf.

We could see that the submarine portion of the great ice-wall was deeply undermined by the action of the waves; but several hundred feet of unseen ice, somewhere below, reflected so much light that the sea was brilliant emerald green. The opal caverns above the surface – from the roofs of which a myriad ice spears menaced the sporting penguins – were all ablaze with turquoise, green and purple, and their inmost recesses were azure. In these wondrous grottoes played hundreds of Peter Pan fairies – rainbow-hued flashes of light, mirrored by the dancing, lapping wavelets.

Such was the Great Ice Barrier – the birth-place of thousands of the icebergs which break away each year in masses some-times many miles in length. The largest berg met with during the Expedition was twenty-three miles long; the ship 'coasted' along it for several hours on the second homeward voyage. Such an iceberg could carry a city the size of London and all its suburbs on its back.

Abutting on the Barrier, a perpendicular wall of rock – two hundred and fifty feet in height – rose out of the sea a few cables' length to the westward of where the *Terra Nova* lay. These were the cliffs of Cape Crozier, and above them towered the black foothills of Mt Terror, whose ten-thousand-feet-high summit was lost, away and beyond, in the clouds. The whole of this region is volcanic rock, the beetling cliffs being faced in places with irregular basaltic columns. Though not so perfect, they reminded me of the beautiful hexagonal pillars on the Fuji river near Minobu, in Japan, which, for a quarter-of-a-mile, are regular in formation as a paling, thirty yards in height.

It had been Captain Scott's fond hope that he might have found a landing-place hereabouts; so he, Dr Wilson and the geologists put off in one of the whale-boats to prospect the locality where the Barrier edge pressed in a series of confused *séracs* against the towering cliffs; but from the ship the

Above left: The outside of the famous 'grotto' in an iceberg.

Above right: The inside of the grotto.

outlook appeared to be hopeless, and the party soon returned corroborating this view.

Captain Scott and Dr Wilson had explained to me the many reasons why Cape Crozier would be a most desirable base to establish winter-quarters, if it were possible to land there. They had both explored the district when on the *Discovery* Expedition. For the main objects of the enterprise the situation would have been admirable in many respects. Shelter from the southern storms would have been afforded by Mt Terror and its foothills; the Barrier edge would have been close at hand for observation; there would have been almost unlimited territory far rambles and for exercising the animals, and there was the additional fascinating prospect of being close to the largest known Adélie penguin rookery, and to the only breeding-ground of the Emperor penguins that had ever been discovered. The Emperors breed, in the winter, at the foot of the Cape Crozier lava cliffs, and the Adélie penguinry was but a mile or two away.

But no landing-place could be found alongside of which to bring the ship for unloading our heavy gear and equipment, and the tempting prospect had perforce to be abandoned. It was a great disappointment to all. The *Terra Nova*'s course was then laid for McMurdo Sound.

Captain Scott had described the Great Ice Barrier to me with great enthusiasm in London; and it had been arranged that, when we reached it, the ship should steam for several miles along its face, so that I might secure photographs and moving-pictures of this eighth wonder of the world. And now it was before us, with the sun shining from an almost cloudless sky, throwing its creviced and caverned precipices into magnificent effects of light and shade; the conditions could not have been more propitious for securing remarkable pictures of priceless educational value. Yet such, it seemed, were the exigencies of our case, owing to the long delay experienced in the pack-ice, that the time could not be spared.

So, hastily securing such photographs and moving-pictures as were possible, with a heavy heart I then impotently watched the bastioned rampart slowly disappear astern – one of the most remarkable features of the earth, to see which, and in the hope of illustrating it, so that others might see it too, I had come over more than a third of the circumference of the globe.

CHAPTER VI

We Land on Ross Island

The *Terra Nova* now headed about north-west, for the northern point of Ross Island. Soon after leaving the Cape Crozier lava cliffs on our port quarter, we passed a berg that had recently calved from one of the glaciers at the foot of Mt Terror – to 'calve' being the geological term signifying the parting of a portion of a glacier from the parent body. The berg had grounded as it took the water, and was hard and fast. As we steamed past this interesting sight, I made a photograph which I named 'The Birth of an Iceberg.' Above the parent glacier's slope there were numerous conical hills of lava – parasitic cones of the great volcano a few miles further inland. Near the stranded berg, there was a smooth, brown stretch of land – perhaps half a square mile in area – sloping to what appeared to the naked eye to be a shingled beach. This excited my curiosity, and I was just about to get my glass to examine it, when Wilson came along and told me that this was the Adélie penguin rookery. He added that the brown appearance was due to the ground being covered with guano.

Then, through the glass I distinguished that what I had taken to be stones were really penguins. For half-a-mile the ground was moving with the creatures, which were in places crowded together so closely as to resemble the pebbles on a sea-beach. Along the shore they were leaping into and out of the water in such numbers that they literally poured into the sea in cataracts, and sprang out of it in streams. For hundreds of yards off shore the sea was alive with them, 'porpoising' through the waves like dolphins; and amongst the multitude Killer whales, or Orcas, fiercest of all sea mammals, rolled and spouted, as presumably they browsed upon them. The penguins seemed to regard these savage monsters with contempt. When porpoising along the surface, if an Orca were bearing in such a direction as to cut across them, they would not deviate from their course, but would go leaping light-heartedly along, in and out of the water, to within a few yards of its evil-looking dorsal fin, and then just dodge astern of it. Though I assume the Orca preys on penguins, yet I never saw one catch a penguin, nor have I heard of anyone who did. Whilst it may be too much of a gourmet to look at penguins when there is a seal to be had for the asking, yet I would not suspect the Orca of being fastidious in its diet, or of prejudices in the matter of food. I surmise that the real reason for the indifference of the penguins is that they know they are too agile for the bulky creature, and can easily elude its jaws. Another possible reason is that the Killer whale does not feed when 'going through its spoutings,' or breathing – for which purpose it comes to the surface. I warrant, however, that the penguins give *Orca gladiator* – to grant him his full scientific designation – the right of way and plenty of elbow-room after he has sounded. Could I have had but one hour ashore amongst the life revealed by my glass, I might have secured such moving-picture marvels as I hesitate to hint of, for fear of being suspected of exaggeration. I pressed to be allowed to have one of the boats for this purpose; but, though in full sympathy with my wishes, Captain Scott considered the danger – from the swell that was breaking on the beach, and of possible attacks from whales – was too great.

In the whole Ross Sea region there is no more favourable place known than the vicinity of Cape Crozier for the study of Antarctic animal life. As this was one of the principal objects that attracted me to the South, it was tantalising to think that if we had been able to land and winter there I might have worked among those abounding zoological wonders at my leisure.

At 8.30 p.m. we were fairly abreast of Mt Terror, which had now shaken off its robe of mist, and rose, an icy cone of lava, many thousands of feet above the glaciers with which the lower slopes were covered. These glaciers descended to the sea, ending in precipitous cliffs of ice, which extended in an unbroken wall to Cape Bird. Midway between Terror and Erebus, Mt Terra Nova was a beautiful sight with the midnight sun shining over its triple-coned summit. We encountered a belt of light pack here, the broken floes composing well into foregrounds for several camera studies.

As we progressed, the towering mass of Erebus now began to rise above the glaciers; and at 11 p.m. I secured my first photograph of the great volcano which was to be so intimately associated with the next year of my life. The mountain was, from this northern aspect, more interesting as a study in vulcanology than remarkable for its beauty. I have seen many volcanoes in many lands, but none that so clearly showed the periods of its life as does Mt Erebus, from the north. The ancient outer crater, a more recent inner crater, and the present active cone were all clearly defined.

At 1 a.m. we rounded Cape Bird – a forbidding-looking promontory of black lava – and entered McMurdo Sound. Erebus now came full into view, presenting a well-balanced contour, with the active, snow-covered cone plumb in the centre of the mountain mass, and the ice-fringed lava skirts of the old, outer crater falling wide on every side. It was a most beautiful and impressive scene.

The midnight sun was shining with such brilliance that I was able to make focal-plane photographic exposures with an aperture of F 11, using a Zeiss Protar lens of sixteen inches focus, with a K 3 colour screen in conjunction with an orthochromatic plate. With this combination I secured correctly exposed negatives, with my 7X5 reflex camera – such was the brilliancy of the light at midnight.

All that night we steamed leisurely along, carefully scrutinising the land, and about 5 a.m. we were passing through loose pack off Cape Royds, where Sir Ernest Shackleton's 1907 Expedition wintered. Through my glass I could see the little hut, nestling in a valley amidst the surrounding volcanic hills, where, in the heart of this godforsaken wilderness of ice and lava, some of our fellow adventurers had lived and done magnificent work two years before. Deep feelings were inspired by the sight of this lone dwelling-place in these ghastly, uninhabited solitudes; and I resolved that this should be the Mecca to which I would make a pilgrimage as soon as chance permitted.

Having now been watching and working with my cameras for twenty-four consecutive hours, I turned in for an hour's sleep. When I awoke there was a strange silence, proclaiming that the engine had stopped. Hurrying on deck, I found that the ship was made fast to a great sheet of ice which extended to the shore, a mile-and-a-half away. The day was calm and bright and warm – the temperature being but a few degrees below the freezing-point – and around me lay a panorama of such austere and desolate grandeur as I had never hitherto seen.

Eastwards, over the frozen sea, in which half-a-dozen weathered bergs were imprisoned, a crenellated ice-cliff rose abruptly for a hundred feet or more of height, and extended northward for several miles. It was the face of the Barne Glacier. Over this formidable rampart there were miles of icy slopes, above which Erebus, the King of the mountains of the South, monarch of all he surveyed, sat enthroned in all his majesty of 13,500 feet of height, spreading his robes far and wide around, reminding me somewhat of the Japanese Fujisan – the mountain by which I judge all others – only Fuji is much more perfect in outline and proportion. Though lacking in symmetry from this western aspect, there was, none the less, a rugged imperfection about Erebus in keeping with this desolate realm.

Far away in the west a magnificent panorama of wild, tumultuous mountains rose in pyramidical formation out of the sea, their rocky scarps and snowy valleys bathed in the morning sun. They were the peaks of the Royal Society Range in South Victoria Land, and though distant nearly one hundred miles from where we lay, stood out so distinctly in the clear, brilliant light, that they seemed scarcely a dozen leagues away. The loftiest of these beautiful peaks was Mt Lister, 13,000 feet in height. No one would dispute the right of this eminent name to the honour thus bestowed upon it, for there are few to whom science and humanity owe a greater debt than to Lord Lister.

Away to the southward was a smaller cone-shaped peak, called Mt Discovery; this name also was both euphonious and fitting. Others of the heights were Mts Hooker, Rikker and Huggins. It might seem to the uninitiated that the geographical nomenclature of the Antarctic was somewhat overburdened with such personal designations; but these were names of those who had been of valuable service to, or had taken an active part in exploration in these regions. Dr Joseph Dalton Hooker was the assistant surgeon and botanist of the *Erebus* of Sir James Ross's Expedition, and became the renowned traveller, Sir Joseph Hooker. Sir William Huggins was, at one time, President of the Royal Society; and Sir Arthur Rikker was once Honorary Secretary of the Royal Society.

I thought, however, that personal appellations, save that of Lister, seemed misfits for these beautiful peaks, and felt grateful that Sir James Ross had not bestowed upon the two most famous Polar mountains the names of his friends or patrons, but had called them after his own two ships – *Erebus* and *Terror*.

Next to Mt Lister, the fairest of the above-named peaks is Mt Huggins, 12,870 feet, which is not unlike the profile of the Aiguille Verte, as seen from Argentière, in France.

Captain Scott, Dr Wilson and Lieut. Evans had gone ashore to prospect, and an hour later they returned greatly pleased with what they had seen. They reported a rocky cape with a gently sloping beach, in a position fairly sheltered from the prevailing winds, and were unanimous as to its suitability as a site for building our Hut. As firm unbroken ice prevented our further progress southwards to the end of McMurdo Sound, it was decided to make this place the headquarters of the Expedition, and the locality was named Cape Evans.

The way ashore being good, over ice sufficiently thick to bear our heaviest equipment, and the weather being all that could possibly be desired, or that kindly fate and fortune could bestow, it behoved us to make the most of these fortuitous conditions; so everyone – officers, scientists and deck-hands alike – set-to with a will and began the unloading of the ship. The ponies were first slung out in a crib, rigged by block and tackle to the yard-arm, and all were soon landed safely on the ice. Ice was almost the natural element of these ponies. Coming from north-eastern Siberia, as they did, they had been accustomed to snow and ice for about six months of the year. Their amazement at finding themselves on their native element once more would have been comical, had it not been pathetic – for they were predestined to spend the rest of their brief existence in the South. Oates, and the Russian groom, Anton, soon had them tethered to a cable anchored in the floe, and for hours the shaggy little fellows seemed scarcely able to believe their senses, and could not stop whinnying and rolling on the ice for joy. It certainly must have been relief beyond measure to them to be freed from their narrow cells and able to rub themselves against the hard rough snow, for they were all badly afflicted with horse lice, from the tortures of which they could now obtain some alleviation by rolling. The dogs, too, were in high spirits, and yelped and whined and howled with delight, as they pawed and scratched at, and dug their noses into the snow. It was all a man could do to hold them back as they were led one by one, or rather as they dragged their leaders, down the gangplank. They were chained to a rope extending from the ship's bow, and no sooner were they all 'ashore' when a company of penguins leapt on to the floe. Immediate pandemonium ensued, for the fierce instincts of the half-wild dogs were instantly aroused by the sight of any living creature. The penguins, nothing daunted, marched up to investigate the, to them, strange visitors; whilst the maddened dogs strained at their chains in the effort to get at such extraordinary-looking objects. The dogs, like our-selves, were quite incomprehensible to the penguins, who know no enemies when they are out of the sea, as there are no land creatures to molest them. No doubt they came forward to the dogs, as they always did to us, not out of curiosity only, but in a spirit of friendship.

On finding their friendly advances met with hostility, several showed fight; but the battle was over in a moment. Before the little innocents could be driven off, more than one bleeding corpse lay on the snow; for, as fast as, with outstretched flippers, they came within reach of the cruel teeth,

Oates with the ponies and dogs.

they were mercilessly slaughtered. Had the dogs not been prevented by their chains, they would have gone off like a pack of wolves, hunting other prey – as indeed they always did when, later, any of them managed to break loose. But Meares and his henchman, Dimitri, were masters of these furies, and they quickly had a couple of teams harnessed and at work – which the dogs seemed to take to with delight.

The heavy cases containing two of the motors were next slung out on to the ice, and unpacked. Our excellent motor engineer, Bernard Day, assisted by biologist Nelson, took them in hand, and their open exhausts were soon rattling out a lively tune. These motor tractors had large toothed wheels fore and aft, round which passed endless chains of flat plates fitted with diagonal cleats to grip the snow. They, so to speak, laid their own track as they rolled along. This is the caterpillar principle, since made so universally known by the 'Tanks.' The machines were made by the Wolseley Company. They had 14 h.p. air-cooled engines, and over a good surface each motor could haul a ton or more of dead weight on trailer sledges. All the timber for the Hut was transported ashore by these two tractors, as well as many tons of hay.

The ponies were given a day's rest, but the dogs were set to steady work at once with light loads until they had become more hardened; whilst officers and men formed teams of four, hauling endless sledge-loads by human muscle as well. Actuated by a common purpose, all worked with such good will and combination, that a constant stream of stores and equipment flowed from the hold of the *Terra Nova* to the shore; so that by the evening of the first day big strides had been made in the unloading of the ship.

Sled dogs.

CHAPTER VII

Some Photographing Episodes

Having decided to establish winter-quarters at Cape Evans, Captain Scott, quick to recognise that fine weather meant every-thing to the success of my work, advised me that it would be as well to take all possible advantage of the exceptionally favourable weather conditions whilst the ice held, as, once it broke up, subjects now easily accessible would then become impossible of approach. I was to consider myself free to devote myself exclusively to my photographic work, and should not be expected to take any part in unloading the ship. Being thus freed from regulations drawn up for the observance of others, I worked almost ceaselessly, for there was no lack of subjects for my cameras.

I had noted some fine icebergs frozen into the sea ice about a mile distant. The morning after our arrival, I was just about to start across the ice to visit these bergs, with a sledge well loaded with photographic apparatus, when eight Killer whales appeared, heading towards the ice, blowing loudly. Since first seeing some of these wolves of the sea off Cape Crozier I had been anxious to secure photographs of them. Captain Scott, who also saw the approaching school, called out to me to try and obtain a picture of them, just as I was snatching up my reflex camera for that purpose. The whales dived under the ice, so, hastily estimating where they would be likely to rise again, I ran to the spot – adjusting the camera as I did so. I had got to within six feet of the edge of the ice – which was about a yard thick – when, to my consternation, it suddenly heaved up under my feet and split into fragments around me; whilst the eight whales, lined up side by side and almost touching each other, burst up from under the ice and 'spouted.'

The head of one was within two yards of me. I saw its nostrils open, and at such close quarters the release of its pent-up breath was like a blast from an air-compressor. The noise of the eight simultaneous blows sounded terrific, and I was enveloped in the warm vapour of the nearest 'spout,' which had a strong fishy smell. Fortunately the shock sent me backwards, instead of precipitating me into the sea, or my Antarctic experiences would have ended somewhat prematurely.

As the whales rose from under the ice, there was a loud 'booming sound' – to use the expression of Captain Scott, who was a witness of the incident – as they struck the ice with their backs. Immediately they had cleared it, with a rapid movement of their flukes (huge tail fins) they made a tremendous commotion, setting the floe on which I was now isolated rocking so furiously that it was all I could do to keep from falling into the water. Then they turned about with the deliberate intention of attacking me. The ship was within sixty yards, and I heard wild shouts of 'Look out!' 'Run!' 'Jump, man, jump!' 'Run, quick!' But I could not run; it was all I could do to keep my feet as I leapt from piece to piece of the rocking ice, with the whales a few yards behind me, snorting and blowing among the ice-blocks. I wondered whether I should be able to reach safety before the whales reached me; and I recollect distinctly thinking, if they did get me, how very unpleasant the first bite would feel, but that it would not matter much about the second.

The broken floes had already started to drift away with the current, and as I reached the last fragment I saw that I could not jump to the firm ice, for the lead was too wide. The whales behind me were making a horrible noise amongst the broken ice, and I stood for a moment hesitating what to do. More frantic shouts of 'Jump, man, jump!' reached me from my friends. Just then, by great good luck, the floe on which I stood turned slightly in the current and lessened the distance. I was able to leap across, not, however, a moment too soon.

As I reached security and looked back, a huge black and tawny head was pushed out of the water at the spot, and rested on the ice, looking round with its little pig-like eyes to see what had become of me. The brute opened his jaws wide, and I saw the terrible teeth which I had so narrowly escaped.

Thinking they might break the ice again, I ran quickly to my sledge, by which Captain Scott was standing. I shall never forget his expression as I reached it in safety. During the next year I saw that same look on his face several times, when someone was in danger. It showed how deeply he felt the responsibility for life, which he thought rested so largely on himself. He was deathly pale as he said to me: 'My God! That was about the nearest squeak I ever saw!'

There were two dogs tethered out on the ice near the scene of this incident, and we came to the conclusion that it was an organised attempt by the whales to get the dogs – which they had doubtless taken for seals – into the water. I had happened on the scene at an inopportune moment, and I have no doubt they looked upon me as fair game as well.

Captain Scott, at the end of his description of this incident in his Journal, stated:

One after the other their huge hideous heads shot vertically into the air through the cracks that they had made. As they reared them to a height of six or eight feet it was possible to see their tawny head markings, their small glistening eyes and their terrible array of teeth – by far the largest and most terrifying in the world. There cannot be a doubt that they looked up to see what had happened to Ponting and the dogs. The latter were horribly frightened, and strained at their chains, whining; the head of one Killer must certainly have been within five feet of one of the dogs. After this, whether they thought the game insignificant, or whether they missed Ponting is uncertain but the terrifying creatures passed on to other hunting grounds and we were able to rescue the dogs.

Of course we have known well that Killer whales continually skirt the edge of the floes, and that they would undoubtedly snap up anyone who was unfortunate enough to fall into the water; but the fact that they could display such deliberate cunning, that they were able to break ice of such thickness (at least 2½ feet), and that they could act in unison, was a revelation to us. It is clear that they are endowed with singular intelligence, and in future we shall treat that intelligence with every respect.

This incident certainly inspired me with a wholesome respect for these devils of the sea, and I never took any chances with them afterwards.

The picture which illustrates this adventure is not, of course, a photograph; but it gives a very good idea of the locality and of what actually happened. It has been drawn from my own description of the incident; from that of Captain Scott; from my photographs of the surrounding landmarks, and from personal study by the artist of models of Killer whales, in the Natural History Museum at South Kensington.

The next day, just as I was about to leave the ship to visit the bergs, a school of Orcas again appeared, heading for the ship in close formation. I leant over the poop rail, with my eyes deep in the hood of my large reflex camera, waiting for the whales to draw nearer, when, as I was about to release the shutter, the view disappeared from the finder, and light flooded the camera; at the same moment I heard something splash in the water. On examining the camera, what was my consternation to find that the lens-board had dropped into the sea, carrying with it the finest lens of my collection – a nine-inch Zeiss double protar, worth about £25, which had been presented to me some years ago by the Bausch and Lomb Optical Company of Rochester, U.S.A. This was a serious loss, as the lens was not only my favourite on account of its superb qualities, but I had used it in many foreign lands, and therefore regarded it with affection. I had none other capable of completely taking its place, and all my subsequent scenic work was done with other and less suitable objectives.

I retailed the story of the loss of the lens – which now lies in a watery grave, 200 fathoms deep, at the bottom of McMurdo Sound – in a letter to the makers, which was duly posted on the return of the ship to New Zealand. When the *Terra Nova* came to relieve us next year, there was a parcel for me containing a replica of the instrument, and a letter from this courteous firm, requesting that I would accept the new lens as a substitute.

The continued glorious fine weather which at this time we experienced, though a godsend to us all, had on me rather an exhausting effect, for as long as it lasted I was loath to take rest. I knew that at any hour it might end, a storm arise, and the sea-ice break up; then there would be an end to my chances of getting any pictures of the stranded icebergs, and other features of our surroundings.

The sun at this season is nearly as high in these regions at midnight as at midday, so if the light was not right on a subject at noon, the chances were that it would be twelve hours later. For the first four nights I scarcely slept at all, as this continuous daylight was too novel and too wonderful to permit of sleep; it seemed waste of precious time to lose one single hour. I determined that lost opportunities should be as few as human endurance would permit. Afterwards I had cause for congratulation that neither time nor chances had been wasted, for the ice was rapidly decaying, and five days later it was so rotten round the stranded bergs that I was no longer able to approach them.

In one of these bergs there was a grotto. This, I decided, should be the object of my first excursion. It was about a mile from the ship, and though a lot of rough and broken ice surrounded it, I was able to get right up to it. A fringe of long icicles hung at the entrance of the grotto, and passing under these I was in the most wonderful place imaginable. From outside, the interior appeared quite white and colourless, but, once inside, it was a lovely symphony of blue and green. I made many photographs in this remarkable place – than which I secured none more beautiful the entire time I was in the South. By almost incredible good luck the entrance to the cavern framed a fine view of the *Terra Nova* lying at the ice-foot, a mile away.

During this first and subsequent visits, I found that the colouring of the grotto changed with the position of the sun; thus, sometimes green would predominate, then blue, and then again it was a delicate lilac. When the sun passed round to the west – opposite the entrance to the cavern – the beams that streamed in were reflected by myriads of crystals, which decomposed the rays into lovely prismatic hues, so that the walls appeared to be studded with gems. Curiously enough, this wonderful effect was only to be obtained when wearing non-actinic goggles. The place then became a veritable Aladdin's Cave of beauty. I was loath to leave it all; but after having made sure of my pictures, I hurried back to persuade Captain Scott to come and see the sight, which he did, and was as delighted as I was with its wonders. Uncle Bill came too, and made some sketches.

The cavern was about forty yards in length, and it had been formed by the berg turning partially over and carrying an ice-floe upwards, about eight feet thick, which had frozen into its present position. The difference of structure of the floe-ice on one side of the cavern, and the berg-ice on the other was very marked. It was great good fortune that I had been able to get the picture showing the ship framed by the grotto's entrance; a few hours later the berg had swung round many degrees in the current, and the ship was no longer to be seen from within.

Taylor and Wright came out to investigate the phenomenon in the afternoon, and with ice-axes cut steps up the floe that formed the outer part of the tunnel, whilst I kinematographed the Alpine feat. It made an excellent film. Then we all explored the cave, which closed up rapidly towards the further end. After squeezing through a passage with a 'Fat Man's Misery' in it, and climbing through a narrow sloping tunnel, we found ourselves high in the open air, near the summit of the berg. As we emerged, Wright had a slip and narrowly escaped falling into the water, fifty feet below. Fortunately he managed to regain his footing – thereby depriving a Killer whale, which immediately afterwards spouted in the pool, of a change of diet for lunch.

This pool was a most alluring feature of the vicinity, and its beauties were perpetuated in many pictures. When unruffled by the breeze, it was a faithful mirror of the sky, and penguins were continually leaping out of it, to rest awhile or roost on the ice. They took little or no notice of me as I made my photographs. Whilst I was engaged on one of them, I heard a sound behind me, and on looking round I saw a Killer whale – with open jaws, and eight feet of its length out of water – leaning on the ice, surveying me with interest. I didn't wait to pack my things. I almost threw them on to the sledge, and pulled off to a safer distance from the water – half expecting, as I did so, to feel the brute burst the ice under me, as I knew it was not very thick hereabouts.

When the temperature was comparatively high, the currents rapidly eroded the ice away underneath, whilst the appearance of the surface changed little. One might be walking along on sound ice; then suddenly tread on a place where it was not an inch thick. One had to feel one's way carefully along, when in doubt, by testing it with a ski-stick. In places the current ran swiftly below, and it was not a pleasant feeling when my legs went through; it made me think how hopeless would be my plight if I went through to the shoulders, and help were not at hand; but such incidents as a leg going through soon became so frequent that they ceased to have the thrill of novelty. I always threw myself flat when I felt the ice giving way under-foot, and I think it saved me a wetting, at least, more than once. Now, I shudder at the risks I took so recklessly in those first days, not realising the imminence of the dangers which, a week later, experience had taught me to hold in greater respect.

During those midnight days, when others slept and only the night watch and I were awake, some of the most memorable of my Antarctic experiences befell me. It was in those 'night' hours, too, as the sun paraded round the southern heavens, that I secured some of the best of my Polar studies. One of these was 'The Death of an Iceberg' – which represents a berg in the last stage of decay, from the action of the sun and currents. This picture always recalls to me one of the most dismaying episodes of my life. The adventure with the Killer whales had been exciting enough; I had relished the thrill of it. But there was nothing either pleasurable or thrilling about the incident which occurred previous to the taking of this photograph.

There was not so much as a zephyr astir, and the 'mercury' stood only a few degrees below the freezing-point, as I started off once more to the bergs that were such a paradise for my work. No sound broke the stillness of the nightless night, save the occasional squawk of a penguin, or the blowing of a whale, perhaps half-a-dozen miles away.

As I neared the bergs, I was perspiring freely from the effort of dragging my sledge; and the yellow goggles, which I wore as protection against snow blindness, became clouded over, so that I could not see. I was just about to stop to wipe them, when I felt the ice sinking under me. I could not see a yard ahead because of my clouded goggles, but I felt the water wet my feet, and I heard a soft hissing sound as the ice gave way around me. I realised instantly that if the heavy sledge, to which I was harnessed, broke through, it would sink like a stone, dragging me down with it. For a moment the impulse was to save myself, by slipping out of the harness, at the expense of all my apparatus. But I went to the frozen South to illustrate its wonders, and without my cameras I was helpless. At all costs, therefore, my precious kit should be saved. I would save it, or go down with it. We would survive or sink together.

A flood of thought rushed through my brain in those fateful moments. I seemed to visualise the two hundred fathoms of water below me, infested with those devils, and wondered how long it would take the sledge to drag me to the bottom. Would I drown, or would an Orca snap me up before I got there?

Though the ice sank under my feet, it did not break; but each step I expected to be my last. The sledge, dragging through the slush, became like lead; and as the water rose above my boots, I was unable to pull it further. Just then, with perspiration dripping from every pore, I felt my feet touch firm ice. With one supreme, final effort, which sapped the last ounce of strength that was left, I got on to it, and managed to drag the sledge on to it too; then I collapsed. I was so completely exhausted that it was quite a long time before my trembling muscles ceased to quake. When finally my knees would hold me up, I took the photograph.

In adventure one never takes anything too seriously. It is strange how quickly incidents of peril are relegated to the limbo of the past. The moment such episodes are over – no matter how imminently life itself may have been at stake – they become mere reminiscences, to be cast aside, and perhaps seldom or never referred to again, until the pen searches them out from the treasure-house of memory.

Having taken the desired photograph, and recorded a very beautiful Polar scene, I lay down on the ice – at the edge of the pool where the reflections appear in the picture – to peer into the profundity that I had so nearly become more intimately acquainted with. A great shaft of sunlight pierced the depths like a searchlight, and, by shading my eyes, with my head close to the water, I could see a hundred feet down into the sea, which was all alive with minute creatures. As I watched, a slim, silvery fish darted by, and then a seal rushed into the field of view, from the surrounding blackness – not in pursuit of the fish, but fleeing in evident terror. The cause of its terror immediately appeared. The horror hove into view without apparent effort, looking like some grim leviathan of war – a submarine; and a thing of war it really was for the seal. It was the dreaded Killer again, in close pursuit of its prey. It came so close to me that I could distinctly see the evil gleam in its eye, and the whole outline of its sleek and sinister shape. For a single second I lay, transfixed with interest at the sight. Then I remembered, and hurried to a safer place.

CHAPTER VIII

We Complete Our Winter-Quarters

For several days after our arrival scarcely a ripple disturbed the surface of the sea. The *Terra Nova* was wonderfully picturesque as she lay berthed alongside the ice; she was of a type nowadays seldom met with on the seas, and her square-rigged masts and rugged hull, mirrored in the water, lent great effect to my pictures. Ever and anon great billowy cumulus clouds would roll up in the heavens, and with almost every changing aspect I felt constrained to get my camera bearing on a fresh impression of the old rover. One day a small iceberg bore towards her, scraping along the ice-foot until its further progress was arrested not a hundred yards away. This berg was all a-hanging with icicles, from the warmth of the sun, and it composed with the ship to add a treasured page to my now rapidly growing album.

Up to the present time I had not visited the shore, as there had been too much to be done in the vicinity of the ship and the bergs, and the shore could wait; but now I loaded up my sledge and made my first excursion there. I did not find it an interesting locality, and it was plain that my sphere of operations would be reduced to very narrow and unlovely limits when the sea-ice broke up; I devoutly hoped it would hold for some time yet. The whole peninsula was of black volcanic rock – Kenyte, our geologists called it. It was not unlike the clinkers of a smelter dump, but very brittle, and full of crystals. Except for a few small glacier formations, the ground was entirely free from ice, and the winter snow had been melted by the heat absorbed by the black lava rocks from the rays of the summer sun, though the temperature was several degrees below freezing.

The site of our future home was an almost level space amidst this lava, just above high-water mark, and well sheltered by low hills from the prevailing south-easterly winds. Mt Erebus towered into the skies a few miles to the east; and the impregnable ramparts of the Barne Glacier, which fringe the skirt of the volcano, pushed a couple of miles northward towards Cape Royds. The bay, formed by this glacier and our promontory, was covered with ice which might any day break up and float out to sea. For a hundred yards along the shore the beach was everywhere scattered with stores, which were being

Above: Terra Nova imprisoned in the ice.

Right: Terra Nova at the ice foot, Cape Evans.

rapidly got into some kind of order under the supervision of Lieut. Bowers, whom Captain Scott had placed in charge of the commissariat. From the hour we landed, this capable young officer became the Leader's right hand in everything connected with the stores; though his old friend and comrade of *Discovery* days, Dr Wilson, was then, as always, his *fidus Achates* in all matters relating to the primary objects of the Expedition.

Rapid progress had been made in the building of the Hut. All the scantling had been numbered in sections, and the whole of the framework had been put together carefully before leaving London, in order to ensure that everything fitted. The match-boarding, too, had all been cut to the correct length, in readiness for nailing to the framework, and the work of fixing it in place was already well in hand. Tents had been erected as sleeping-quarters for those who were now living ashore.

On wandering further afield, I found a remarkable phenomenon for these latitudes – a cascade of running water, which owed its existence to three causes: the exceptionally fine weather; the fact that the 'mercury' was only a few degrees below the freezing-point, and to the heat of the sun radiated by the black rocks, which were warm to the touch. The melting snow water was caught in hollows in the hills, forming ponds, one of which we named Skua Lake, because of the numbers of Skua-gulls that bathed and gambolled in it. It was the overflow from this lake that formed the cascade, and its water was perfectly fresh. This waterfall was destined soon to be hushed by the resistless grip of Jack Frost.

A little company of Adélie penguins were paying our camp a visit. They strolled about, for all the world like a party of tourists taking in the sights. I was glad to notice that my camera came in for a share of their interest, and was deservedly examined and discussed. Some of the ship's officers started a game with them, and endeavoured to catch them; but they were far too wary, and easily avoided capture. The agility they exhibited when necessary was amazing.

As I should have ample opportunities for further investigating our surroundings later, I thought it as well to get out on to the ice again. On rounding the cape, I found Dr Wilson at work skinning Weddell seals. It was gratifying to know that animals providing such excellent food frequented the locality. There were usually plenty of seals lying in the lee of the icebergs, where they would sometimes sleep for days on end. Our zoologist, more intent on securing skins for specimens than meat for the larder, would sally forth on his mission armed with a pick-handle, and a murderous-looking hunting knife, which had a roughened horn-handled grip with a guard to prevent the hand from slipping, and a slender blade some fifteen inches long. Approaching the unsuspecting victim, he would stun it with a blow of the pick-handle; then, as the floppy creature rolled over, exposing its quivering belly, the lethal steel would slide between its ribs, and, finding the heart, a steaming geyser would spout from the wound, dyeing the snow deep crimson. Before the carcass began to stiffen – as it does rapidly in a freezing temperature – he would strip it of its covering; if this were delayed too long the carcass would freeze, and skinning be rendered quite impossible. Then he would sling the heavy pelt across a device called a 'flensing table,' a sloping board held in place by two supports, on which he would quickly cut the blubber from the hide— the blubber being a blanket of fat, from two to three inches thick, lying between the skin and the flesh. Blubber as food is a taste that takes a good deal of acquiring; but it makes excellent fuel.

Then I met the Norwegian, Gran, out on the ice. He had been putting in some strenuous work in a man-hauling team, pulling heavy loads, and was now having an hour or two 'off' to keep his hand in, or rather his feet in, with his ski. He told me he was going to ascend the Barne Glacier, and ski down a long slope that he pointed out to me. He pressed me to come and kinematograph the feat; but I declined, as I considered it was too dangerous an experiment to try on such an enterprise as this, where any accident might seriously hamper our programme. He ridiculed the idea of danger with such scorn, however, that I finally consented to accompany him, after exacting from him a promise that he would not expose himself to any unnecessary risk. We duly arrived at the spot he had selected – a long slope of ice, covered with snow, leading to the top of the glacier, which was at this point about two hundred feet in height. Gran then explained that he would ascend by an easy incline, and that it was his intention to ski down a very much steeper place, which he pointed out; I therefore took up my position on the sea-ice a slight distance beyond the proposed terminus of the course, and waited.

Our ski expert then laboriously 'herring-boned' up the slope, and, having reached the summit, shouted to me that he was about to descend; I thereupon began to take the picture. He swept like a meteor towards the edge of the cliff; and I drew my breath sharply as he seemed about to precipitate himself into space. But with consummate skill he turned about, almost on the overhanging cornice itself, and then, in a wild swoop, described a great curve to the other side of the slope, which was nearly a hundred yards in width. Turning about once more, with arms outstretched and knees well together, he then came straight for the camera, down the steepest part of the slide, at something approaching a mile a minute, until he encountered the change of surface as he struck the sea-ice – when he suddenly ascended, or was projected, five yards upwards. There was an impression of revolving arms and legs; of a spinning catherine-wheel in the air; of ski flying off at a tangent; a thud and – silence! Not knowing whether this spectacular manoeuvre was part of the performance, or unpremeditated – as Gran had foretold nothing of so dramatic a nature – I went on turning the handle of the camera for a few seconds; but becoming alarmed at his not moving, I ran to see if he was hurt. For a long time he lay ghastly white and motionless; then, to my great relief, his eyes opened and he slowly came-to. He was badly blown and very sore; but there were no bones broken, and, after recovering his wind by a good rest, he managed to limp home. He told me that it was part of the training of a ski-runner to know how to fall, when a fall was unavoidable, with the minimum risk to limb. Hence, when he found a spill was inevitable, he had let all the muscles of his body and limbs relax and become limp, and had thus saved himself from serious hurt. Even so, he had had a nasty shock, and felt the effects of it for some months afterwards; but in the end he was none the worse for the experience.

The work of unloading the ship was going on merrily, and there was now a clearly defined trail on the ice from the ship to the shore. This trail was well beaded with sledges at intervals, either coming from or returning to the ship, all returning sledges carrying loads of kenyte rock, for ballast to replace some of the weight we were taking from the hold. The ponies were now working well, with two obstreperous exceptions: one, Christopher – a vicious little beggar who persistently refused to work, and tried his best to kill anyone who came near him – was being disciplined by Captain Oates; and another, Hackenschmidt, was living up to his sporting name by having a bout with his driver, Captain Scott, every hundred yards. It was wonderful how well the work was going, but I noticed signs of deterioration in the ice, which was sodden in places, showing that it was rotting underneath.

The third, and last, of the three motor tractors was now slung overboard from the yard-arm, and a dozen pairs of arms started to haul it well away from the ship before starting up the engine; when, to the consternation of all, the ice sank under its weight, and the machine disappeared. Frantic efforts were made to save it, but as the sinking motor broke the ice back to those who were hanging on to the ropes, they had to let go. Petty Officer Williamson was dragged into the water up to his armpits, and the current immediately swung his legs away; but he was quickly pulled out of danger by his comrades.

This accident to our transport equipment was considered a grave calamity at the time; but as we became better acquainted with the two surviving motors and their habits, we regarded this incident in retrospect with less regret. Some even deemed it a stroke of luck; whilst others went so far as to bemoan the fact that the other two had not sunk as well. My own feeling in the matter was strictly neutral, as I must give the two motors that were left credit for doing a good deal of heavy work in the earlier stages of the adventure, and for providing some excellent subjects for my films – even if, later, their principal achievement was to provoke remarks for which there may be pangs of regret when Gabriel blows his horn.

I now decided to get some of my gear ashore, and made several lone trips, hauling some hundreds of pounds of photographic and dark-room equipment, and my personal belongings, on a sledge. I fixed up a tent for my sleeping-quarters; but so warm was the sun that night, even at midnight, that I spread my reindeer-skin sleeping-bag on the ground in the open air. The warmth of the bag compelled me to keep my head out, and then the brilliant sunlight and the discordant cries of the Skua-gulls, which swarmed about our camp, made sleep well nigh impossible; so I had to retreat to the stuffy tent after all, for shelter from the sun.

The climate of these regions in fine summer weather is magically invigorating, and though the temperature of the air was below freezing, the heat absorbed from the sun by the black lava made the ground quite warm. By 'ground' it must not, however, be inferred that I mean mould, or other earthy matter. There is no soil anywhere on Ross Island. The whole island is volcanic rock, ice and lava. The nearest approach to earth, in the agricultural sense, is sterile volcanic detritus and sand, eroded from the rocks by the weathering process of the frost, and by the wind which is almost incessant for a great part of the year. Since our arrival we had, so far, experienced almost complete freedom from wind; but though it was now the height of summer, we knew that, even so, we might consider ourselves favoured of the gods for the smiles that Fortune had bestowed upon us.

The next day, the sixth after our arrival, this fine weather showed signs of breaking up. During the morning I had been ashore helping the carpenters at work on the Hut, and early in the afternoon had started back for the ship, when the wind veered round to the south-east, and with the change of direction the whole summit of Erebus became hidden by driving scud.

I had read in *The Voyage of the Discovery* how quickly blizzards worked up and swept these Antarctic wildernesses, and that members of the 1901–4 expedition had lost their way in snowstorms within hailing distance of help; so that it was found necessary to rig a life-line for guidance between the ship and the shore. In their case, the distance was less than half of that which lay before me; and as I looked back at the lowering heavens and then at the mile of featureless and now deserted ice, I realised that there was little to guide one if the track became obliterated. The threatened storm did not break, however, until some hours later. It continued until the evening of the next day, and whilst it lasted the air was so full of finely powdered snow – which was driven like thick mist before the wind – that one could see nothing a few yards distant.

The morning after the blizzard broke fine and clear. Having established myself ashore, I was free to work at either end of the trail, and therefore alternated between the ship and the shore for sleep. The vicinity of the ship was to me the more attractive locality; I knew that ere long there would be no alternative to the shore, as the ice might go out any day. The view of Erebus was foreshortened from the Hut, but from the ship it was very fine, and was always changing as the light illumined the mountain from different aspects. There was neither rising nor setting of the sun. Day and night the orb meandered round the heavens, in the morning shining against the mountain, throwing it into silhouette; whilst in the evening the whole great mountain mass and its leagues of glaciers reflected the full brilliance of the rays, and was dazzling to behold. The crater now began to show signs of considerable activity, a trail of smoke streaming from the summit for miles away to the south-east, until it was lost behind the rise of the glaciers. A volcano in any land is always interesting; but few are more so than the great fire-mountain amidst these desolate wastes of eternal ice.

Hut Point, a promontory near the end of the Sound, was the headquarters of the *Discovery* Expedition. Captain Scott, anxious to renew old associations there, set out one day across the frozen sea to cover the intervening fifteen miles by dog-team, accompanied by Meares. On reaching the old hut, after sundry checks, due to streaks of open water which had to be circumvented, they found it perfectly sound and undamaged; but on endeavouring to enter, to their dismay the interior was nearly filled with hard frozen snow, blown in through a window which unfortunately had been left open by some member of the Shackleton Expedition, who had used the building for shelter. This necessitated some weeks of hard labour with pick and shovel by several men later on, as this hut was of the utmost importance in connection with our own operations. Captain Scott returned from the journey much depressed over the thoughtlessness of those who had entailed this labour upon us.

We now had several breaks in the fine weather, and ten days after our arrival a cold snap gave us some idea of what we might henceforth expect. The temperature fell to zero, and it was intensely cold in the ship; even the water in the unused boiler froze. We had also snow and bitter winds; but these conditions alternated with sunny days for several weeks.

All the shore party, with the exception of myself, had now taken up their abode in the Hut ashore; but I still spent much time on the ship. The sea had been making rapid inroads into the ice of late, and one night a heavy swell came up from the north, causing the *Terra Nova* to bump heavily against the floe. The engine room staff worked anxiously to get up steam and put to sea, for, with a stiff north wind rising rapidly and thick ice close under our lee, the ship was not in a happy situation. As soon as steam was raised she put out into the Sound. The next afternoon, as she came up to the ice again, we found that a large tabular berg had borne down upon our old position, and had run aground where the ship had yesterday been berthed. We heard from our friends that this berg had sailed in soon after we departed. Had the ship not steamed out when she did, the berg would probably have wrecked her. In manoeuvring for a fresh position, the *Terra Nova* ran on to a rock. I was in my lab' at the time, and the jar was sufficient to make me stagger. She was firmly held by the forefoot, and reversing the engines failed to back her off. All hands were piped to lighten her for'ard; and for a couple of hours everyone aboard worked like slaves, piling heavy bales of hay and sacks of fodder on the poop, so as to lift her bow. But this expedient not availing, Lieut. Pennell, who was now in command, decided to try the experiment of 'rolling ship.' All hands were marshalled on one side of the waist, and then ran to the other, and at given periods ran back and forth in the endeavour to rock her loose, the engines going full speed astern the while. This experiment was effective at last, and with thankful hearts we felt her slide off the ledge and ride easily on the waves. Whilst we were in this unpleasant fix, a crew came off from the shore in the whale boat to offer help; but they could not get alongside owing to the swell, and, as it proved, their services were not needed. This accident, which would have made a hole sufficient to sink an iron vessel, meant nothing to the sturdy *Terra Nova*. When she was dry-docked on her return to New Zealand, it was found that a furrow, a foot deep and several yards long, had been gouged into her bottom; but she did not spring an additional ounce of water, of such massive timbers was the ship constructed.

One day Captain Scott had accompanied me to see about photographing a heavy cornice which hung from the Barne Glacier, with icicles depending therefrom. But I could not do the work at that time, as the light was not right; the sun was shining full on to the face of the glacier, which for ice photography is useless. One must work half against the light to get correct effects of shadow; I should, therefore, have to return some morning. The cornice was a heavy one: there must have been many tons of overhanging ice, and I saw that there would be a fine picture to be made if I could get my camera behind the icicles, and photograph through them. But I considered the danger too great, as there was a large crack in the cornice, and I feared that any movement might precipitate the avalanche which, to me, appeared imminent. I know how the Swiss guides respect overhanging cornices, especially when there are cracks in them. Three years previously, with two guides and two porters, I had narrowly escaped being buried in a falling cornice on the Eiger, so I hesitated to take the risk. Scott, however, scorned the idea of risk, saying that the cornice might last for months.

We returned home without securing any photographs. Two days later, I proceeded to visit the place again, accompanied by a shipmate. There were neither icicles nor cornice to be seen; instead there was a mass of hundreds of tons of debris where the avalanche had fallen.

As I announced my intention to do some camera work further along the glacier the next day, my companion suggested leaving the sledge and apparatus on the sea-ice, where we were, as we were both very tired. But tired as I was, I decided the sledge must be pulled home to certain safety. I had cause to congratulate myself that I had adopted this prudent course, for, the next morning, to my amazement I no longer looked out on to a vast expanse of ice, but the blue sea! The entire sea-ice north of the cape, instead of gradually breaking up, had gone out during the night en bloc – a mass several miles in area.

Many a time I found, whilst in the South, that such travel-begotten discretion was not a bad asset in these latitudes.

CHAPTER IX

Exploring Operations Commence

Since the completion of the Hut, most of the Shore Party had been busy getting sledges into order, and preparing provisions, pony fodder and various gear for the southern depôt-laying journey.

The day fixed for the departure of the Southern Party was January 25th, 1911; but as the ice was breaking up rapidly the start was advanced a day. On January 24th, eleven men with eight ponies and two dog-teams set out from Cape Evans across the sea-ice for Glacier Tongue, where Captain Scott with more dogs would meet them, going thence by the *Terra Nova*.

The value of that single day gained was realised when we found that most of the ice between Cape Evans and Glacier Tongue broke up within twenty-four hours. Thus, had the start not been made on the 24th, the operations of the Expedition would have been delayed for one year; for we could not have got the ponies on to the ship again, and there was no way of getting them to Glacier Tongue by land; almost the entire coast is a region of impassable glaciers that fall from Mt Erebus.

I went in the ship to the Tongue – a peninsula of ice, ten to one hundred feet in height, which jutted out into the sea for some five miles. It was a mile wide at the coastal end, whilst it tapered to less than half a mile in width at the snout. Glacier Tongue is one of the mysteries of the Far South. It is a relic of the ancient ice-sheet which originally covered the whole of McMurdo Sound; but it is remarkable that a narrow strip of the Barrier ice should have remained floating in such a stormy arm of the sea for years after the rest of that part of the Polar ice-cap, which formerly filled the Sound, had disappeared. It was all the more surprising when we found that the glacier was networked with deep crevasses. The only rational explanation of the phenomenon is that it is held by some shoal or reef.

The *Terra Nova* berthed alongside this natural wharf, and in due course the ponies arrived, having thus safely accomplished about half of the journey to Hut Point.

On the south side of the glacier there was a crack in the sea-ice, several yards in width and filled with frozen slush. As the ponies were conducted out

Captain Scott,
Captain Oates,
Lieutenant Bowers,
Dr Wilson,
Lieutenant Evans.

on to the floe, the first two negotiated this place safely, struggling through the heavy slush and across to the firm ice well enough. The third was less fortunate; his leader, instead of taking him across a fresh place, followed the preceding two, with the result that the frightened animal got stuck, plunged, and then broke through. Fortunately, though his body was submerged, he kept his forelegs and head above the icy bog. We managed to get ropes round him and hauled him out; but he had experienced a very uncomfortable ten minutes, and was a pitiable object until he had been warmed by vigorous rubbing and a run on firmer footing. The other ponies were taken to a safer place, and got across without further mishap.

Though exhibiting signs of decay, the ice was holding well south of the Glacier Tongue, so for the next two days all the party were hard at work transporting some tons of fodder, dog biscuit and supplies, to the Great Ice Barrier edge at the south-east end of Ross Island, where the 'Southern Road' begins. These supplies were to be depôted at intervals along the route that the Pole party would take next year – as far as it was found possible to transport them ere the winter set in.

Here I must leave the Southern Party, as my work now lay in other directions. After discussing matters with Captain Scott, I had decided to abandon my original arrangement to go with the Western Geological Party, and to work instead in the neighbourhood of Cape Evans and Cape Royds for the remainder of the summer. The western journey would not have enabled me to take my own time over my work, and photography in these regions is too important and difficult to be done in haste. Moreover, I should not have been able to take my heavy kinematograph apparatus and equipment, and Captain Scott was in complete accord with me as to the desirability of securing typical scenery and animal life records, rather than geological details, which Debenham, the most painstaking of my pupils, was fairly competent to deal with.

The *Terra Nova* remained at Glacier Tongue for two days, until our friends had removed all their supplies from where they had temporarily depôted them on the ice, to Hut Point. During this time the weather could not have been more favourable to our plans; the sun shone from an almost cloudless sky, and there was no wind. Biologist Lillie, who never missed an opportunity to procure specimens from the deep, got busy with his nets, and he secured many prizes. The rarest of all his finds were some catches of *Cephalodiscus*, which are colonies of minute creatures that live in semi-transparent, gelatinous structures resembling branches of trees. Only half-a-dozen fragments of these domiciles of pelagic life had previously been available for the eye of Science. Lillie was, in his quiet way, the most elated of men when he saw the priceless nature of that particular catch, for it alone meant fame for himself and the Expedition. Once, Lillie dropped his biggest trawl overboard. We steamed dead slow and let the great net scour the sea-bed for a couple of miles; then the winch was started and the trawl was hauled aboard. It bulged and overflowed with the abundance of the catch – *Crustacea*, star-fish, sea-urchins, great worms, anemones, molluscs, etc.; but the bulk of the mass of strange creatures from the deep were large siliceous sponges covered with long glassy spines. The best of the various genera were sorted into jars of spirit, and the whole operation provided another fine subject for the kinematograph.

Sometimes, as we lay at the glacier edge, ice-floes closed in around us and drifted away again on the turn of the tide – though the rise and fall of the tide in McMurdo Sound is very slight. Occasionally seals came up and blinked and snorted at the ship in wonder, and penguins eyed us critically; whilst frequently whales rose and spouted in our vicinity. These great creatures were to me a never-ending wonder. The last whale that I saw in the Antarctic excited in me almost as much awe as did the first, and I spent many interesting hours trying to secure moving-pictures of them – which is anything but an easy task.

It is a matter of common, though erroneous, belief, that whales spout water from their heads; but it is no more possible for a whale to blow water from its lungs than for any other mammal to do so. (Elephants refresh themselves by blowing water over their bodies, but it is only such water as they can secrete in their trunks.) Whales, being mammals, can only remain under water for a limited time. Periodically they must come to the surface to breathe, and it is the vapour they exhale when breathing – which resembles a jet of spray in the air – that is known as the 'spout.' The lower the temperature, the more plainly visible is this breath of the whale; I have often seen whales blowing in the warm waters of the Pacific, but their spouts were much greater in these Polar seas.

We saw several different species of whales in McMurdo Sound. As, however, it is not my mission to embark upon biological dissertations, but simply to describe interesting phases of the animal life of the South which came within my province to observe and illustrate, I will confine my remarks to the two most interesting – the Blue whale, and the Killer whale.

The family, *Cetacea*, is a large one; it comprises all those ocean mammalia ranging from the smallest porpoises and dolphins to the leviathans of the sea. The Killer whale, or Grampus, which comes midway between these extremes, is a huge carnivorous dolphin which preys on warm-blooded animals, such as seals and penguins. Full-grown members of the order run to thirty feet in length, and their upper and lower jaws are filled with a terrible array of teeth, two to three inches long.

There is a model of a small Killer whale in the Natural History Museum at South Kensington, about which the following information is given: 'The members of this genus are distinguished from all their allies by their great ferocity, being the only cetaceans which habitually prey on warm-blooded animals. Though fish form part of their food, they also attack and devour seals, and various species of their own order, not only the smaller porpoises and dolphins, but even full-sized whales, which they hunt in packs, as wolves do the larger ruminants.'

Many of these 'wolves of the sea' – as they are called by whalers – now appeared around us, and great Rorquals were seen as well. The Rorquals are fish-eating whales; they have no teeth, but their upper jaws are filled with comb-like layers of the horny, flexible substance known as baleen, or whale-bone, through which they strain their food. Cruising open-jawed into a shoal of fish, or *Crustacea*, the Rorqual gathers a cavernous mouthful; then it ejects the water through the baleen – which acts as a sieve – and swallows the catch that is retained. The Blue whale is the largest of the Rorquals, and is said to be the greatest of all mammals, individuals having been known to considerably exceed one hundred feet in length.

The Rorquals almost invariably hunted alone; but we did not regard these huge fellows with the same morbid interest that attached to their smaller, bloodthirsty cousins. The Killers, more often than not, hunted in pairs, or even, with devilish cunning and combination, in schools; and in these schools we sometimes observed a female spouting with a baby bobbing up and down by her side – the baby doing about three blows to the mother's one.

A whale 'going through its spoutings' is a profoundly interesting sight. One first becomes aware of the presence of one in the vicinity by a loud, hollow-sounding blast, which can be heard for miles. On a perfectly calm day the stillness of the Antarctic is so vast that the voices of men talking in ordinary outdoor tones can he heard for a mile or more, and the blow of a whale can be heard for several. From Wind Vane Hill, Cape Evans, I frequently watched great Rorquals pass two miles behind Razorback Island, which is about three miles away, and heard them blow; and on one occasion, through my Zeiss glass, from the same vantage-point I saw one some distance beyond Cape Royds, which is seven miles away, and distinctly heard it breathing – the sound of each expiration reaching me many seconds after the appearance of the spout.

The larger the whale the greater the spout and louder the blow; and the blow of a Rorqual has quite a different note from that of a Killer. Each blow of a full-grown Killer whale lasts for a second – it takes exactly sixteen pictures on the kinematograph to illustrate it, and the machine runs at sixteen pictures to the second – but a Rorqual's blast lasts half as long again. The evolutions of a large Rorqual when breathing are very regular and rhythmical. First, the top of a huge black head appears above the water; this is instantly followed by the warm breath spout, which rises ten or twenty feet, and then spreads out and quickly condenses away. According to the distance of the whale, the spout is sometimes seen a second, or many seconds before it is heard. Following the spout, as the great animal describes an arc of half a circle with its body, one sees the upper part of the neck and back just tip the surface; then a small, black dorsal fin emerges and disappears, and that is all, until the process is repeated some seconds later. Rorquals sometimes spout without showing the dorsal fin at all, and the flukes, or caudal fins, never appear; doubtless they are depressed during the process to act as steering-planes.

The period between the expirations varies, according to the size of the whale, from twelve to thirty seconds, and I have counted as many as thirty-five spouts in succession. The period, however, is not governed only by the size of the whale, but also by its proximity to ice. Out in the open water the interval is longer than when the same whale is skirting ice-floes.

Once, I saw an eighty-footer Blue whale rise by the glacier edge, and then coast along so close to the ice that part of its bulk was in the undercut. It headed straight for the ship, and, as the water was crystal clear and the sea unruffled at the time, I could see it below the surface nearly a hundred yards away. It blew twice as it approached, and appeared to be travelling at about six knots an hour. As it swerved away from the ice to avoid the ship, it passed almost under the counter, and I leant well over to observe more closely. It was swimming not two yards below the surface, and rose right under my eyes to blow again. I saw the blowhole open, and felt the blast of its fishy breath in my face, and vapour with a strong oily smell enveloped me. I noticed that the spiracle (blowhole) was divided by cartilage into two sections, like the nostrils of any other mammal. It opened the moment it broke surface, and I could hear the loud hiss of the inspiration that followed; then it closed and the head was immersed. The total period of exhalation and inhalation was about three seconds. After watching this operation at such close quarters, I surmise that spray is frequently mingled with the breath, as in agitated water I have no doubt the spiracle opens before it actually breaks surface, and any water above it is blown upwards. Hence, no doubt, the origin of the old whaling term 'spouting.'

The big creature had beautiful, clean-cut lines, the greatest breadth not being more than eight feet – about a tenth of its length – and I could not detect the slightest movement of its propelling members; it seemed to glide along without any effort whatever. As it reached the edge of the firm ice ahead, it rose higher than usual – as whales always do before sounding – and then disappeared. There was a long opening in the ice, about thirty feet wide, just south of the Tongue, and here, a minute later, the whale rose to continue its spoutings, as though revelling in the sunshine and exhilarating air. When it had reached about the middle of the lead, it humped its back, as though about to sound, and submerged, as I thought for good. But not so. It suddenly appeared again, not, however, to blow, but to 'breach,' or leap into the air. The huge creature shot clean out of water, all dripping and shining in the sun, and fell back into the sea with a splash that could be heard for miles, sending waves far and wide over the ice.

I rushed my kinematograph as near as I could to the scene, in the hope that the sportive monster would repeat the exploit. What a subject for a moving-picture! A hundred tons of living, glistening flesh, projected twenty feet into space through an opening in the ice! But though I waited expectantly and hopefully, with my camera focussed on the lead for nine consecutive hours – never stirring from the spot from noon till nine p.m. – the whale did not appear again.

I never succeeded in getting any moving-pictures of a Rorqual spouting near the ship, but some fine records were secured of Killer whales doing so. Though the Killer is so much smaller than the Blue whale, its dorsal fin is much larger, that of the male being of isosceles triangular shape, tapering to a point, and sometimes as much as five or six feet high. The dorsal fin of the female is much smaller, less pointed, and slightly curved. Killers will frequently swim just below the surface, with only their dorsal fins showing above water. Once we saw a pack of them cruising thus, their menacing fins looking like murderous weapons mysteriously moving along the surface of the sea. It was a sinister sight – knowing, as we did, the evil record of the owners below.

I have made further remarks about these Huns of the ocean in my observations 'Concerning Seals.'

We saw a great number of Lesser Rorquals, which are fish-eating whales, about thirty feet long, with hooked dorsal fins. They lacked, however, the interest of either of their congeners above described.

To those who may be interested in the great sea mammals I would advocate a visit to the Whale Room at South Kensington, for one may there learn much about them. One may see how the Right whales – which are the only cetaceans bearing whalebone in sufficient quantities to pay for hunting them for the commodity – are fitted by Nature to feed only on the smallest sea creatures; whilst the Cachalot, or Sperm whale, can prey on some of the most fearsome monsters of the deep. The jaws of the Sperm whale are filled with enormous teeth, and it lives on the gigantic cuttle-fish that exist in the ocean depths. But we saw neither Sperm nor Right whales in the Antarctic; they frequent more northern waters.

The *Terra Nova* now proceeded to the western side of McMurdo Sound, to disembark the party who were to examine the geological structure of the mountains of Victoria Land. They were geologists Taylor and Debenham, physicist Wright and Petty Officer Edgar Evans. We landed them on the ice near the Ferrar Glacier, at the base of the range of mountains which are seen in such magnificent panorama from Ross Island. The sloping cliffs of the foothills, eroded by the glacial action of ages, were an impressive sight as we drew near them. But so high were these lesser hills, that Mt Lister and the other giants, which brush the skies fifty miles further inland, sank inversely as the foothills rose, and were lost to view ere we had crossed much more than half the Sound. I should much have liked to visit this region; but to illustrate these fine mountains with justice would have taken many weeks, and there was equally important work awaiting me at Ross Island.

Taylor and his merry men were in high spirits with the weather, the scenery and their prospects as they started for the Ferrar Glacier. Their programme was to explore it and the bordering hills for fifty miles inland; then travel round the south end of the Sound and finish at the Discovery Hut, to which the Southern Party would also return after completing their depôt laying.

Having landed the Western Party, the ship returned to Cape Evans, where I disembarked for good, my work on board now being finished. There was yet another party to be considered, the Eastern Party. They were under the leadership of Lieut. Victor Campbell, and numbered six all told, the others being surgeon Levick, geologist Priestley, and Petty Officers Abbot, Dickason and Browning. They were to proceed to, and endeavour to land and winter on King Edward VII Land – some four hundred miles to the eastward, at the other end of the Great Ice Barrier.

Ten days later the *Terra Nova* returned to Cape Evans, and Campbell reported that on sighting King Edward's Land they had found the way barred by impenetrable pack and bergs, with inaccessible ice-cliffs beyond. Thus, landing there being impossible, he had decided to prospect for a suitable wintering place on the Barrier itself. On rounding a promontory and entering the inlet which Shackleton had named the Bay of Whales – from the numbers of these creatures which frequent that locality – to their amazement they found Captain Amundsen's ship, the *Fram*, berthed alongside the ice. On boarding her, they learnt that the Norwegian explorer had established winter-quarters on the Barrier, some three miles from its edge. After spending a day with the Norwegians, as two rival expeditions could not advantageously operate simultaneously from the same base, Campbell had decided to return to Cape Evans to report this information, and then to proceed northwards to Cape Adare, in Victoria Land, and winter there.

Captain Amundsen's Expedition left Norway with the expressed intention of exploring the North Pole. It was not until after it had proceeded to sea, and all Scott's plans were known to the world, that the news was received that the Norwegian explorer had changed his, and would endeavour to anticipate Scott in reaching the South Pole. Even so, it was Scott's belief that Amundsen would endeavour to reach the Pole from the western side of the continent, instead of coming into his own sphere of operations. It was therefore a great surprise to us when the *Terra Nova* returned to Cape Evans with the news that Amundsen was on the Great Ice Barrier.

Before proceeding northwards the ship came in as close to the shore as was advisable, to disembark two ponies which had been allotted to Lieut.

Campbell's party, as he would now have no need of them. Owing to the shallowness of the water, the ponies were lowered into the sea some distance out, and had to swim ashore with a boat to tow them. The shivering animals were each made to drink half-a-bottle of neat whisky on landing; but one of them never recovered from this, and his previous experience in the gale in the Fifties, and had to be shot a few weeks later.

There was no time to be lost; so, as soon as the ponies had been landed, our shipmates bade us all farewell, and pulled off. We stood on the shore watching them until the boat was hoisted aboard. Then the good ship dipped her ensign, and, with three blasts of her whistle in salute, she stood away to the northward.

With mingled feelings we watched her disappear into the distance, for we should see her no more for nearly a year. With what keen expectation we should then look for her again! The old ship was our one connection with civilisation and home, and those dear ones from whom we were now cut off by thousands of miles of the most perilous of the seas. With what tidings would she come again? Momentous events might happen in a year. History would be made; kingdoms might even fall in that great striving world so far away. But our friends would look for news of us as anxiously as we should later look to hear of them. That fine old vessel, now northward-bound, would relieve as much anxiety on her voyage homeward as she would allay for us when she came south again. It was now her mission to bear tidings of a little band of adventurers, who, in one of the most remote corners of the earth, strove to maintain the honour of their country in the cause of Science. May it be the destiny of the *Terra Nova* ever to serve as deserving a cause.

The adventures of the Eastern Party – which henceforth became known as the Northern Party – and of the Southern and Western Parties are set forth in the second volume of *Scott's Last Expedition*; but there is room for many books about an enterprise such as this: each separate party has experiences and adventures quite different from those of others.

My object must now be to recount my own experiences on and about Ross Island, whilst the three exploring parties were radiating in various directions.

CHAPTER X

The Barne Glacier and Cape Royds

The direct route from Cape Evans to Cape Royds, when the sea is frozen, is only a matter of seven miles across the ice; but the sea was now open and the waves were washing the foot of the Barne Glacier ice-cliffs. I decided to make this journey immediately, and the only alternative was to go via the glacier itself, which had been traversed but once previously. The distance by way of the glacier is about twelve miles, but it was not my intention to make the journey in one day, as, besides photographing, there was other work to be done en route.

The party now at our winter-quarters Hut numbered eight. They were meteorologist Simpson, biologist Nelson, engineer Day, mechanic Lashly, Clissold the cook, Hooper the steward, Anton the Russian groom, and myself. It was arranged that Nelson, Day and Lashly should accompany me; so we made our preparations that evening for a ten days' absence, and the next morning started off after an early breakfast.

At the base of Cape Evans there is a steep glacial moraine, two hundred feet high with a slope of about 45°, which Captain Scott had named The Ramp. Our sledge and some 700 lbs. of equipment had to be portaged up the slope, which has a loose surface of rough volcanic rock; this was fairly hard work, so some of the others lent a hand. The summit of the moraine is of broken blocks of lava for a distance of a quarter-of-a-mile, amongst which there are many glacial debris-cones ten to twenty feet in height. At the edge of this moraine we planted a twelve-foot bamboo pole, with a silvered glass ball at the top – the object of the ball being to reflect a bright spot of light from the rays of the sun, which could be seen for miles. This was the base-pole from which we were to lay out a row of stakes across the glacier, the purpose of which I will later explain. Leaving the moraine, we struck out on to the ice, and the first three or four miles being easy enough, we made good headway with the laying of the stakes, one of which was planted every two hundred yards and carefully lined up with its predecessors.

As the sun alternately shone brightly and then passed behind clouds, it helped or impeded our progress over the uneven surface of the snow-encrusted ice. In the sunshine, any rise or hollow, no matter how slight, was clearly indicated by its shadow; but when the sun was obscured the whole surface became dead, shadowless white, so that it was difficult to tell whether the next step would be on higher or lower ground. We were continually dropping into holes a foot deeper than expected, or else striking sudden, unexpected rises, either of which caused uncomfortable jolts and stumbles. One's sensations on these occasions were exactly the same as, when descending stairs in the dark, there is still another step when one thinks the end of the flight has been reached; or vice versa, when ascending, one thinks there is yet another step when there isn't. But a ray of sunlight transformed everything. With the passing of each cloud such perplexities disappeared, and the going was easy enough, except when periodically we encountered heavy *sastrugi*, which are irregular raised patches of hard wind-swept snow. The runners – which slipped easily enough over smooth snow or ice – would cling tenaciously to these patches, so that frequently we had to put forth our utmost united effort to move the sledge.

Eastwards, lay miles of icy slopes, above which the smoking Erebus squatted complacently, its lofty crest gleaming in the rays of the sun. As we gradually rose to some seven or eight hundred feet above sea-level, the views over the Sound were magnificent, with bird's-eye aspects of Cape Evans and Cape Royds, which are rocky promontories about half-a-mile, and a mile in length. At the end of Cape Barne there is a remarkable volcanic formation terminating in a lofty pillar of lava, which is the core that solidified in the vent of a once active crater. We found, later in the season, that this pillar was a much more striking sight when viewed from the frozen sea.

In the middle of the afternoon we got into trouble. The ice was badly crevassed in places, and we found ourselves in a maze of dangerous pitfalls – blind chasms bridged over with snow. Some of these bridges were very thin, and I became aware that I was on one when, leading and piloting the sledge, I suddenly broke through to my armpits. It is not a pleasant sensation when the ground under one's feet gives way, and one brings up with a jolt that nearly dislocates the shoulders, and finds body and legs dangling in space which may terminate perhaps a hundred yards below. Lashly – who is an old Antarctic traveller, having been with Scott on the *Discovery* Expedition – seemed to think I had broken through out of inexperience. He asked to be allowed to take the lead, which I handed over to him; but he also broke through a few minutes later. The bridge – or 'lid,' as it is called – of a crevasse usually has quite a different appearance to a snow surface on firm ice; but one cannot afford to be off one's guard for a moment when amongst them.

Should one member of a team disappear – as happened more than once to the Southern Party – the strong sledging harness invariably holds him up until he is hauled out by his companions.

Covered crevasses can usually be distinguished easily enough when the sun is shining; but it is vastly more difficult to detect them in cloudy weather. They should always be crossed at right angles. Sometimes these bridges are yards thick, and then they are safe enough; but often they are only of a foot or two of snow, or it may be a matter of inches only. One tests this by probing with a ski-stick. If a crevasse be only a few yards wide and the bridge be strong, a sledge-team may string across it in single file quite safely; but if it be wider and the stability of the bridge open to suspicion, a narrower place must be sought. To attempt to cross a wide crevasse obliquely is to court disaster; should the heavy sledge break through, it would precipitate the whole team to the bottom of the abyss. We had to proceed with caution, and it took the best part of an hour to get clear of the place. Another half mile then brought us to the north edge of the ice.

Having crossed the glacier, two miles of undulating lava hills lay between us and Cape Royds. Here we fixed another twelve-foot bamboo pole with a glass ball, as before. There was now a continuous line of stakes across the glacier, the object of which was to test the movement, or flow of the ice. Observations made a year later showed that all the stakes had moved forward, those in the centre of the line having advanced nearly twenty feet. The face of the glacier, however, presented no apparent change during the fifteen months that we had it under observation, though masses of it, but not bergs, broke away from time to time.

The forward movement of a glacier is caused by the intermittent precipitation of snow, the weight of which forces the front of the glacier bodily into the sea, and masses of it fall away, or float off periodically in the shape of icebergs. Not all the icebergs met with in the Ross Sea and Antarctic Ocean are born of the Great Ice Barrier; thousands of bergs are discharged annually from other floating ice-shelves and from the numerous land glaciers, such as the Barne, which line the coast of the Antarctic continent wherever there are mountains.

We pitched our tent that evening just beyond the edge of the ice. To have hauled the sledge any further would have ruined the runners, as the rest of the journey was over rough lava.

The next morning we portaged our baggage and equipment – transporting everything save the tent and camping gear, which we should not require, on our shoulders. Back Door Bay is well known by name to readers of Sir Ernest

Shackleton's *Heart of the Antarctic*; it lies between the base of Mt Erebus and Cape Royds. Could we have crossed this bay we might have saved ourselves a lot of trouble; but we had to carry our burdens laboriously around it, as it was now open water. We came across plenty of evidence of the late human occupation of the vicinity; but the hut itself lies in a sheltered valley, and we were almost on it before it came into view. The photographs that I had previously seen of it had impressed themselves on my memory, and when I saw the hut for the first time I seemed to have known it for years. A fair-sized 'cabin,' as one would call it in America, littered around with packing-cases, in a valley sheltered by black lava hills – with a frozen lake, a stranded iceberg in the offing, and a distant view of the Western Mountains – was the picture that met our view as we stood on the summit of the rise.

As I passed through the doorway into the place that Shackleton and his comrades had known as 'home,' I thought of that wonderful journey – the greatest feat at that time in the annals of Antarctic exploration – on which Sir Ernest, with three companions, Dr Eric Marshall, Frank Wild and Lieut. J. B. Adams, had, without any support after the first week, penetrated the Great Unknown to 88° 23' S. – ninety-seven geographical miles from the Pole – having traversed a distance of about seven hundred and fifty miles in seventy days; and I entered this simple dwelling-place with a feeling akin to awe.

The interior was all disarranged – things thrown about in confusion, showing that the former occupants had left in a hurry. So, as we were to make this our abode for the next ten days, we set to work to get the place shipshape and more comfortable. There were stores of food of all description in and around the building, and Lashly soon had a welcome hot meal steaming on the galley. Though we kept the stove going, we found the hut very cold, for it was badly planned; the floor being raised several feet above the ground, the biting winds and frost had access to every side of the structure. We realised that the 1907 Expedition had lived under conditions of discomfort unknown to us in our snug, commodious house at Cape Evans – which was all the greater credit to them for the splendid work they did there.

I have read in books that there are no germs in the Polar regions; that colds and such afflictions are unknown. My confidence in such reports was somewhat shaken during the ensuing twenty-four hours; for, whilst lying in my thick reindeer-skin sleeping-bag that night, I caught an awful cold, and for the whole of the next day, which was dull and stormy, I suffered from paroxysms of sneezing. After that experience no one will ever convince me that microbes cannot stand the rigours of those regions. No doubt they had been imported there, perhaps in some clothing, and had been disturbed, and perhaps annoyed, by our moving things about. In such latitudes only the fittest germs survive, and those that made of me their unwilling host that day were certainly the most robust and energetic of their kind I have ever entertained. A day later I had recovered from their onslaught sufficiently to get on with my work.

It was now the middle of February, and we found very few penguins on the rookery that Shackleton's biologist, James Murray, had made so well known. It was too late in the year; the breeding season was over, and the young chicks were shedding their down and just about to take to the water, whilst such of the old birds as still remained were beginning to moult. I should have to revisit the place in November, when thousands would return here to breed again.

We found Cape Royds a more interesting locality than our own cape – which was comparatively featureless. The end of the promontory is quite rugged and picturesque, with steep volcanic cliffs, and an icy coating which must vary in aspect with every storm that sends the waves dashing against the rocks, to fall in spray, and freeze as it falls into ever-changing ice-forms. There were fine views from the end of the cape, and during the time of our visit one Barrier fragment – the vertical cliffs of which were clean cut as though sliced with a knife – remained aground about two hundred yards off the point. I imagine that in spring-time, when the ice is breaking up, this place must be a fine vantage-point from which to view the procession of bergs that march past daily, a few hundred yards from the land. None passed during our stay, as this was not the time of year for bergs to parade these waters – most well-regulated icebergs being by this time well on their northward voyage to dissolution. Only two, the one now off the point, and another in Back Door Bay, remained; these, fortunately for me, having added a further year to their existence by stranding on the rocks. I felt duly grateful to these sole survivors, for they helped out well in the composition of several pictures.

There were many interesting localities and sights at Cape Royds. Sandy Beach, a rock-bound bay with a sloping shore, a mile away to the north-west, was a place where seals loved to roll about in the breakers that curled and thundered into foam on the smooth volcanic sand; and there were frozen lakes embedded in the desolate hills. One of these, Blue Lake, had been so christened by Shackleton's Expedition because of the vivid colour of the ice – which was bright ultra-marine, and resembled a frozen pool of water that had been coloured with washing blue. Green Lake was of an almost equally brilliant hue, but emerald. Then there was Clear Lake, which was frozen solid, and both ice and water were of crystal purity. A fine curved reach of coastline had been named Horseshoe Bay, and was rugged as the wildest parts of Cornwall. Another small indentation in the shore, by the penguinry, had been named Dead Horse Bay, because one of Shackleton's ponies had died there. Strange to relate, the body of that pony was still there on our arrival – coated with ice and floating amongst the rocks. Stranger still, when, the day after I discovered it, I went down to make a snapshot of that pony's body, lapped by the waves, to my amazement it had disappeared! For three years it had remained. Not even the wild storms of this tempest-tossed arm of the sea had carried it away, yet the night of our arrival the corpse departed! It seemed incredible; and, half doubting my own senses, and wondering if I had dreamed about the pony, I enquired if my companions had seen it. They had; and Day, who had been a member of the Shackleton Expedition, informed me that this was the unfortunate that had given the bay its name. This strange circumstance can only be accounted for by the long-reaching arm of coincidence, or by reasoning that the sea is open here for only a few of the calmest (!) months of the year, and that the previous night had been very stormy.

On a Polar expedition any fresh specimen of animal life that may be discovered is an event of importance. When, as I was prospecting with my camera one morning at the end of the cape, I espied a weird-looking creature in the shallow water near Dead Horse Bay, I was therefore not a little elated. Shouting excitedly for assistance to Lashly, who was some distance away, I scrambled down the rocks to endeavour to cut off the visitor's retreat into deep water. But it made no effort to escape; it seemed to be in a comatose condition, as though half-frozen. It was a pink, pulpy-fleshed creature with a number of tentacles, which I recognised as a small octopus, about five feet from 'tip to tip.' We had no difficulty in capturing it with our ski-sticks, and bore it back triumphantly to Nelson, who welcomed it as a valuable addition to his biological collection. He had discovered a large jar of spirit in the hut soon after our arrival; and in this the find was immersed for preservation.

The Back Door Bay iceberg provided us with a fine entertainment one day. We were all in the hut having our mid-day meal, when we were startled by a loud rumbling sound, like the roll of distant thunder. We rushed headlong out into the open, and up to the summit of the hill, fully expecting to see the great volcano, twenty miles away, bursting into action. But the crater was at peace. The thunder was coming from the tabular berg aground in the bay, which was slowly crumbling into pieces. As we watched, great slices slipped one by one from its sides and, as they fell, smashed up the sea-ice that had formed since our arrival. Crack after crack opened up in the berg, and slab after slab of ice fell away from it as though some unseen, resistless force were at work sending the great cube to its destruction. As they fell into the water the fragments rolled over and over, bursting asunder again and again, until the bay for hundreds of yards around was scattered with a mass of floating debris, whilst a mist of ice crystals floated o'er the scene. The final phase of this remarkable phenomenon was a mere truncated obelisk with a few sculpture-like formations around a spreading base – all that was now left of what, a few minutes before, had been an immense cube of perhaps a million tons of ice.

What would I not have given to have known that such a spectacle was about to occur, so that I might have had my kinematograph bearing on the wonder? But it was all over in five minutes – five minutes of one of the most remarkable sights I had ever witnessed.

We found scores of magazines and illustrated weeklies in the hut. In some numbers of the *Sphere*, and the *Graphic*, and the *Illustrated London News*, I came across many reproductions of my pictures of tropical lands. Little had I imagined, when I took those photographs, that I should one day find them under such different conditions of climate, in a part of the world which at that time I had no thought of ever seeing, I brought those pages back, as souvenirs of my visit to one of the most famous places in the Antarctic.

It was now time to be off home again. So we 'packed' our gear on our shoulders the two miles to the sledge; slept that night in our tent on the moraine, and in fine weather the next morning made an early start, reaching Cape Evans after an uneventful journey the same evening.

CHAPTER XI

The Freezing of the Sea

Stormy weather, which developed into a southerly gale, followed on our return from Cape Royds; when the blizzard ceased there was a remarkable marine effect to be seen at the end of our cape.

The gale had blown much water out to the open sea; but the water was now filling the Sound again, coming in with a great swell which, as it neared the shore, worked up into long rollers that curled over and dashed with a thunderous roar against the stranded ice-blocks. The waves were coming in from the north – against the wind, which was in the south – and as each incoming roller began to feather, a long mane of spindrift streamed out yards behind in the breeze. It was a beautiful sight; but it did not last long, and we never saw anything like it again.

The spray from the breaking waves was blown far and wide, and as this mist froze as it fell, the end of the cape soon became filigreed with arabesques of ice and fringed with icicles. These effects provided some beautiful subjects for the camera.

My wanderings were now confined to circumscribed limits until the sea should freeze again, and I had to make the most of such chances when they occurred. It was not easy to find material for scenic compositions. One could not walk more than half-a-mile in any direction except the Barne Glacier, which was featureless and uninviting; and on the cape there were only hills of coarse black lava, and a few uninteresting snowdrifts.

There were curiosities, however, amongst the distorted volcanic rocks. Some of the kenyte blocks had been weathered into remarkable forms by the cutting action of the particles of sand that are constantly being driven by the wind; and by the erosion of the climate, which has a disintegrating effect on the rocks as they become warmed by the summer sun after the extreme cold of winter. One of the most grotesque of these shapes was a monolith of kenyte, fashioned by these agencies into the similitude of some weird prehistoric animal – an antediluvian beast half bird, half toad, which had wings, legs, a head, beak and eyes. It resembled an armadillo more than any other modern creature, and we christened it The Polarosaurus.

The geologists were much interested in this curiosity, and, as kenyte lava is very brittle, exhorted all not to injure it.

Other curious features were a number of conical hillocks, not unlike the dolmen mounds of the Stone Age to be found in the British Isles. These were at first thought to be parasitic cones of Erebus, or offshoot blowholes from the main vent of the volcano. But investigation of several of them proved that they were either heaps of morainic debris, carried and dumped off at these places by some glacier ice that had long since disappeared, or the remains of huge weathered boulders.

There were several ponds among the hills on the cape, where the Skua-gulls had been accustomed to bathe; but these were now frozen solid, and the cascade, to which I have previously referred, had trilled its silvery lay for a few days only after our arrival. Ten months hence, when these waters were free again, I hoped to find some camera subjects there.

The sea was perfectly clear round the coast, and in places off the cape ice had formed on the sea floor, whilst there was none on the surface. Some of the rocks that lay several fathoms deep were thickly covered with white ice, yet others adjoining them were free from it. Captain Scott was much interested when, later, I reported this information, as he never had an opportunity of observing this phenomenon.

There were plenty of seals about. From the cliffs, I often watched them gliding sinuously along, searching for the fish that lurked among the rocks. Whenever ice-floes drifted in under the lee of the land, or there was no wind, the clumsy creatures would laboriously work themselves on to these rafts, and snooze for hours in the feeble sunshine. There was a sandy stretch of shore at a place we called West Beach, where seals sometimes came to loaf and bask and sleep – occasionally remaining dormant in the same spot for a day or two.

About ninety yards from the Hut there was a hill, about seventy feet high, on the summit of which Simpson had arranged a meteorological screen with some of his instruments – a barograph, a thermograph, registering thermometers, wind gauges and a sunshine-recorder. This latter was a glass ball which focussed the sun's rays to a point of light. Whenever the sun shone, this point of light burnt a hole in a paper record, marked with the hours, which encircled the ball. The paper remained intact during such periods as the sun was obscured by clouds; but the intervals of clear sky were duly burnt into the paper in a series of dots and dashes. From now onwards this instrument was certainly not overworked, and in a few weeks it would be free to take a vacation of about four months.

The anemometers, however, had a strenuous time of it. They attended strictly to business, and were seldom idle; their cups when not whirling madly were at least spinning merrily for the greater part of the year, for Antarctica is the most wind-swept zone of the earth.

The registering thermometers showed little variation now between maximum and minimum each twenty-four hours; by the middle of March we were enjoying (?) zero temperatures night and day.

Wind Vane Hill, as this elevation was named, commanded a wide prospect. I visited it daily, and from this vantage-point, one day early in March, I observed a long string of icebergs sailing up from the south. This was such an unprecedented occurrence, that I searched with my glass to find from what part of the Sound they were originating. To my astonishment, I discovered that Glacier Tongue had broken away for about half its length. I ran down to the Hut with this remarkable information, which was received with incredulity. All hurried to the hill, only to find, however, that my report was correct. Two miles of the ancient ice peninsula, which had existed in its former state for unknown years— perhaps for ages – had broken away, and was drifting out to sea. As we watched the fleet of bergs slowly cruising northwards towards the Ross Sea, with Killer whales spouting around them, we thought of what might now have been our predicament if an error of judgment had been made.

Captain Scott had seriously considered establishing winter-quarters on Glacier Tongue, when it was found impracticable to land at Cape Crozier. But the idea had been abandoned in favour of Cape Evans, because in his opinion the latter locality offered better shelter, and also was in other respects more suitable for our purpose, as well as being safer.

Had we built our house and landed all supplies on Glacier Tongue, the whole Expedition might have perished, either by drifting out to sea, or else, having lost our house and stores, from exposure and starvation. Fortunately for us all, our Leader's judgment had been sound.

There are some volcanic islands south of Cape Evans – the Delbridge Islands. One of these, Inaccessible Island, was so named because it can only be approached when the sea is frozen, and is not easy of ascent even then, as its coast is exceedingly steep. Another, Tent Island, looks not unlike a tent, but was so named because a party once camped on the ice under its lee, during the *Discovery* Expedition. A third, Razorback, is a long, narrow ridge of rock with a sharp, serrated summit. The most distant was Lesser Razorback, about four miles away. These islands are not picturesque; but the vicinity of Razorback became of much interest to me eight months later, as seals frequented the sheltered side of the island to bring forth their young.

About this time the Sound began to show signs of freezing, and it was interesting to watch the process. As the cold wind smote the water, which was of a much higher temperature than the air, clouds of vapour arose therefrom, as though the sea were steaming. This phenomenon is known as 'Frost-smoke.' The vapour, as it condensed, froze in the air, and fell back in minute particles of ice into the sea; also, as the wind agitated the water into spray, this, too, froze and formed into slush, which speedily congealed into solid ice as soon as the wind subsided. Then again, when the sea was still, needle-like crystals could be seen forming under water, and tiny flat crystals also; these would float to the surface and quickly freeze to each other, forming thin frozen discs. If no wind came to disturb them, these little discs – about the size of a dollar – would rapidly increase in size and become 'pancakes', which soon froze together, forming larger ones. As the pancakes grew bigger and lay in contact with each other, crystals would shoot across and knit them firmly, until the whole surface of the water was covered with a mosaic of little floes – like the parts of a jig-saw puzzle – gradually fitting themselves together. So, Jack Frost worked; and in calm, zero weather, in a single hour I have seen an inch of ice grow over a mile of the sea. Then would come the wind, and break up all this delicate fabric before it had gained sufficient strength to offer any resistance. When the wind subsided, the process would begin all over again; and so it went on until there came a day when the whole of McMurdo Sound was locked in the embrace of the Frost King. But for weeks the ice kept forming on the sea and breaking up again.

Early in March, I made this entry in my diary: 'Owing to the wind last night, all the new ice has gone this morning.' Then followed a three-days blizzard from the south-east. When it ceased I proceeded to the south side of the cape with my camera, prospecting for subjects showing new ice-features along the shore. I found that the spray from the waves, which, during the blizzard, dashed against the ice-foot in South Bay – as an indentation in the coast hereabouts was named – had frozen into very beautiful forms: deep, irregular furrows, as though the ice had been turned over by a gigantic plough. It was impossible satisfactorily to account for this strange formation: why the spray should have been deposited and frozen so irregularly, seeing that the surface had been comparatively even before the gale. Beautiful though the ice furrows were, they were anything but a blessing in other respects. Several feet deep, and exceedingly difficult to traverse, they completely barred the way to carrying heavy apparatus further round the shore. It was not easy to move amongst them even with hands free, as they all sloped towards the sea and narrowed at the bottom, so that one's feet got wedged in them, and the ankles badly wrenched. Thus, my peregrinations became still more circumscribed, and I was more than ever anxious for the sea to freeze, so as to have wider fields for exploration with my cameras. Besides, too, the light was rapidly failing, and before the end of April the sun would disappear altogether for a third of the year, putting an end to all such work until September.

During March, from time to time large icebergs would sail into the Sound, and as often sail out again with the change of the tide; but occasionally individuals would cruise about for a day or two before departing. To my gratification, towards the end of the month several picturesque specimens took the ground half-a-mile off our cape. They had probably stranded on a submerged reef, for our soundings had shown the depth thereabouts to be two hundred fathoms. I observed them anxiously each day, fearing they might drift away before the ice was strong enough to imprison them. If they were held, they would later provide some fine photographic subjects. Though occasionally they swung a few degrees with the tides and currents, the jagged rocks had bitten deep and retained their hold. It was not, however, until the middle of April that the ice, which alternately formed and broke up again, was strong enough to enable me to walk out to visit them; but by that time the fast disappearing daylight was too weak for such photography. I should have to look forward to dealing with them when the sun came back in the spring.

During the weeks that the Southern and Western Parties had been away, we had frequently wondered and discussed what might be befalling them. Each day I ascended Wind Vane Hill, to search Hut Point for any signs of life. Near the end of March I detected, with my Zeiss 12 X glass, several figures moving about on the snow, and was able to announce to my companions in the Hut, that some, if not all, of the party were there. They would have to wait until the ice was strong enough to enable them to traverse the intervening fifteen miles of sea that separated them from us. As previously stated, it is not possible to reach Cape Evans from Hut Point by land, as a great part of the coast is impassable glaciers.

We endeavoured to signal to them by means of a smoke cloud, made by burning wet hay, to let them know we were aware of their presence, and that all was well with us; but at the time we made the signal, no one appeared at their end, and the effort failed. Further attempts were made later, when the weather was clear, but these, also, were unsuccessful.

There was still much open water between Cape Evans and Hut Point; but we knew that if the ice held these open spaces would soon close, and then it would only be a matter of a few days for it to become sufficiently firm to enable our friends to attempt the journey.

The direct route over the sea-ice would take them at least eight hours, with all conditions in their favour. We knew that, however anxious they might be to get home, they would not risk such a dangerous journey lightly; for one never knows what weather a few hours may bring forth in these regions. We considered they would not make the attempt until the ice was of a minimum thickness of ten inches inshore, as, should a blizzard overtake them on the way, their predicament might otherwise be perilous.

On the 12th April, with the 'mercury' at zero, a south-easterly blizzard raged, with thick drifting snow. In the comfort of our well-conditioned home we were glad to think that the ice – which close to the beach in our sheltered bay was not yet nine inches thick – could not be strong enough out in the Sound for our comrades at Hut Point to have made the attempt to reach us, and to have been caught in the storm. What, therefore, was our amazement? when, just after breakfast the next morning (the blizzard having ceased), Lashly, who had gone outside, burst into the Hut, shouting excitedly: 'There's a large party coming round the cape!'

The incredulity with which this announcement was received was speedily dispersed by his earnestness, and, rushing in a body out into the open, to our astonishment we saw nine bulky figures approaching the Hut, dragging two laden sledges behind them. With their unkempt beards, they presented so remarkable a change of appearance that we recognised them with difficulty. We greeted them warmly as we peered into their bronzed faces; they were Captain Scott, Lieutenants Evans, Bowers and Gran, geologists Taylor and Debenham, physicist Wright, and Petty Officers Evans and Crean. It was good to hear their voices again and to know that all were well, and that the rest of the Southern and Western Parties were safe at Hut Point, waiting for the ice to get strong enough for them to bring the dogs and ponies across the fifteen miles of sea.

Greetings over, the party exhibited no bashfulness about expressing their immediate wants, which, as they had, hours ago, exhausted the rations with which they had started out, not unnaturally centred in the direction of the larder.

Clissold, the cook, as soon as he heard of the party's approach, surmising that the call upon his resources would not be a light one, got busy with his pots; and, with a rapidity that did him much credit, prepared great dishes of porridge and scrambled 'Truegg,' jugs of steaming cocoa, and plates of bread and butter for the famished wayfarers, who lost no time in disposing of this goodly fare. Then, their tongues loosened by tightened waistbelts, their interests became less self-centred; and, in response to the hail of questions to which they were subjected, they related something of their doings and adventures. They had a remarkable tale to tell, and first we extracted from them the story of their most recent experiences. It seems they had started two days previously; but owing to the insecure state of the ice near Hut Point – which region is swept by strong currents – they had made the first eight miles of the journey (as far as was possible) by land. They had then descended on to the sea-ice, and proceeded to Lesser Razorback Island, where, the difficulties thus far having been much greater than expected, they had been compelled to camp for the night.

Being overtaken by the recent blizzard, they had perforce to remain there for thirty-six hours, until the storm abated. It had been an anxious time, for, in the expectation of making the entire journey in a day, they had not provided themselves with any emergency rations. During the blizzard they had been compelled to strike camp, and change its site from the ice under the lee of the land, to a shelf on the weather side of the island, where they would at least be safe from the danger of being precipitated into the sea in the event of the ice breaking up. There, they had spent a second night, during which, Captain Scott told us, 'the noise of the wind sweeping over the rocky ridge above our heads was deafening; we could scarcely hear ourselves speak.' Fortunately, in the latter part of the night the gale abated, and they got under way soon after daylight; hence their appearance just as we were finishing our morning meal.

Temporary camp.

During the recital of these experiences, I had contemplated the picturesque and unkempt appearance of the party with satisfaction and approval, as suitable for richly enhancing my growing photographic collection. As soon, therefore, as I was able to lure them from the table, I took a group of them all, minus their windproof overalls. Having dealt with them thus collectively, I proceeded to gather them in individually in full Polar kit. To my intense disgust, however, Petty Officers Evans and Crean had clipped off their bushy, black beards before their turn came round, leaving only a lot of bristles that were sufficient to dismay any self-respecting camera.

Immediately these portraits had been taken, harsh sounds of razors scraping stubbly chins and cheeks filled the Hut; and the galley stove was kept busy during the greater part of the ensuing twenty-four hours melting ice for hot baths. The next morning, the party, clean and in clean clothes, presented such a conventional, well-groomed appearance that they were no longer of any photographic interest. But Griffith Taylor, with a lofty scorn for gibes, which added greatly to my regard for him, declined to sacrifice his 'Keir-Hardie' whiskers for anyone.

That evening was an interesting and memorable one. Over and over again, the newcomers were called upon to repeat the tale of their achievements and adventures. The Southern Party had experienced very severe weather, with frequent blizzards and low temperatures. Often the 'mercury' fell to 40° F. below zero, and these low temperatures had told severely on the ponies. The party had depôted a ton of stores on the Great Ice Barrier, at a place about 150 miles south of Hut Point, which they named One Ton Camp. They had returned to the *Discovery* hut, all well, on March 5th.

On the return journey, one of the dog-teams had escaped disaster almost by a miracle. In the uncertain light the team ran on to the snow bridge of a crevasse, which gave way under the weight, and the middle dogs disappeared. Osman, the leader, exerted all his great strength, and, digging his feet into the snow, managed to keep his hold until the sledge was dragged back to safety and securely anchored, when he was released. Scott told us that they had been actually travelling along the bridge of the crevasse; the sledge had stopped on it, whilst the dogs hung in their harness in the abyss, suspended between the sledge and the leading dog. Why the sledge and they themselves didn't follow the dogs, they never knew. He thought a fraction of a pound of added weight must have taken them down.

On peering into the depths, they could see the dogs hanging in all sorts of positions, and howling dismally. Two had dropped out of their harness, and could be discerned on a snow bridge, far below. After the strain on Osman had been relieved, Meares was lowered into the crevasse, to secure an Alpine rope to the end of the dog-trace. The animals were then hauled up, in pairs, until eleven of the thirteen had been recovered. The remaining two were 65 feet down. Scott himself was then lowered into the chasm; he found the snow bridge firm, and secured the two dogs, which were in turn hauled up, and then he was pulled to the surface. It had been a miraculous escape for him and Meares, and some of the dogs never recovered from the internal strain to which they had been subjected whilst dangling on the rope.

On March 1st, when within sight of Hut Point, another disaster had occurred, which, to quote Scott's words, 'bid fair to wreck the Expedition.' Bowers, Cherry-Garrard and Petty Officer Crean had left the Barrier to cross the sea-ice to Hut Point, when they found cracks ahead of them. It was necessary to retrace their steps, but the ponies were too done-up to return the two miles to the Barrier that night; the party therefore camped. They woke up in the night to find themselves adrift on a raft of ice which was splitting under them, and one of the ponies had disappeared. Packing the sledge in haste, they jumped the three remaining ponies from floe to floe until they reached a bigger floe near the Barrier edge – 'Killer whales meanwhile expectantly pushing their heads up on all sides. Luckily they did not frighten the ponies.'

In the morning Crean requested permission – which Lieut. Bowers granted – to endeavour to get across the heaving floes, to summon help. It was a desperate venture, but luckily successful. He met Captain Scott and Oates, who returned with him to the scene of the disaster. With the aid of an Alpine rope they dragged Bowers and Cherry-Garrard and the sledges up on to the Barrier. Then the ice began to move out again, before anything could be done to rescue the ponies. All that night they floated about on their ice-raft; but the next morning the floe had drifted near to the Barrier again. The rescue party then descended and tried to rush the ponies to safety; but one, Punch, in trying to leap a gap, fell in, and had to be killed with an ice-axe. Two ponies were left. 'We saved one, and for a time I thought we should get both; but Bowers' poor animal slipped at a jump and plunged into the water. We dragged him out on some brash ice – Killer whales all about us in an intense state of excitement. The poor creature couldn't rise, and the only merciful thing was to kill it. These incidents were too terrible!' – so our Leader told us, and wrote in his Journal.

Before they had finished the tale of their own adventures, the new arrivals were anxious to hear of what we had seen and accomplished. It was good to see the pleasure and satisfaction with which they 'took in' the comforts of the Hut (it had been a mere shell when they left), and I was glad to note that all were much interested in my dark-room, which I had built and equipped in such spare time as I had been able to devote to the purpose.

Four days after the return of the party, Captain Scott and seven others went over to the *Discovery* hut with supplies for those who had remained there. They soon came back, reporting all well, and Dr Wilson returned with them. But not until three weeks later was the ice strong enough off Hut Point for the dog-teams and the two ponies to be brought across. Meares showed excellent judgment in declining to take any risks with the surviving transport animals, on which so much now depended.

CHAPTER XII

Farewell to the Sun

By the middle of April, the sea had frozen from Cape Evans to Hut Point, and nearly to the snout of the Barne Glacier, a league to the northward. We were, therefore, no longer confined to the limits of our promontory; but were free to investigate the scenery and phenomena for many miles about us. Whenever the weather was clear, the dominant feature of the region was the great volcano at the hem of whose flowing skirts stood our home. The mountain was a never-ceasing source of interest to us. Rising from the Ramp – the steep scarp of moraine, about half a mile from our door – Erebus glided, at first almost imperceptibly, and then by a rapidly steepening slope up into space, until its rounded, snow-clad crest seemed to brush the sky. In the sunlight the mountain was sometimes a marvellously beautiful sight. During the fine weather which prevailed for a week after our arrival, the precipitous glissade below its crater rim, polished by the rays of the sun, had gleamed each evening like a beacon in the cobalt heavens. Now, in the rapidly waning daylight, as the red orb dipped behind Victoria Land, and, unseen, traversed the western arc of the horizon, the lofty dome of the great Erebus – two and a half miles above us – caught and held the rays for hours after its lower slopes had become all pink and violet and silver-grey. As the sun sank lower, the brilliance of this radiance dimmed, until it became a glowing ember in the darkening skies. Then, late in the afternoon, this ember would suddenly dwindle to a spark, which burnt for but a moment; and when this dying glimmer was extinguished, we knew that Mt Lister, Erebus' rival in the Western Mountains, had intercepted the rays of the sun, and that the beacon would shine no more that day.

With the sinking of the sun, the massive substance of the great volcano dissolved into a ghostly outline in the purple ether: a shadowy mist-like shape which, with the fall of night, would often slowly change again to matter – a coal-black silhouette – as the silvering east foretold the rising moon. And then the moon crept up and sat awhile upon the mountain's crest.

But Erebus was an interesting neighbour, not only because of its grandeur. The steam-cloud, that perpetually hovered above its crater, was, to our meteorologist, a vane which infallibly indicated the direction of the higher air-currents. Sometimes this cloud drifted away to the southward, and sometimes it bore to the north; at other times its course was eastward, but only once I saw it blow to the west whilst we were on Ross Island. When the cloud bore eastwards, it was, of course, invisible to us, as we were at the mountain's western base; when, therefore, no steam cloud could be seen, it was safe to assume that the wind at the crater's lip was westerly.

In summer the volume of this vapour was greatest, for, as the weather became colder, it diminished by reason of the rapid condensation. Often billows of grey smoke would mingle with the steam, forming wondrous lights and shadows, and occasionally great convolutions of deep black fumes would swirl up from the crater's lungs, and roll fifty miles towards the Pole.

But, interesting as Erebus was as a wind vane, Dr Simpson had brought scientific equipment for observing air-currents, upper as well as lower. He had provided a number of small balloons made of gold-beater's skin, of a capacity of one cubic metre when fully inflated. Periodically, he would fill one of these balloons with hydrogen gas, which was made by immersing hydrate of calcium in water, in a generator of his own design. The ends of two strands of fine black silk (wound on reels containing ten miles) were tied to a small black parachute, to which a very light instrument was attached for recording the temperature and altitude. When all was ready, a slow-match fuse was ignited, the object of which was to burn through a short thread which held the parachute to the balloon, after a certain time had elapsed, and detach it, so that it fell. As the balloon ascended, it unwound the two silk threads from the conical reels, which were contained in a box with holes on the top through which the thread paid out. The balloon was then watched through a telescope, and its course recorded. When in due time the match detached the parachute, the little instrument was borne safely to the ground, and was easily discovered by following the trail of the black thread over the ice.

By means of these balloons, the air-currents were investigated to a height of as much as five miles. Although on more than one occasion the parachute was lost, the experiments were generally successful; the little instrument was usually recovered, and proved to have done its work, having recorded the temperature and pressure. The course of the balloon sometimes showed that the upper air-currents were directly contrary to those at lesser altitudes, and on one occasion the balloon's movements were so erratic that, after zigzagging about to all points of the compass, and unwinding several miles of thread, the parachute dropped within a few hundred feet of the spot from which it had started.

Simpson was the wizard of our little community. In a cave in a small glacier at the foot of Wind Vane Hill – which he and his assistant, physicist Wright, had excavated with the object of obtaining a more equable temperature – he had installed one of the most interesting of his instruments, the magnetograph. This apparatus was operated by clockwork which, once in each twenty-four hours, revolved a drum, round which was rolled a band of sensitised bromide paper. The grotto was lighted by a small electric lamp, the rays of which were projected on to three small mirrors (suspended from magnets), and, being reflected therefrom, penetrated through a slit in the instrument, forming points of light on the paper band. As the drum slowly revolved, an inch per hour, these points of light, influenced by the three magnets swinging on horizontal and vertical axes, made a latent photographic record (in the bromide paper) of the lines of magnetic force. Simpson accepted my offer to relieve him of the daily task of developing the records, and I always looked forward expectantly to seeing what form the curves would take. These magnetic records were probably the most valuable of all the mechanical scientific data secured by the Expedition.

Similar observations are made in the principal observatories of the world; for why the earth is a magnet, and why its magnetism is constantly changing, are problems as yet unsolved, as also is the mystery of magnetism itself. These problems can most profitably be investigated nearest the Poles.

In addition to his cave, Simpson had also a small hut at the foot of his hill. It was divided into two compartments, in one of which he charted the form and movements of clouds with the aid of a *camera obscura*; and in the other, which was heated with a small coal stove, he incarcerated himself for several hours each week to make 'absolute' calculations with a magnetometer, to check the instrument in the ice grotto. These researches, however, by no means marked the limits of our meteorologist's activities. Besides his apparatus on Wind Vane Hill, he established three other screens with self-registering thermometers: one on the Ramp; a second out on the sea-ice, half-a-mile to the north; and a third on the ice about two miles to the west of our cape. These instruments were examined and their readings taken daily, freedom from blizzards permitting.

Simpson also established telephone communication between his cave and the Hut, and later with Nelson's shelter at his biological hole out in the ice; still later in the season, he laid a telephone wire on the frozen sea, connecting our Hut with Hut Point, fifteen miles distant.

When Dr Wilson returned from the *Discovery* hut, he had reported wonderful colouring in the sunsets he had observed there, of which he had made a number of coloured sketches. We certainly saw no such vivid sky effects at Cape Evans, though the two points were only fifteen miles distant from each other. There was colour in our sunsets, but it was much more delicate than he described. We had, however, some lovely afterglows.

Messrs Lumière & Co., of Lyons, had presented me with a number of boxes of Autochrome plates for photographing in natural colours, though they did not hold out much hope that the plates would retain their qualities for more than a few months. The plates were really too old to obtain satisfactory results by the time I had an opportunity of using them on the beautiful afterglow effects we had in the autumn, and they had deteriorated in the slow journey through the heat of the Tropics. But though the cloud formations were unfortunately nondescript, I secured some very interesting records of after-glows with these plates.

Dr Wilson's modus operandi, when sketching, was of interest. In zero temperatures he could not, of course, work with the brush, either in water-colour or oil; and he had little affection for pastel. He therefore used his pencil. Even so, this necessitated the use of bare fingers; so, removing his thick dog-fur 'mits,' he would work for a few moments in woollen mittens, until his fingers began to chill; then he donned his mits again to warm them, and this process was repeated until the sketch was complete. Memoranda for colouring were pencilled on the margin of each sketch, and indicated by pointers. These sketches were by no means rough, though they were always drawn again from the original, in much fuller detail, before being coloured at leisure in the Hut, by the aid of acetylene light. Wilson's pencil work, not intended for colouring, was always finished in detail on the spot. Many of his drawings were artistic gems.

It was not until the third week of April that the ice was safe enough to enable me to walk out to inspect the icebergs that had grounded three-quarters of a mile from the end of our cape. By rare good fortune, one of these bergs was the most picturesque we saw during the Expedition. I had contemplated it with interest each day since its arrival: at first with the apprehension that it might slide off the reef that held it, and sail away before the sea froze; then with the fear that the storms, that broke up the ice, might free it, and blow it out to sea. Now I had the satisfaction of knowing that it was frozen in fast; but there was no longer sufficient light to photograph it successfully. There were two main portions of the berg, separated by a bridge of ice, the span forming a perfect arch. I walked through this arch, and found that it framed an enchanting view of Erebus. One part of the berg resembled a mediaeval castle – keep, bastions, crenellated parapet and all. As I carefully took in all its structural beauties, I realised that it would form material for many a fine camera study when the sun came back.

Near the berg I came upon a solitary Emperor penguin, wrapped in meditation. I regretted having to intrude upon his reflections; but the demands of science and the larder were inexorable. So, after we had exchanged short speeches and a few ceremonious bows, I apologetically slipped a noose about his chest, and conducted him protestingly hutwards.

On April 22nd, the reluctant sun peeped begrudgingly over the top of the Barne Glacier, slid along the ridge for half a furlong, and set. That was the last we saw of old Sol for four long months! The next day was the date of his actual departure, but the glacier hid him from our view. The disappearance of the luminary marked the advent of a brief period of soft, semi-twilight days – days that are a lasting recollection to every Polar traveller. The sun, as he meandered below the horizon, caused a blue earth-shadow to envelop the Sound – a pallid, cadaverous shade, which turned the spectral icebergs green. Above this chill, mysterious, rayless dimness – which was neither morning, afternoon nor evening, but near akin to those sweet moments which in the Tropics intervene between the dawn and sunrise – soft, timid, pellucid hues – blue-grey, and rose, and pink, and amber – merged and intermingled; then slowly metamorphosed into night.

Such transitory daylight hours as now we enjoyed were shyly iridescent with this colouring; and it was on such a day Gran ciceroned Taylor and me to see the wonders of some caverns he had discovered in the ice-cliffs in South Bay.

On arriving at the scene, Gran pointed out his find with elation. The glacier face hereabouts was 150 feet sheer, and Taylor at once pronounced the caverns to be the exposed ends of crevasses; then naively remarking: 'This seems a more sensible way of entering a crevasse, than dropping into it,' he and I followed Gran through one of several gashes in the precipice, and found ourselves at the bottom of one of those deadly pitfalls, to keep out of which has hitherto been the endeavour of all who ever visited these regions.

Although the ice floor of the grotto was level with the frozen sea, the walls exhibited no signs of recent water-action; they were broken and irregular, and encrusted with ice crystals. Above us, the chasm was almost closed by masses having fallen in from the walls, but it extended further into the glacier than any of us cared to venture. There was little if any colouring, except the most delicate of green in places; but, on cutting with an ice-axe into some pockets near the entrance, the most beautiful blue light imaginable filtered through and filled the cavities. They glowed and flamed with colour. If the bare hand were held in one of these cavities for a moment – one could not hold it so much longer – the hand turned azure.

Our visit to this remarkable grotto was so interesting that I conducted Captain Scott and Wright, our ice-investigating physicist, there next day. They were both delighted with this latest find in Jack Frost's wonderland, and I photographed them examining it, with the aid of flashlights.

As soon as the sea was permanently frozen, biologist Nelson established an experimental station about a mile out on the ice. Here he spent much of his time, weather permitting, repeating each day unpleasant, wet and messy operations, which involved lowering various devices to the bottom of the sea, and then hauling them up again. The hole, through which he carried out these experiments, froze at least a foot per day, and the ice had first to be removed with a pick. As it was very hard, this took time. It was unfortunate for Nelson that the warming exercise thus entailed came at the beginning, instead of at the end of his job, as the ensuing operations were not exactly of a blood-circulating nature.

Having opened the hole, he would first drag up the net he had set the previous day, and strain and bottle such diatoms and animalcule as it contained; next, he lowered thermometers to test the temperature at the sea floor and at various depths; then he dropped his 'water-bottle' to secure a sample from the bottom, and, finally, before departing, set his nets preparatory to repeating similar operations the next day. Later, in comfort in his lab', he would submit the result of his catch to microscopical examination, and write his reports. Nelson's experiments showed that the sea-water maintained a constant temperature of +29° F., even when the ice was many feet thick, and the temperature was seventy or eighty degrees lower above it.

Amongst his numerous appliances, 'gadgets,' he called them – windlasses, water-bottles, current meters, sounding devices, nets, townets, trawls and other things – Nelson had brought the essentials for a fish-trap. These, when assembled, formed a long, cylindrical-shaped affair, made of a framework of iron rods covered with wire netting, the ends being truncated cones turned inwards, with a hole in the centre – like a fly-trap. Baited with some scraps of seal-meat, this snare was lowered through a hole in the ice to the bottom, about half-a-mile off the cape, and left there for twenty-four hours. Such fish as entered the trap and were unable to find the way out again, were captured. A number of a genus named *Notothenia* were so caught, occasionally as many as forty. When fried, they tasted not unlike whiting, and were a welcome addition to our table. Finding, however, that the catch soon fell off in numbers, we assumed that the seals had found the vicinity of the trap good hunting-ground, and gobbled up the fish that were attracted to it, before they were ensnared. Consequently, the location of the trap had to be changed frequently; each new hole being pierced about half-a-mile from its immediate predecessor.

Dr Atkinson took charge of these fishing operations – excavating the hole; opening it each day; securing the catch and rebaiting the trap, and then re-setting it. But one of the afterguard or the men always accompanied him to lend a hand. Sometimes I assisted at this operation myself, as it was exceedingly interesting; and once I took out my camera in the midst of the winter night, and made some flashlight photographs of Atkinson and Clissold hauling the trap to the surface. It was an intensely cold job, with the 'mercury'[1] at 42° F. below zero, as the preparing of the flashes necessitated the removal of my thick fur mits. Immediately after taking the picture, I had to hurry back to the Hut to restore the circulation in both hands, which had gone white and bloodless.

The trap sparkled with phosphorescence as it was pulled to the surface, and the catch was instantly frozen to death on reaching the air, which was at that time about seventy degrees colder than the water.

The Polar night crept upon us imperceptibly. With the departure of the sun there followed three weeks of gradually deepening twilight days, until, inversely as in December there had been little difference between day and night; now, the middle of May, there was little difference between night and day. Darkness encompassed the earth. We had witnessed the summer glories of the midnight sun. Now we were to behold the winter wonders of the midday night.

CHAPTER XIII

The Polar Winter

With the return, on May 13th, 1911, of the rest of the Barrier Party who had remained at the Discovery hut, our number was once more complete. There were now twenty-five, all told, in our abode, which was tenanted to the comfortable limit of its capacity. We had a full house. So, as henceforth we spent nearly six months in closest association under its single roof, I will endeavour briefly to describe our Polar home.

It was always called the Hut; but the usually accepted meaning of 'hut' conveys a somewhat misleading idea of our habitation. Certainly no such house had previously been built in the Antarctic. It was fifty feet long; twenty-five feet wide; eight feet to the eaves, and sixteen feet to the ridge. The framework was lined with two thicknesses of tongue-and-grooved boards, between which was a layer of dried seaweed, quilted in sackcloth. The outer side was also covered with two thicknesses of boarding, with seaweed insulation between. The roof was double-boarded, with a layer of a rubber and cork composition (called 'ruberoid'), and a layer of seaweed quilting between; it was covered with a thicker layer of ruberoid, and was lined with a single thickness of boards. In the centre there was a large ventilator.

The floor was double-boarded, with layers of felt and quilted seaweed between; it was covered with heavy linoleum, and volcanic sand was well piled up round the base of the walls to keep out draught. We certainly spared no pains to make our dwelling-place weathertight.

The Hut had two double windows, and at the west end there was a porch with two doors; in this vestibule there was an acetylene-gas plant which furnished light for about ten burners. The south and west sides were piled six feet high with a wall of stores; and a covered alleyway from the porch gave the cook access to these stores – which were of the commodities in most frequent demand – without going out into the open. There was a door in this wall of stores also, so that it was necessary to pass through three doors to enter the Hut; and it was customary to remove snow from boots and garments in this outer alley. From time to time, this storehouse was replenished by excavating replacements from the snowed-up stacks of goods outside. On the north side was the stable, the walls of which were made of bales of hay and rectangular briquettes of coal, and it had a 'lean-to' roof.

The interior of the Hut was divided by a wall, shelved for stores, into two large apartments, the second being about twice the area of the first. The first room, in which were the men's quarters and the galley, was known as the Mess-deck. Nine men lived and messed in this room; which was the warmest part of the building, as it was comfortably heated by the cook's range.

The second apartment, or Ward-room, had a long dining-table in the centre, on either side of which there was a three-feet passage-way. On the outer sides of this passage were open compartments, or cubicles, with sleeping-bunks – the bunks being light iron-frame spring-beds, with wool mattresses and blankets. Captain Scott and fifteen of his staff lived in the ward-room.

At the far end – the east end – of this room, I had been allotted sufficient space to erect a photographic dark-room. Being fairly handy with carpenter's tools, I had brought my own, so as to be independent of others, and during the summer I had built and equipped my laboratory when the weather was too stormy to work outside. It was eight feet long, six feet wide, and eight feet high. After boarding the framework, I covered the walls with ruberoid left over from our building operations, to keep out all light, and lined the room all round with two or three tiers of shelves. On one side I built a bench, covered with ruberoid, and at the end of the bench a thirty-inch, lead-lined sink was fitted. On the roof of this room – which was eight feet below the ridge of the roof of the Hut – a thirty-gallon iron tank was fixed, that I had brought for the purpose. A lead pipe, terminating in a swing tap, connected this tank with the sink – the fall from the tank to the tap being four feet, which gave an ample head of water for rinsing plates.

Under the sink were racks for developing-dishes, etc. Various things were also stored under the bench, including the kinematograph developing-machine, when not in use; and a small carbide-gas plant which generated my own light, independent of the Hut supply. Every available inch of stowage space was utilised, even the ceiling being covered with racks in which photographic gear was stored. My bed was so arranged that it could be folded up in the daytime against the lower part of the wall on the opposite side to the bench, where it was out of the way.

To obtain water, I would go out daily and get ice from the little glacier at the foot of Wind Vane Hill, melt it down in a 'cooler' on the stove, then mount a ladder and empty the water into the tank, through a funnel. Thus,

I always had plenty for photographic purposes, if used with care. The sink drained into a pail, which was emptied when necessary.

I devoted much care to building and equipping my compartment, and it was not only a comfortable laboratory and living-place for me, but it proved useful for other purposes. This room was always kept spotlessly clean and neat, for though I cannot claim excessive orderliness in other respects to be one of my redeeming points, yet in matters photographic untidiness is abhorrent to me.

On the south side of the dark-room was Dr Atkinson's parasitological laboratory, with a bench covered with test-tubes, microscopes, etc.; and on top of my room he had incubators for the culture of bacteria. Adjoining his bench was the physical laboratory, presided over by Dr Simpson.

Simpson's Corner, as we called it, was of constant interest to all, for there were self-registering instruments scattered about the numerous shelves, by which we could, at a glance, learn all about everything in connection with the weather. Clockwork ticked everywhere. There were barometers, thermometers, thermographs and a bewildering array of other scientific apparatus; and there were rows of electric batteries, and a petrol engine for running the dynamo which charged them – the petrol being fed to the carburettor from a tank outside the Hut.

Perhaps the most interesting, and certainly the most popular of all Simpson's apparatus was 'Dine's Anemometer,' a wonderful self-registering instrument which recorded each separate gust of wind, whether gentle as a zephyr, or of hurricane velocity – not that many zephyrs favoured us from now onwards. It had a vane at the top of a two-inch pipe which projected several feet above the eastern end of the Hut roof. This vane kept a nozzle at the end of the pipe, which revolved on a swivel, constantly pointed into the wind. The wind, rushing into this opening, passed through the pipe, which pierced the Hut wall and terminated in a closed cylindrical tank in Simpson's Corner. This tank was two-thirds full of paraffin oil; the end of the pipe rose above the surface of the oil, and over the pipe there floated a long, hollow, bell-shaped drum. A gust of wind, however light, entering the pipe would raise this floating drum, and also a rod attached to its upper end, which worked up and down through an opening in the top of the tank, like a piston. At the top of this reciprocating rod a barograph pen recorded its every movement on a chart on a cylinder, revolved by clockwork, which was graduated vertically and horizontally into hours and velocity. If for a moment it was calm, the pen so stated; and if a gust of eighty miles an hour raged over the cape, the moving finger leapt up to eighty, and recorded it.

This instrument was christened 'The Blizzometer,' and during the first gales that followed its installation, Sunny Jim, as we nicknamed our meteorologist, watched it closely, and was eager to inform us about the velocity of every violent gust. Blizzards became so frequent, however, and the instrument was so infallible, that its novelty soon wore off. There came an inevitable day on which, when a more than usually fierce gust shook the Hut, and a chorus shouted 'Where did that one go?' (although in those days we had not yet heard of Bairnsfather), Sunny Jim lost his customary luminosity, and exhorted us to go and see for ourselves.

The pipe through which the air passed to the blizzometer was just outside my own compartment, and when blizzards raged, the sighing and moaning and utterly unearthly sounds emitted by this tube at night were most depressing. They frequently rendered sleep impossible, and during the winter calm weather was the exception.

I have stated that my dark-room was at the eastern end of the building. Whenever the door was closed – as was necessary when developing, or changing plates – it became exceedingly cold. As no warmth could enter, the temperature would rapidly drop to about 36° F. Foreseeing the likelihood of difficulty in heating my room, I had brought a small oil-stove for that purpose; but I presented this stove to the sailors of the *Terra Nova*, as their mess-room in the ship was inadequately heated. For lack of sufficient warmth when the door was closed, the lower part of the wall at the end of my room speedily became a mass of ice, due to warm air condensing on the cold wall. I had to chip this baby glacier away with an ice-axe whenever it became six inches thick, which it did about once a week throughout the winter.

As the galley stove failed sufficiently to heat the ward-room, a coal stove was started in the space between the end of the dining-table and my dark-room. This was a great comfort to me, as several times before this stove was inaugurated my water-tank froze. Now, however, we were able to keep the Hut at about 52° F.; we found that any higher temperature was uncomfortable.

The corner opposite Simpson's, at the east end of the Hut, was inhabited by Dr Wilson, who spent most of his time throughout the winter months working up his sketches. Lieut. Evans also berthed there. He spent the winter drawing maps from local surveys, which he had made with the help of his Norwegian friend, Gran.

Because of the kindred nature of our work, I was drawn into closer contact with Wilson than with any other of my comrades. He would often submit his sketches to me, and sometimes he would seek my advice when he experienced difficulty in getting the effect he wanted. I remember how puzzled he once was over one of his studies of Mt Erebus. He could not get the mountain to look high enough. My experience in photographing mountains showed me what was wrong. He had given the sketch too much sky. Taking a sheet of paper I placed it across the top of his drawing, cutting off three inches, and immediately the mountain rose. He was quite pleased, and thought it remarkable that he had not thought of such a simple expedient himself.

It was my province to illustrate, amongst other things, the animal life about us. When, later, I was engaged on this fascinating work, my own affection for it was no greater incentive than the knowledge that the man whom I held in such high regard would be able to invest my pictures with the maximum of scientific information. Some of the animal habits recorded would have been a revelation to him – as they are to every zoologist who sees them – and I know what delight they would have given to Uncle Bill, had he lived.

Captain Scott's cubicle was the next. His 'den' was about eight feet by six; it had several shelves of books, which included a number of volumes on Polar exploration given to the Expedition by his friends Sir Clements Markham and Sir Lewis Beaumont. These were in demand by all. I shall have more to say about our Leader's environment later.

The most ornate of the cubicle compartments was that occupied by Nelson and Day, on the elaboration of which they spent a lot of time. The least pretentious was the large one where slept Bowers, Cherry-Garrard, Oates, Meares and Atkinson; it was conspicuous by its lack of any attempt at anything more than necessary comfort, and was christened The Tenements.

Opposite The Tenements, on the south side of the dining-table, was a compartment occupied by Taylor, Debenham and Gran. Whilst we were in Christchurch, I had cast longing eyes on a curtain in Mr Kinsey's laboratory, as likely to be useful in the South, and he had given it to me. Gran, seeing this curtain stowed away on one of my dark-room shelves, in turn fell in love with it, and begged it of me for their cubicle. I therefore lent it to them, and it was hung on a wire across the entrance to their abode whenever the occupants desired seclusion and freedom from the gaze of those in The Tenements opposite. Whereupon, Oates, scorning privacy and such 'effeminate luxury', as he characterised this fitment, compared their cubicle to an 'opium den', 'a ladies' boudoir', and various other things expressive of his contempt. To these gibes the tenants listened with grins of delight, and retorted that he needn't be envious because he hadn't got the only curtain in the Antarctic for himself.

Such good-humoured banter attended every domestic happening during the long months of darkness that we lived through together.

When the Hut had been finished, it was found that there would be room for the 'player' piano, and it had accordingly been unshipped from its cabin in the *Terra Nova*, and brought ashore in sections to be re-erected in our home. From now on it was in frequent use in the evenings; but, owing to its proximity to his bunk, Sunny Jim insisted that all music should cease by 9.30 p.m., as it was his habit to retire early, to enjoy a good book and a good cigar, a well-earned indulgence which, next to his work, he loved more than anything.

It was unfortunate that there was so little musical ability amongst us. Nelson could play the mandolin by ear; Anton, the Russian, occasionally gave us selections on the balalaika, and I had brought my banjo and a number of banjo-and-piano duets. As no one could play the accompaniments, however, these were never used.

Few seemed to have much idea of playing the pianola piano, and the audience were caused some occasional suffering, which was borne in silence. Two or three, however, notably Debenham and Cherry-Garrard, manipulated the controls well, and played with feeling and understanding. The piano, with its fine assortment of music rolls, was, in their hands, a source of enjoyment to all. It had been given to Captain Scott by the Broadwood Company; and, on the return of the Expedition, Lady Scott generously suggested its presentation to Lieut. Rennick, as a wedding present from his comrades.

We had also a fine His Master's Voice gramophone, which had been donated by the makers, together with several hundred excellent records. Only those who have lived away from civilisation and its comforts can realise the pleasure such an instrument gives to those in exile.

One of the indispensable members of our community was the cook. Clissold was a good cook; he was also a clever mechanic, and was called into consultation by our meteorologist whenever his electrical apparatus got out of order. When not engaged in his culinary duties, Clissold was sure to be absorbed with some ingenious device or other. The most remarkable of his inventions was a contrivance which he introduced in connection with the making of bread. Having mixed the dough, he would deposit it in a large pan near the galley stove to rise, and then retire to his bunk. On top of the dough he had placed a small metal disc, the object of which, when the contents of the pan rose to the requisite height, was to come into contact with another piece of metal, thereby completing an electrical circuit which rang a bell by his bed. Clissold then got up to do his baking.

As, for some reason known only to himself, he preferred to bake his loaves in the small hours of the morning, this bell roused not only the cook, but it also woke everyone else as well. Under these circumstances it was scarcely to be expected that the device would be popular for very long. It was tolerated for a time because of its ingenuity; but it was finally suppressed by a majority vote, only the cook polling in its favour. Not to be beaten, however, Clissold substituted for the bell a red electric lamp – which he wheedled out of Simpson – and henceforth it became part of the duty of the night-watchman to rouse the chef when this signal began to glow.

I am reminded to give some account of how we fared under Clissold's care. We certainly laid no great tax upon his skill, for our diet was as simple as it was wholesome. During the winter the steward called us at 8.30, and we breakfasted at 9, on porridge, bread, butter, marmalade and cocoa. Sometimes we had scrambled 'truegg'; and, whenever sport had been good with the fish-trap, we had fried 'notothenia', which, as I have already stated, taste like whiting.

For lunch we had bread and butter, cheese and cocoa – cheese being substituted by jam on alternate days – and we had sardines and canned lambs' tongues twice a week. For dinner we had always soup, of which there was an abundant assorted supply in tins; and seal meat appeared on

His Master's Voice gramophone and sled dog.

the table six days out of every seven, as a rule. The meat is quite palatable if well cooked and the seal be young, but it is dark and coarse-grained when full-grown. A young seal-steak, nicely grilled, is really excellent; the coarser meat always went into the stock-pot, and the joint was usually a roasted saddle. This was sometimes varied by seal steak-and-kidney pie, or slices of fried seal's liver, which was a delicious dish; whilst as for seal-liver curry – like Kipling's cinnamon stew of the fat-tailed sheep, 'He who never hath tasted the food, by Allah! he knoweth not bad from good.'

On Sundays, we always had roast mutton, from the New Zealand supply stored in an ice-cave at the base of Wind Vane Hill. Occasionally, too, the cook would pleasantly surprise us with mutton during the week; or with a ragout of stewed penguins' breasts, which, when served with red-currant jelly, savours of hare. Neither seal nor penguin flesh tastes fishy if all the fat be carefully removed before cooking. We grew very tired of seal meat, however, as we had so much of it, and were always glad when the seventh days came round.

We had a fine assortment of dried and canned vegetables – potatoes, sprouts, peas, beans, etc. – and two were always on the menu. The dried potatoes were especially good. There was always an excellent sweet of some kind – canned fruit and rice, rice and prunes, or milk pudding, or jelly. Our commissariat was remarkable for the vast quantity of pickles it contained. There were sufficient to supply ten times our number for about as many years. Most of those condiments are there still. One's taste does not run overmuch to pickles in such latitudes.

As it was imperative that every precaution should be taken against scurvy, lime juice and water was our only beverage – except on birthdays, when the non-abstainers were treated to a glass or two of champagne in which to drink the health of the 'guest,' who was allowed a bottle for himself and had to make a speech. A record was carefully kept – to ensure that no one had more than one birthday during the winter!

The night-watch had been started on the return of the first contingent of the Barrier Party from Hut Point. The after-guard took it in turn. The duties of the watchman were to stoke the galley fire; visit the stable occasionally to see that all was well with the ponies; attend to the acetylene-gas plant; and every two hours to record in the meteorological log the readings of the barometer in Simpson's Corner, and of a thermometer outside the south-east corner of the Hut, which was that most exposed to the prevailing winds. These meteorological duties had previously devolved upon Simpson, who, hitherto, had been roused every two hours by a reminder from an alarm

Captain Scott's birthday dinner, 6 June 1911.

clock. All were as glad to relieve Sunny Jim of this tax upon his slumbers, when their turn came round, as they were to be relieved themselves, during the intervening two weeks, of his alarm clock's toll upon their own night's rest. The night-watchman usually regarded the occasion as favourable to have a 'tub', for which he brewed hot water from ice on the galley stove.

Another, and often less pleasant obligation of the watchman was to keep a heedful eye upon the blizzometer. When blizzards raged, the nozzle of this instrument sometimes became clogged with snow, thereby shutting off all pressure on the floating drum, and causing the recording pen to fall lifeless to the bottom of the chart. The watchman would visit the instrument anxiously on stormy nights, for if the pen were 'dead' he had to clothe himself warmly, and, heading out into the driving blizzard, make his way round the Hut, climb a ladder, and with a wire brush clean out the snow that plugged the pipe. This was not exactly a joyful task, with the thermometer below zero, and gusts of sixty to eighty miles per hour buffeting his ribs. But it had to be done. If the job were shirked, the recording pen told a visible tale of neglect to Simpson, who knew well enough that, though a blizzard might burst upon us and work up to hurricane velocity in the space of ten minutes, it always died out gradually. Unless, therefore, he visited the blizzometer frequently, the night-watchman risked laying himself open to the charge of having been caught napping.

Still another of the watchman's duties was to take notes of Aurora each hour, and describe its appearance in the log. Long before continued darkness settled down, we had witnessed some fine displays when the sky was clear; and during the winter we often saw this bewilderingly beautiful phenomenon, the enchantment and mystery and awe-inspiring grandeur of which it is impossible to convey in words.

I was quite unable to secure satisfactory photographs of Aurora, though I had equipped myself for the purpose with the most rapid plates and lenses obtainable, and also with plates specially sensitised to green rays. With exposures of half-a-second stars of the magnitude of those of the Southern Cross developed out, but no trace of Aurora appeared. A fraction of a second exposure would have been necessary to secure a clear impression of the restless rays; but even exposures of a minute showed no sign of them, though the stars appeared as little streaks. Exposures of five minutes sometimes revealed a nebulous glare, of no scientific interest whatever.

I knew that photographs of Aurora Borealis had been secured by Professor Störmer in Lapland, with short exposures. When, several years after returning from the Antarctic, I visited the north of Norway in the autumn, I realised the reason of my inability to secure similar results in the Antarctic. The Aurora Borealis that I witnessed in Norway, though not so beautiful in its formations, was more luminous than the Aurora Australis we saw at Ross Island, and it seemingly took a higher spectroscopic line. I think we were perhaps too far south, in 77° 40', to see the displays at their brightest.

The investigation of Aurora has long engaged the attention of scientists in the north; but we were able to contribute little to what is already known about the phenomenon. The finest displays occurred when Simpson's instruments recorded periods of unusual magnetic activity, and it was interesting to note that they almost invariably originated in the south-east – opposite the Magnetic Pole, which is north-west of Cape Evans.

I have so frequently been asked how we managed to 'while away' the winter months, that I am convinced few, besides those who have been intimately associated with a scientific expedition such as this, have any conception of the work entailed. Never at any period, summer or winter, was there lack of employment for the energies of all.

The Petty Officers had sleeping-bags and tents to overhaul; sledges to assemble and repair; hundreds of provision-bags to make for the sledging journeys; footgear to make and mend, and a score of other jobs which kept them fully occupied from day to day, and every day the winter through. Anton had his 'hands full' to care for ten ponies under the superintendence of Captain Oates; whilst Meares and Dimitri found the care of two dozen dogs, and the preparation of their rations for the big journey before them, no easy task. Harness for both ponies and dogs had to be repaired, and new parts made; and a great deal of work was involved in protecting the dogs from the ravages of the blizzards. It was necessary that the ponies should be exercised each day, weather permitting. Each man who was gazetted to lead one on the Polar Journey in the spring looked after his own particular steed in this respect, so that man and beast might better know each other.

The cook was never idle. Hooper, the steward, kept the Hut swept and tidy; and had an interminable job in setting and clearing tables, in helping the cook with stores, and in lending a hand with his other messmates in continually replacing the water supply, by digging ice from the small glacier at the foot of Wind Vane Hill.

Taylor, our head geologist – or physiographer as he preferred to be styled – spent most of his time writing his diary and reports. He must have written volumes, in addition to working out maps from Debenham's plane-table surveys. He was also a ravenous reader and a merciless literary critic. Debenham, his associate – a quiet, tireless worker, beloved by all – was continually grinding and polishing specimens of rocks and lavas which he had collected on the Western Journey. It was interesting to watch the gradual transformation, in his careful hands, of a rough uninviting-looking fragment of stone into a beautiful section, with a surface worthy of enrichment by the carving of a cameo.

Physicist Wright spent most of his time investigating ice problems. I went into the subject of photographing frost crystals with him, showing him how to secure illustrations of his specimens by the aid of magnesium wire, and, later, coaching him in photographing ice-crystal formations in situ.

I have already mentioned the meteorological screens – with maximum and minimum thermometers, which Simpson had erected on the sea-ice and on the Ramp – and that these were visited daily, freedom from blizzards permitting. It was impossible for our meteorologist personally to inspect these stations daily, in addition to his manifold other duties; therefore all the afterguard assisted in visiting one or other of them. As these visits were not infrequently accompanied by some risk, it was scarcely to be expected that the uninteresting designations by which the methodical Simpson had classified the stations – A. B. and C. – would prove popular.

The unscientific ones speedily improved upon this alphabetical labelling, and personified the objects of their calls by christening them 'Archibald,' 'Bertram' and 'Clarence.' Archibald resided half a mile out on North Bay; Bertram a mile away on the Ramp, whilst Clarence sojourned on the ice, half-way to Razorback Island.

If the weather looked threatening, it was especially risky to visit Clarence, as, should a blizzard suddenly break upon anyone two miles from home, the chances of finding the way back to the Hut would be uncertain, to say the least. Clarence therefore received less frequent visits than did Archibald and Bertram. Our calls on Bertram entailed many a frostbitten nose, for the wind was keen where he rusticated at the summit of a debris-cone, 250 feet up, on the Erebus moraine above the Ramp. On reaching the screen, the 'highest' and 'lowest' temperatures were read by the visitor by the light of a fusee. Once I carried my camera up there, and by flashlight photographed Bowers and Wilson examining the instrument. It was a fearfully cold job, in a temperature of - 50°. One day in May, when Taylor and I walked out at noon to inspect the Arch Berg that lay about a mile off the cape, it was creaking somewhat ominously; we therefore considered it prudent not to approach too near, nor to pass under the arch. I examined it with a view of estimating the chances of successfully making a flashlight study of so huge a structure with such appliances as I had at my command. I thought it would be possible, if three or four separate flashes were fired to illuminate it. In view of the possibility of the arch collapsing, I decided to essay the feat at the earliest opportunity the weather presented.

That same afternoon at 5 p.m. a resounding crash was heard. Apprehensive of the worst, I ran out of the Hut, and could dimly discern in the gloom that my fears had been well-founded. The bridge had fallen, and the Arch Berg was no more. Somewhat dejected over the passing of this magnificent subject for the camera, I went to have a look at the ruins, and was greatly cheered to find that, though the arch had gone, the portion of the berg that resembled a castle was now a more perfect mediaeval fortress than ever. I decided to take no chances of further disaster to this fine subject; but it was a month later ere the weather was clear and calm enough to attempt to photograph it with any hope of success. A breath of wind would scatter the magnesium flash-powder (which was necessary to illuminate the picture) before it could be ignited.

On a comparatively mild day in June – that is to say when there was only about 50° of frost, and it was a dead calm – I took out my camera, and fired two flashes of eight grammes of powder, about one hundred feet distant from the part of the berg I desired fully lighted, and one flash for the part I desired to be more or less in shadow. This photograph proved a complete success, and is probably the only example in existence of a magnificent iceberg photographed by artificial light in the depths of a Polar winter.

That evening, at dinner, Captain Scott related, with much ardour, to us all, and more especially to our meteorologist, how, when he had been walking round Tent Island, he had seen three exceedingly brilliant flashes of lightning to the northward. As such a phenomenon was unprecedented, he wished Simpson to record the fact in his log. I listened with attention, and then asked him at what time he had witnessed the manifestation. As the time synchronised with my firing of the flashlights, I was reluctantly compelled to tell him so. He was disappointed to be 'done' out of being able to record a remarkable happening, but he enjoyed, as much as anyone, so good a joke against himself.

It is interesting to note that, at the time, he was about four miles away from where I fired the flashes, and on the far side of an island several hundred feet high. He considered the incident of interest, as illustrating the possibility of signalling at long distances with such a simple contrivance.

Early in the winter, the subject came up for discussion as to how we could employ our evenings in the most popular and profitable manner. Captain Scott was of the opinion that a series of lectures would be of interest to all. This suggestion was received with approval, and a programme for a 'lecture season' embracing a wide range of subjects was drawn up, after volunteers had been called for and had offered their services.

Dr Wilson led off after dinner one evening, with a discourse on 'Antarctic Flying-birds,' a subject on which he was one of the foremost living authorities. He illustrated his remarks on gulls and petrels, great and small, with diagrams and sketches, and told us many interesting things about them. Other talks that he gave us from time to time were on 'Penguins,' 'Whales,' and 'Sketching'. Simpson lectured on various subjects, the study of which came within his province – 'Halos,' 'Aurora,' and other meteorological phenomena; Taylor gave us some splendid chats about 'Geology,' and so did Debenham. Wright discoursed on 'Physics'; Nelson on 'Biology'; Atkinson on 'Parasitology'; Evans on 'Surveying'; Oates about 'Horses'; and Meares gave us a wonderfully interesting yarn concerning his travels in Lololand, in Central China. Bowers told us all about 'Polar Clothing' and 'Sledging Rations,' and was remarkable for the amount of humour he got out of such prosy subjects.

Simpson always managed to make his lectures entertaining to all, by practical demonstrations showing how certain physical phenomena could be produced artificially. And Taylor could tell us more in an hour about Physiography and Glaciology than we could have absorbed in months of reading on such matters. Moreover, he had a very interesting way of telling his story.

Captain Scott's contribution concerned his plans for the Polar journey; he also gave us a masterly essay on the Great Ice Barrier, which showed how deep was the thought and study he had devoted to the subject.

Scott always took the chair when others lectured, and afterwards he invited all in turn to comment on any points they might desire elucidated. There was often a good deal of banter in these discussions; and the comments frequently brought forth more information which it had not occurred to the lecturer, being thoroughly au fait with his subject, to impart.

My own co-operation in these evenings consisted of half-a-dozen lectures about my travels in foreign lands, illustrated with lantern-slides. I had brought my own lantern with me – a most ingenious and compact one that I had bought in California several years before – and about five hundred lantern-slides of the Far East, made from my own negatives, and coloured by Japanese artists during my long stay in Tokyo. I was glad to find that these slides were much appreciated; and I believe getting back into the world again, for an occasional hour or two, had a healthy effect. My first lecture was on 'Burma and Ceylon.' It was good, amidst all this eternal snow and ice, to see palm trees nodding to pellucid, tropical seas; 'Elephants a pilin' teak in the sludgy, squidgy creek'; Burmese girls smoking their 'whackin' white cheroots'; golden pagodas gleaming in the noonday sun, and a hundred other scenes aglow with the colour of that fascinating East that always called me so strongly – and calls me still – to remind us that all the world was not ice and snow and science.

Subsequently, I gave other lectures on 'Peking and The Great Wall of China'; 'Flower Festivals and Customs of Japan'; 'Japanese Temples and Scenery'; 'Across Northern India' and 'Switzerland.' Scott and Wilson were particularly interested in my story of Japan, and they resolved to visit that charming country at the earliest opportunity. Uncle Bill even got me to make out his itinerary, and he spent a lot of time studying my book,[1] *In Lotus-Land*, as a preliminary.

In May, a notice had been posted up announcing that the third volume of the *South Polar Times* would be published on Midwinter Day – two previous volumes having appeared during the *Discovery* Expedition. All were invited to send in anonymous contributions in the form of prose, poetry or drawings, which were to be deposited in the 'Editor's Box' under the notice. From that time onwards there was a noticeably more studious and preoccupied air about the occupants of the ward-room, and it was not difficult to divine who of our number had literary aspirations, dissemble though they might. Cherry-Garrard, the Editor, had a strenuous time for three weeks in June, carefully typing the MSS. he had accepted.

Midwinter Day, June 22nd, was our 'Christmas,' and it marked our sounding the depths of the Polar night – for it was now two months since the sun had deserted us. This day – which was of course night so far as light was concerned – came in the midst of the only week of continuous calm we had throughout the winter. The mercury stood at 37° F. below zero.

At tea that afternoon, Cherry-Garrard – whose kind ones at home had furnished him with boxes of all sorts of delicacies, which from time to time he generously brought forth for the enjoyment of all – produced a colossal cake, which was freely sampled by everyone with expressions of gratitude and approval. Cherry's masterpiece was then disclosed, *The South Polar Times*, on which he had spent weeks of patient, unremitting care. It was a Crown Quarto volume, cleverly bound by Day with 'Venesta' three-ply board, carved with the monogram S.P.T., and edged with silver-grey sealskin.

Cherry had typed its fifty pages faultlessly, and many of the contributions were beautifully illustrated with water-colour sketches by Uncle Bill. Most of the prose took a comic turn; but some of the verses were of a serious nature. Some photographs which I sent in had been accepted; also the following lines – with the idea of which I had been inspired whilst listening to an argument on the best way to use a sleeping-bag:

> There seems to be a difference of opinion amongst us as to the most satisfactory way to use a Sleeping-bag. It may almost be said that there are 'Sides' on the subject, hence the following:

> On the outside grows the furside, on the inside grows the skinside;
> So the furside is the outside, and the skinside is the inside.
> As the skinside is the inside, and the furside is the outside;
> One Side likes the skinside inside, and the furside on the outside.
> Others like the skinside outside, and the furside on the inside;
> As the skinside is the hard side, and the furside is the soft side.
> If you turn the *skinside* outside, thinking you will side with *that* Side,
> Then the soft side, furside's inside, which some argue is the wrong side.
> If you turn the *furside* outside, as you say it *grows* on that side,
> Then your outside's next the skinside, which for comfort's not the right side;

For the skinside is the cold side, and your outside's not your warm side,
And two cold sides coming side-by-side are not right sides one Side
decides.
If you decide to side with *that* Side, turn the outside, furside, inside;
Then the hard side, cold side, skinside's, beyond all question, *inside-outside*.

Captain Scott read each article aloud, and there was much guessing over the authorship of the contributions. Gran was, I believe, the only one to suspect me of having perpetrated the above infamy.

Space forbids me to quote other articles that concerned my comrades. Moreover, to do so would be to trespass too much on the kindness of Messrs Smith Elder & Co., who published an edition of the entire volume in facsimile.

Before dinner, a brisk walk on the sea-ice, in the crisp invigorating air, gave some of us a pleasant perspective in which to view our cook's efforts to do honour to the occasion; and he had risen to it nobly.

The Hut had been entirely transformed from its customary appearance, by the draping of Union Jacks and sledging-flags, and we sat down under festoons of bunting and coloured and embroidered silks to a feast, the bounteousness of which seemed almost incredible after our customary simple fare. A specially excellent brew of seal soup was followed by a huge sirloin of roast beef (from our store in the ice-cave) and Yorkshire pudding, with Brussels sprouts and potatoes. Those who have never been deprived of it for many months have never relished the national dish of Old England as we did that day. It was food for the gods! Then a huge plum-pudding, all a-fire, was borne in, arm high, to a chorus of joyous shouts. There were hot mince-pies, raspberry jellies, pine-apple custards, crystallised fruits, bon-bons, chocolates and other dainties galore; and, for that one evening only, champagne followed ad lib. We toasted our Leader, who replied in a short and appropriate speech, emphasising the fact that this day we had reached the 'half-way house' in the plans of the Expedition. Then we drank to the Northern Party, and lastly to Sweethearts and Wives!

A Christmas tree was then brought in from the mess-deck, where it had been produced that morning by Bowers and the Petty Officers, safe from prying eyes behind a tent-cover. It was cleverly constructed of sticks and Skua-gulls' feathers and coloured paper, and was decorated in the customary manner and hung with presents for all – for which kind thought our thanks were due to Dr Wilson's sister-in-law, to whom many a hearty good wish went out that day. Bowers rose to the occasion finely, and distributed these little gifts amongst us with many humorous remarks, amidst uproarious merriment. Then, after the company had been photographed, the table was moved aside, so that I might show about a hundred lantern-slides which I had prepared from my negatives of the Expedition. The company were in a mood to receive each of these topical pictures with a generous round of applause. They were a real 'hit.'

Great dishes of snapdragon next came on the scene, and when we had enjoyed them to the full, the gramophone started up a dance, which – if the truth must be told – was performed by some with underpinning more than a trifle unsteady. Under the influence of rum punch the fun became fast and furious; but two of the afterguard, who were suffering from over-indulgence in the pleasures of the table, had retired to their bunks and were now lost in slumber.

The cook, becoming romantic, had burst into song somewhat early in the festivities; but under the stress of the occasion his remarkably comprehensive repertoire had narrowed down to a single ditty which ran to two lines only, repeated over and over again, and of which the chorus – which nobody joined in – was the same:

And while he was chasing the girl round the room,
He was chasing the girl round the room.

And while he was chasing the girl round the room,
He was chasing the girl round the room.

After calling out 'Chorus. Fifteenth verse,' and getting as far as 'And while he was chasing' somebody stopped him; otherwise he might still have been 'chasing the girl.'

Petty Officer Evans became reminiscent; whilst the mind of the Irishman, Keohane, ran to his native politics, and he sought vainly for either an opponent or a sympathiser with whom to exchange views. Growing over vehement, he was taken in hand by Oates, who tactfully led him to more timely subjects. Another Petty Officer who, before turning in, had wandered outside – perhaps for a moment's solitary meditation under the stars, on the folly of human weaknesses – was found reposing on the snow, clad only in his underclothes and sleeping-suit, in 40° below zero, and had to be resuscitated. Fortunately for him, he had been in this predicament for a few minutes only.

It was nearly 1 a.m. when someone reported: 'There's fine Aurora beginning!' Hastily donning my warmest clothing, I left the now waning saturnalia and went out into the sweet fresh air, and was immediately followed by Captain Scott and several others. We stood together, spellbound, as we watched the grandest and most awesome spectacle the heavens paraded during the entire time we were in the South.

A greenish glare was growing out of the east, silhouetting the snowy Erebus into a black, forbidding mass. From the midst of this glare great rays shot upwards to the zenith, and wandered, like searchlights, among the constellations – incessantly moving, never pausing for a moment in any particular spot. Then yellow flames came out of the eastern fire, streamed above the ridge of the Barne Glacier, and trickled along it for miles. They leapt up into the skies and sank again, and rolled in billows down the great volcano's slopes – just as molten lava might have rolled; then suddenly they flickered out, and all was dark once more. But only for a minute. Out of the darkness came forth light again. The ghostly beams flared out and searched the vault of heaven, and from the skies above us luminous tasselled curtains unfolded, whilst resplendent streamers softly grew, and beckoned to each other. Again and again they came and went, and waxed and waned, and ebbed and flowed in waves; then a delicate flush suffused the flowing draperies, rippling from end to end along their undulating fringes, and timidly dissolved away. In the final tableau of this lovely transformation scene the draperies, too, broke up, and, dispersing into little groups, hung from the shimmering firmament in clusters. Never for a moment still, the mystic, evanescent radiance came from nowhere, crept and pirouetted about the arch of heaven, and vanished into nothing, leaving only the faint lustre of the stars to pierce the indigo of the Polar night.

It was a marvellous inauguration of a season, which, as Scott wrote: 'For weal or woe must be numbered amongst the greatest in our lives.'

CHAPTER XIV

The Return of the Sun

Just before the rise of the new moon on the 27th June, at eleven o'clock in the morning, three of our number set out into the midwinter gloom on one of the bravest adventures ever undertaken in the cause of science. They were Dr Wilson, Lieut. Bowers, and A. Cherry-Garrard; and their objective was the region where the Great Ice Barrier joins the precipices of Cape Crozier. This place was known to the *Discovery* Expedition to be a breeding-place of Emperor penguins; and the object of the present journey was to study the nesting habits of these primitive birds, about which no information had, hitherto, been available to science.

The gales, which had made our Hut tremble during the preceding weeks, had failed to shake the determination of these stout hearts to embark upon this perilous enterprise. They were provisioned for two months and expected to be away about six weeks. They lined up beside their heavy sledge for a flashlight photograph to be taken; then they bade us a cheery farewell, and, with several willing volunteers to help them on the first few miles, they pulled off into the darkness.

But for that new moon which was to light them on their hazardous way – But I must tell the story in its proper sequence.

You will remember the previous mention I have made of the meteorological screens which Dr Simpson had erected in several places, for comparison with the readings of the instruments at the main screen on Wind Vane Hill. We were inclined to regard somewhat lightly the risk of visiting these stations in 'thick' weather. One evening we missed Surgeon Atkinson at dinner, and enquiry revealed the fact that he had told Taylor at 6 p.m. that he was going to visit Archibald – the screen in North Bay. Taylor advised him not to do so, as the drift was beginning to blow; but Atkinson had persisted, saying he would easily find his way back by facing the wind.

Fresh snow does not necessarily fall during a blizzard. The gale, sweeping over the vast plains of *nevé* (hard wind-beaten snow), picks up and carries along minute particles of old snow – finer than powdered salt – and it is these minute particles that form the blinding clouds of 'drift,' in which it

Lieutenant Bowers, Dr Wilson and Apsley Cherry-Garrard.

is frequently impossible to see anything more than a few feet distant, even in broad daylight. Sometimes this drift is not more than five to fifty feet in height, and the sky may be perfectly clear and the sun shining brilliantly above it.

As, at the time we missed Atkinson, he had been absent two hours, we were thoroughly alarmed; fortunately, however, the blizzard had quieted down. Search parties were at once organised, and for three hours they scoured the cape and the sea-ice in vain, whilst flares were frequently lighted at the top of Wind Vane Hill, to guide the wanderer or the searchers home. Taylor and I went about two miles along the Barne Glacier, but saw no signs of anyone. On returning to the cape, we met Captain Scott. He looked pale and dejected, and was in a state of great anxiety, for he had about given Atkinson up for lost. We then started out again in another direction, but by now we had almost given up hope of again seeing our comrade alive. At 11 p.m., when we were some distance out, a rocket recalled all the search parties home.

We learned that Atkinson had returned. It seems that he had gone about half way to Archibald; then, as the weather was so thick, he had given it up and turned back, but had failed to find our cape. In the swirling drift he had lost all sense of direction, and wandered for miles, knowing that only by constantly moving could he keep his circulation up, and so remain alive.

He had reached – as he believed – Tent Island, and, almost exhausted, had attempted to find safety by burrowing into a snow-drift for shelter until the blizzard should cease. Fortunately, in this dilemma the weather cleared sufficiently for him to see the moon. Knowing it would then be over Erebus, he at once started off in the right direction and reached the Hut unaided.

It was 2 a.m. before the last of the search parties returned home, and all were immensely relieved to know that Atkinson was safe. He came back in a dazed condition and badly frost-bitten, especially in one of his hands, and certainly owed his life to the lull in the blizzard which enabled him to see the moon.

The incident might have jeopardised more lives than one, for the blizzard increased to almost gale force soon after the last search party returned, and it raged all the next day.

It was my watch that night, and I can testify to Atkinson's fortitude. Though he lay awake writhing with pain all night, never a murmur escaped his lips. The next morning his fingers were covered with blisters, almost as big as the fingers themselves, but with careful treatment he soon recovered.

The thoughts of all in our comfortable Hut turned frequently to our gallant absent comrades during the following weeks, for in July we had lower temperatures and fiercer gales than any we had hitherto experienced. The blizzometer was seldom idle; but whenever it became unusually energetic, such activity was generally accompanied by a rise of the thermometer to the region of the zero line. This rule, however, had notable exceptions, and the blizzard which followed on Atkinson's adventure attained a wind velocity of sixty miles per hour with a temperature of - 35° F. This is a pretty awful combination, for no man could expose his bare hand for half a minute to so shrivelling a blast without its being frozen to the bone.

On venturing outside in the height of that storm, I was blown off my feet and rolled over by a sudden terrific gust, and lost one of my woollen mits. Recovering myself, I was completely at a loss, in the smothering drift and pitch darkness, to know which way to turn. Taking the wrong direction, I stumbled over something and fell again, this time measuring my length in a bank of snow. On floundering to my feet, I found my mitless hand was numbed and feelingless, and, having no wind-proof clothing on, I was shaking with the cold. The situation struck me as being absurd and ludicrous, for though I could not be more than ten yards from the Hut, I was quite lost as to my whereabouts, and my shouts to those indoors for help were borne impotently away and stifled by the hissing and drumming of the blizzard. Plunging about in this awkward plight, with my bare hand tucked into my coat for protection, hope revived joyfully when I came in contact with a packing-case, the location of which I knew. This gave me my bearings, so, backing against it, I took six paces forward and six diagonally, and brought up against the bales of hay that formed the wall of the stable. Feeling my way along this wall to the Hut door, I was indeed thankful to see the inside of our cheery home again. My hand was quite bloodless, and I had carefully to massage it back to life.

I mention this trifling incident to show how a moment's lack of care in this land, where danger lurks everywhere, may involve one in a predicament which might easily cost a life.

The following is an extract from Dr Simpson's report about this storm: – 'The worst blizzard experienced, though not the highest velocity of wind, was on July 8, 1911. It was fairly decent weather in the morning until 9 o'clock, when the temperature was minus 35° or 67° below freezing point. Then it started to blow, and by noon was blowing forty-three miles an hour, not in gusts but continuously. Between 3 p.m. and 4 p.m. it blew fifty-two miles an hour, and between 9 p.m. and 10 p.m. it blew sixty-three miles, with the temperature - 31°. That gale continued to blow at over gale strength for six days, and between 10 and 11 a.m. on July 12 it blew sixty-six miles in the hour. Records of gusts up to eighty miles an hour were recorded.'

Captain Scott made the following entry in his Journal at this time:

July 10. We have had the worst gale I have ever known in these regions, and have not yet done with it. The wind started at about mid-day on Friday, and increasing in violence reached an average of 60 miles for one hour on Saturday, the gusts at this time exceeding 70 m.p.h. ... The extraordinary feature of this gale was the long continuance of a very cold temperature. Needless to say no one has been far from the Hut. It was my turn for duty on Saturday night, and on the occasions when I had to step out of doors I was struck with the impossibility of enduring such conditions for any length of time. One seemed to be robbed of breath; the fine snow beat in behind the wind guard, and ten paces against the wind were sufficient to reduce one's face to the verge of frostbite. To clear the anemometer vane it is necessary to go to the other end of the Hut and climb a ladder. Whilst thus engaged I had literally to lean against the wind, with head bent and face averted and so stagger crablike on my course.'

Who shall describe the beauty and the glory of a calm, moonlit day in the depths of the Polar night? Its serenity is almost as uncommunicable as are the fleeting glories of Aurora. I never fully realised the wonder of it until once, when the moon was full, urged by the rarity of a windless day and the exhilarating influence of 70° of frost, I walked rapidly over the frozen sea until I was well beyond the precipice of ice that towers 200 feet skywards at the end of the Barne Glacier. Then I paused, for the prospect that opened out was of arresting grandeur. The face of the great rampart on my right had, until then, been in the shadow; but on rounding the snout of the glacier, the northern wall was softly illumined by the moon, whose beams gleamed brightly on innumerable polished facets in the cliff, and coruscated from a myriad crystals at my feet. Her radiance shed for miles along the coast, and I could see that the glacier swept northwards in a mighty curve towards Cape Barne, at the point of which promontory a great black column of lava stood like a sentinel in the night.

But it was not so much the austere beauty of the scene that so dominated me, as its utter desolation, and its intense and wholly indescribable loneliness. I stood awhile beneath the shivering stars, with every sense alert, striving to detect some sound; but the stillness about me was profound. Concentrate the faculties as I might, I could hear nothing but the beating of my heart.

I knew then what Service meant when he wrote:

Were you ever out in the Great Alone, when the moon was awful clear,
And the icy mountains hemmed you in with a silence you most could hear?

An eerie feeling crept over me in the presence of this majesty of silence: a feeling of exhilaration and awe, as I thought of my remoteness from that great pulsating throng of life so many thousands of miles away. The desire to break the magic spell was irresistible, so I shouted a loud 'Coo-ee!' To my astonishment the precipice immediately responded, and shouted back 'Coo-ee!' It was thus I discovered one of the finest echoes I have heard in any land. I have listened to some of the most famous echoes of the Alps, mocking the yodellers and the Alp-horns; but I have heard none so wondrously clear and ringing as the voice of this Antarctic glacier. I sang to it, and joked with it, and, if the sentences were short enough, it reproduced them perfectly; but longer phrases sent it all a-chattering with a babel of voices that became pandemonium.

So it was here dwelt the spirits of the Great White South! I found they lurked elsewhere, too, along the glacier wall, and, now that I had by chance discovered their hiding place, I often went out to exchange a few words with them.

It was greatly to my disadvantage during this winter season that I am so light a sleeper. The slightest sound made by the night-watchman would wake me; and the melancholy droning of the blizzometer pipe outside the wall of my compartment often kept me awake all night, or until sleep came from sheer inability of the brain longer to resist. It was curious how certain thoughts would persistently recur during those wakeful hours. The mind would dwell on waterfalls and rivers in distant, temperate lands; and it seemed incredible, in that world of perpetual ice, that I could actually have seen men squirting water – water that was not frozen – out of great hose-pipes, in the dead of night, to cleanse the streets of London.

I think these long weeks of comparative inactivity in the Hut were more irksome to me than to any of my comrades; for the very nature of my life of continuous travel, in search of the picturesque during the preceding ten years, had made constant change of scene almost a necessity to me. My spirit chafed impatiently for the reappearance of the sun, so that I might get on with the work for which daylight was essential.

Long walks over the frozen sea when the weather permitted, and a vigorous series of exercises in the open air before turning-in, now failed to have the effect of inducing sleep; so, in the absence of Uncle Bill – who was away at Cape Crozier – I consulted Atkinson. He suggested a change of muscular effort by excavating holes in the ice for the fish-trap; but, though I tried it fairly regularly, this produced no result. I never had a good night's rest until the sun came back, and day and night alternated once more in a properly-regulated manner.

The piercing of a fresh hole for the fish-trap entailed many hours of work; it was done with pick and shovel and a crow-bar. The ice was now about eight feet thick, and of flinty hardness. Each shaft sunk had to be about four feet in diameter, in order that one might freely work in it, and the deeper one delved the harder became the labour. Ere the digger neared the end of the task he was well overhead in the hole; and in windy weather he had to cast each shovelful to leeward, or risk a shower of the lesser fragments about his head. The holes were excavated by the light of a lantern, and the digger could tell by the black appearance of the ice when he was nearing water. Then he had to proceed with care, for if he worked too deep and drove the pick through, it behoved him to look lively, for a fountain of water would spurt upwards and fill the hole, and all his labour might be lost. The correct modus operandi, when nearing water, was to leave the centre alone, and gingerly pick a trough evenly all round the bottom, until only a few inches of ice remained. Then throwing his tools out, the digger himself was assisted out by a companion – for two always worked together on the last stage – and a long crow-bar was used to cut away the disc. This, too, had to be done with care, for if one struck too hard and punched through unexpectedly, he might commit the unpardonable crime of losing the heavy crow-bar, and such implements were too valuable in these parts to take risks with; it was necessary to pierce all round the gutter gently. The hole would be full of water long before the last remaining ligament was tapped away, and then the 'pancake' floated to the surface.

Such spells of necessary exercise were grateful enough, so long as the weather was calm. No matter how great a desire the 'mercury' exhibited to shrink into the bulb, one could defy the cold if properly clad. Seventy or eighty degrees of frost can be endured by any healthy individual if seasonably clothed and there be no wind. But if a breeze, be it ever so gentle, gets astir in such a temperature, it behoves one to be well alert, for Jack Frost is ever on the watch to take his toll, and he will bite as often and as deep as he gets the chance. Consequently, in the winter time it was nothing unusual to see the tips of half the noses in the Hut 'hanging in rags.'

In bad weather there was always ample for me to do indoors. A great amount of monotonous work is entailed in developing kinematograph films in these latitudes. On account of the difficulty of getting sufficient water, the tank system cannot be used. Therefore the films have to be developed, fixed and washed in strips of fifty feet on a revolving drum; by which method the necessary quantity of the solutions, or of water, is reduced to the minimum. But it is exceedingly slow. Fifty feet of film lasts for less than a minute on the screen; but to develop, fix and wash that quantity of negative took about an hour and a half. As several thousand feet of film had been exposed in the summer, it took over a hundred hours during the winter to develop and wash the negatives. These were dried by hanging them up in the Hut on frames. In addition, there were many hundreds of glass negatives to be developed; so, as space in the ship had not permitted my bringing an assistant to do all this work, my hands were seldom idle.

For some time past, when the weather was clear, we had seen, about midday, a beautiful rosy glow in the north, foretelling that joyous hour when we should welcome the reappearance of the sun. This harbinger of coming springtime grew brighter daily; and by the middle of August a soft ethereal twilight, which fell from blue, and pink, and lilac skies, prevailed for several hours before and afternoon. The daily increasing brightness of this twilight had an uplifting effect on the spirits of all. Each worker went about his task with a nimbleness and effervescent light-heartedness that had not been exhibited for many weeks; for three months of continual darkness, almost constant blizzards, and detention in a crowded building – following on months of glorious activity in the most exhilarating air in all the world – have a sluggish effect on the energies. I hailed the approach of daylight with a feeling of gladness such as I had not known since those wondrous summer days and nights when sleep seemed almost waste of precious hours.

The rapidly brightening skies were an equal source of gratification to Nelson, for during the dark months his job had been anything but a pleasant one – though no one ever heard him say so. If by any human possibility he could carry out his daily experiments at his 'hole,' he did so; and when he came in with his monotonously regular records of temperatures and samples of water obtained from various depths, and a great mass of ice about his helmet, I often saw him quietly nursing his fingers back to life.

Wright, too, must have been glad to see the end of continuous night. He seemed to be impervious to the elements, and used to kneel for hours beside his transit telescope, observing the occultation of stars – with a telephone transmitter at his lips and the receiver at his ear, by which means he communicated the exact moment of contact to his confederate, Simpson, at the sidereal clock inside the Hut. Wright was the possessor of a vocabulary of Canadian expressions that was the envy of all his comrades. If by chance he should breathe upon the eye-piece of his telescope at a critical moment, thereby causing it to fog – or anything else went wrong – the remarks that our 'Silas' addressed to the particular heavenly body under observation were of such a wrathful nature that it was reported a star was once seen positively to wobble.

I cannot vouch for the accuracy of this assertion; but Silas was, at all events, no wobbler. Never did mortal man persevere at so frigid a task with more consistent resolution. Zero or 'fifty below,' it was all the same to him. If the skies were clear, Silas knelt in the darkness, scrutinising the heavens whenever an occultation was due, whilst Simpson counted half-seconds to him through the telephone.

Shortly after dinner on August 1st, someone dashed into the Hut shouting excitedly that the Cape Crozier Party were returning. A rush was made to meet them, just as they came staggering in, with helmets encrusted with ice, and with pounds of ice massed around their mouths. Being masked to protect their cheeks and noses, we could not see their faces; but we could see their eyes sparkling in their icy visors, and their voices sounded cheery enough. We were all anxious to help them out of the armour that encased them – for their helmets and wind-blouses were literally frozen on to them

– and some one suggested getting a 'can-opener.' We had to excavate them carefully, and when finally they were exposed, their faces bore unmistakable evidence of the terrible hardships they had endured. Their looks haunted me for days. Once before, I had seen similar expressions on men's faces – when some half-starved Russian prisoners, after the Battle of Mukden, were being taken to Japan.

We did not press them overmuch to recount their adventures that night, for it was obvious they were almost at the point of exhaustion for want of sleep. So, after they had eaten their fill, they were permitted to turn-in to their beds – which must have seemed paradise to them after five weeks camping under conditions such as never had been endured, hitherto, by any human beings, with only a thin tent to cover them. Next day we drew from them the whole splendid story. Low zero temperatures had prevailed during the entire period of absence, and at one time the 'mercury' had fallen to - 77° F. (109 degrees of frost). They had encountered all the gales that we experienced; but under what different conditions! In one terrific storm, when the wind reached hurricane velocity, their tent was blown away, and they lay in their sleeping-bags buried under the snow for forty-eight hours without food. Then the gale had abated, and providentially they recovered the tent, which was found some distance away in a crevice in the rocks. Had they not recovered it, they must inevitably have perished, for shelter was necessary to operate the Primus stove on which they were dependent for hot food.

Undismayed by hardships and mishaps, these Stoics had persevered in their task, only to find that almost insuperable difficulties confronted them at the goal. Crevasses and appalling pressure-ridges lay between them and the sea-ice where the Emperor penguins nested; but, nothing daunted, they had struggled down by the help of ice-axes and an Alpine rope, to find only about a hundred birds, instead of the thousand or more that Wilson had expected.

The spoils of the adventure were three fine skins and three eggs. Skins and addled eggs had been secured on the *Discovery* Expedition; but these were the only fresh Emperor penguins' eggs that had ever been found. They were 10 centimetres long, by 7 centimetres in diameter, and appeared to be of a bluish white shade, much discoloured by stains; but beyond their scientific value they did not look of any special interest. Only those who had risked all to find them could realise their import.

The biological value of the eggs was greatly enhanced when Wilson found, on examination in the Hut, that they were in an advanced stage of incubation. Information as to the birds' past history and development, unobtainable in the adult, might be acquired by study of the embryo. When, therefore, Uncle Bill found the eggs were in the very condition he had hoped for, his joy was great, for he now looked forward to being able to prove something about the evolution of this strange creature. Thus, though the adventure was not productive of all the results expected, it was successful in its main object. It was, beyond question, the most arduous ever undertaken in the interests of ornithology.

To some, it may seem incredible that men should forego the comforts and luxuries of civilisation, and, leaving the joys of home and all that many consider most worth living for, venture to the most forbidding ends of the earth to suffer inconceivable hardships, and to risk health and limb and life itself in order to study the breeding habits of a bird. Yet ought we all to be thankful that our race produces such men; for the thirst of science for knowledge is insatiable, and Britain has ever been foremost in the van of those who have not hesitated, if needs be, to sacrifice all to satisfy it.

Scott wrote:

> To me and to everyone who has remained here the result of their effort is the appeal it makes to the imagination as one of the most gallant stories in Polar history. That men should wander forth in the depth of a Polar night to face the most dismal cold and the fiercest gales in darkness is something new; that they should have persisted in their effort in spite of every adversity for five weeks is heroic. It makes a tale for our generation which I hope may not be lost in the telling.

When I think of the enthusiasm with which they prepared for the colossal task they had voluntarily set themselves; the lighthearted manner in which they met the hour of their departure, and the quiet and modest way they told of their adventures and achievements, I feel it has been a great privilege to have known these men as comrades.

I have made further reference to their journey elsewhere in this volume, under my observations on Penguins. With the return of the Cape Crozier Party we resumed our evening lectures, which had been abandoned during their absence. No one ever played cards in the ward-room, though in the mess-deck the men played frequently. Chess, backgammon, draughts and dominoes were our only games; and at all these Nelson was easily champion. Meares and Oates were very keen on backgammon. Captain Scott was fond of chess, but as Nelson always beat him, he preferred to play with Atkinson, when he invariably won. Nelson, though one of the most argumentative of men, was also one of the most even-tempered and good-natured. He would argue for the love of argument; take any side about almost any subject, and usually reduce his opponent to silence from sheer ability in the art of controversy. He ought to have been a barrister.

All manner of subjects came up for discussion at dinner time, and were thoroughly thrashed out in the no-lecture evenings. One of the most interesting was on Travel, for it brought out the fact that the ward-room members had, between them, visited almost every part of the habitable globe. Scott, Evans and Gran scored the highest in actual countries visited. But Simpson, Meares and I maintained that sailors ought not to be regarded as bona fide travellers; as in the majority of cases they only touched at sea-ports, and seldom went inland. It seemed to us disproportionate that a day's call at Rio Janeiro, or elsewhere, should rank equally with Meares' two years in Siberia, Simpson's year in Lapland, or my three years of travel in Japan.

A good deal of banter continually passed between the scientists and the non-scientist members. This led to Oates one day classifying those who held scientific degrees, as 'Scientists,' and those of us who did not, as 'Gentlemen.' Henceforth Titus – as he was nicknamed by someone, but whether after his historic or sporting namesake I never knew – who possessed a rich vein of repartee and dry humour, was always the warmest champion of the Gentlemen in these bouts with the Scientists.

Of course many good stories were told from time to time, and not unnaturally those most appreciated were such as concerned travel and exploration. We discovered some excellent humorous incidents recounted in Polar books. The best Polar story that I ever read, however, appeared in a London daily paper a few years later. Here it is:

The strangest 'bunco game' in American police annals has come to light at Minneapolis, Kansas, where Homer Hograth, a farmer, applied for a warrant for the arrest of a man who sold him £4,000 worth of shares in a company to bring ice from the North Pole for use in Kansas.

The man, states our New York correspondent, first interested the farmer when he found him engaged apparently in making astronomical observations on Hograth's farm. He said he had been to the North Pole with Peary, and discovered that it was really a pole of magnetised steel projecting upward from the centre of the earth, and the source of all electrical energy.

The man claimed that he had invented an enormous electrical shovel capable of scooping up thousands of tons of ice. This shovel, he said, would be held suspended in the air through a secret process in connection with the electrical energy in the North Pole. As the world rotated the shovel would gradually drop back, and astronomical calculations showed that it would land on Hograth's farm, and an immense profit could be realised by selling the ice.

Hograth and the stranger agreed to form a company. Hograth subscribed £4,000, the stranger took the money, and said he intended going to the North Pole. He has not been seen since.

Of books we had any number, and of all kinds, so that with reading, games and lectures our leisure hours passed pleasantly and profitably. It is worthy of note that Oates, as becomes a soldier, read little else but Napier's *Peninsular War*. Occasionally he would dip into a novel, but he looked upon such literature as trifling, and soon returned to the beloved volumes. Near the head of his bunk he had hung a picture of his one hero, Napoleon.

Every Sunday morning Captain Scott read the Church Service, and the day was as far as possible regarded as one of relaxation.

On August 17th (1911) the sun gilded the summit of Erebus and the highest peaks of the Western Mountains, and on the 20th was said to be above the horizon, but the mountain slopes obscured him from view. The 26th broke clear and calm, with a temperature of - 12° F. It was a glorious day; and half an hour before noon Captain Scott invited me to accompany him to witness the first sunrise of the season. We walked out to the icebergs, climbed to the summit of one that had an easy slope, and breathlessly waited. Scott had timed things to a nicety. Within a few minutes a flame seemed to burst from the serrated lava ridge above Cape Barne; then the upper rim of the sun crept out, not rising but sidling along the slope. A few minutes more, and the blazing orb had cleared the land, and for the first time in more than four months we were bathed in his grateful rays. The world was once more golden. It was one of the moments of our lives, and we could not restrain our joy.

Scott wrote: 'We felt very young, and sang and cheered.' With what admirable constraint he always wrote, as becomes the great man that he was. 'Felt very young, and sang and cheered.' I should think we did! We felt like boys again, and acted, too, like boys. We shouted and sang for pure delight, and cheered and cheered again. Had we been on a more secure footing I believe we should have danced, from the superabundance of our spirits. As it was, we sat long on our icy pinnacle, and rejoiced more decorously in the birth of the Polar Spring.

CHAPTER XV

The Early Spring

When a little band of men live through an Antarctic winter in intimate association under a single roof, the character and true purpose of each become bared to his comrades, almost to his inmost soul. In the crowded throng of life 'make-believe' is too often a disguise that remains uncloaked; but in a Polar hut no man could hide behind a mask. The Antarctic is no place for drones, and he who is not animated by genuine love of his work had better remain at home, for he would be a burden unto himself and others. Lukewarmness for the cause, or any shirking of difficulties or discomforts would be intolerable.

That twenty-five men passed through this test without friction must be held to the credit of all. That this result could only have been attained by the possession of the most sterling qualities in others besides the Leader, will be granted. Such qualities stood out most prominently in the two men who stood at Scott's right hand – Dr Wilson and Lieut. Bowers. These two were inseparable friends. In physique they were the strangest contrast – Wilson, tall and lean, clean-cut and aquiline of feature, with thews of steel, and without an ounce of superfluous flesh on his slim, athletic frame; Bowers, short, thick-set and round, with body and limbs as tough as teak, yet devoid of ugly knots or ridges of muscle.

Scott had proved the quality of Wilson's ability, spirit and wisdom in *Discovery* days. Ripened by ten years, these attributes, combined with added richness of learning and incomparable tact, had produced one of the most lovable of men. Like his Chief, Wilson had learnt the true philosophy of living – that happiness is not to be attained in the pursuit of riches; but in the contentment of spirit born of knowledge, congenial occupation, and a useful and well-spent life. It was this splendid man – the Head of the Scientific Staff of the Expedition, and one of the most eminent Polar zoologists of his day – on whom all leant at times. Because of the sheer force of his resolute character, his outstanding personality, and the sympathetic and selfless nature of his disposition, Uncle Bill not only stood foremost at the right hand of the Leader of the Expedition, but was beloved by every member of it.

Dr Wilson and the pony 'Nobby'.

And so was Bowers – who was nicknamed Birdie, because of his unusually prominent nose. No more cheery, joyful soul ever lived than he, nor any more disdainful of hardship; the word was unknown in his vocabulary – and here let me state I never heard it mentioned by any member of the Expedition. Bowers was our Commissariat Officer, and from the hour we disembarked in the South he was Scott's privy counsellor in all matters relative to the important work of provisioning the various exploring parties. To Birdie's never-failing good humour and kindly nature we owed almost as much as to Uncle Bill's sagacity and tact for the smoothness of our domestic life.

The fine example set by these two in devotion to their Chief, and of their Chief's reliance on them, was one of the strongest bonds that united the enterprise. Another of the outstanding figures of our little community was Captain Oates. Oates had a personality that could be felt. He was a man of few words; he spoke with deliberation and never loosely, and he had a fund of dry humour, and a store of anecdote from which gems would drop at the most unexpected moments. Scott described him as a 'cheery old pessimist' – because he was never known to express himself in superlatives about anything. He always delivered his considered judgment on any matter that came under his jurisdiction calmly, decisively and positively. Unwavering strength of purpose was written on Oates' firm face; and his sturdy frame was a foundation on which Scott largely built his hopes later – in the great final effort. His devotion to the indispensable animals in his charge was not only one of the most inspiring examples of the Expedition, but was one of the main factors to which the success of the primary object of the enterprise must be attributed. His precedent was ever before us, for the

Soldier (another of Oates' nicknames) was more conspicuous by his absence from our midst, than by his presence amongst us. He spent the greater part of his time in the stable, and had little use for the Hut except as a convenient place in which to have his meals and to sleep.

He would pass hours on end in the frigid temperature of the stable – often, I am convinced, merely because of his desire to be near the ponies. There was a blubber-burning stove at the far end, and when he was not otherwise engaged in something connected with the welfare of his charges, he could usually be found beside that stove, cooking bran-mashes for them.

One of my most vivid recollections of our winter life is of Oates, pipe in mouth, and arms on the ward-room table, poring over his inseparable *Peninsular War*. During such evening hours as he spent amongst us, that was how we almost always saw him, except when occasionally he substituted a backgammon-board for the familiar volumes.

In the mess-deck, Petty Officer Evans was the dominant personality. His previous Polar experience, his splendid build, and his stentorian voice and manner of using it – all compelled the respect due to one who would have been conspicuous in any company. He, also, was one of the Leader's towers of strength. More than once I heard Scott tell him that he did not know what the Expedition would do without him.

It is worthy of remark – though by no means remarkable – that the party selected by Captain Scott to accompany him on the last stage of the Pole journey were the four men who possessed the most striking personalities in our community.

Petty Officers Evans and Crean, and mechanic Lashly, too, were old friends of Scott's, of *Discovery* days. Evans and Lashly had, amongst other risks, been concerned with him in a famous crevasse adventure on the Ferrar Glacier, on the western side of McMurdo Sound. Scott and Evans were both precipitated through a snow bridge into an abyss, and hung there, dangling on the rope, in space. It was due to Lashly's resource, strength and presence of mind that they escaped with their lives. Such experiences make for lasting friendship.

The staunchest tie of all that bound the Expedition was the incentive for each to do his utmost, born of esteem, respect and fellow-feeling for the quiet and unassuming yet masterful man on whose broad shoulders rested the grave responsibilities of leadership. Animated by the common purpose – to attain success in each branch of the undertaking – all recognised that the pangs of any failure would be keenest in our Chief, for it would be on him that the gaze of all the world would focus.

There were times when one's whole soul went out to him in sympathy – as when his chances of success were jeopardised by the irreparable losses of the ponies the preceding summer. But one honoured him the more for his admirable attitude over such blows of Fate. There was no repining or lamentation in adversity. Scott simply cast aside misfortunes that could not be helped, and seldom if ever referred to them again. He looked always forward, with hope and confidence in his destiny.

Captain Scott was a man of splendid physique: five feet, nine inches in height, broad and deep-chested, and slender in the flanks. His eyes were deep blue, and his face was a faithful index to the resolution and courage that dominated his soul. He possessed in a marked degree the organising ability indispensable to the leadership of a great scientific enterprise. Though each member of his staff was an expert in some branch of science or art, he would meet these specialists – physicist, geologist, biologist, or zoologist – on their own ground, and discuss intimate details of their work. Sound in his judgment, and just in his criticisms, he was always quick to appreciate and generous in praise; and on those whom he trusted, he relied as on himself. He took the most keen and kindly interest in all about him; and his most prominent characteristics were determination, self-reliance and inherent modesty.

He had kept much to himself during the winter. He read a great deal – generally books on Polar exploration, relieved by an occasional novel. He worked a great deal on his plans for the future; he wrote much in his diary, and smoked incessantly. Almost invariably he took his exercise alone. Once, during the winter, I asked him if he had yet started on his book. His reply was: 'No fear! I'll leave that until I get home.' From which I gathered that his Journal was to be used merely as notes which later would be elaborated into his official account of the Expedition. Though a great part of it was written under conditions of extreme discomfort, and much of it in the face of unparalleled hardship, when Scott's Journal ultimately became known, it was manifest to the world that his literary ability was of a high order, though readers of his previous work, *The Voyage of the Discovery*, knew this already.

Our Leader had created a characteristic environment about him. Besides the numerous books to which I have referred, there were many photographs of his wife and little son, Peter, about the walls of his cubicle; there was also a rack of pipes, and a jumble of Polar clothing. On his bunk lay his naval overcoat. When he told me the history of that coat, he revealed such a lovable trait of character – a warm affection for old and tried friends – that I quote its story as told by its owner in his Journal:

I must confess to an affection for my veteran uniform overcoat, inspired by its insistent utility. I find that it is twenty-three years of age, and can testify to its strenuous existence. It has been spared neither rain, wind, nor salt sea spray, Tropic heat nor Arctic cold; it has outlived many sets of buttons, from their glittering gilded youth to green old age, and it supports its four-stripe shoulder-straps as gaily as the single lace ring of the early days which proclaimed it the possession of a humble sub-lieutenant. Withal, it is still a very long way from the fate of the 'one-horse shay'.

A man of moods himself, Scott respected those of others. Sometimes he was so light of heart that every inhabitant of the Hut felt the influence of his spirits. At other times he was morose and reticent. It was obvious on such occasions that he was silently weighted with the problems of the future – so infinitely increased by the heavy losses to his transport. When this mood was upon him I felt instinctively that he was oppressed by the sense of obligation to his country to push the venture to success, be the enhanced difficulties what they may.

Moreover, as he told me more than once, he was troubled by the fact that the cost of the enterprise had greatly exceeded his estimate, and that there would be a considerable deficit to face. I thought he was inclined to let this worry him overmuch. During the winter, he had on several occasions come to my room, closed the door, and opened out his heart to me in the matter. Each time I was able to reassure him greatly, for I well knew that the photographic department would prove to be a considerable asset to the Expedition.

During these intimate talks I discovered how totally inexperienced Scott was in dealing with the Press. He seemed to have little idea of the value of photographs made at so remote a part of the earth. I warned him that, if the Expedition should remain in the South for a second season, it would be advisable for him to instruct members, who would return the first year, that on no conditions should they release any photographs, which they might have taken, otherwise than through his Press Agent. He gave instructions to that effect, and, as I should be returning, he wrote a letter to his agent stating that he was to consult me about all press matters, adding that I had his entire confidence, and the right to arrange details of such matters on his behalf. (Notwithstanding this, I found, when I reached home, that injudicious contracts had already been entered into – in 1910 – by which a considerable sum was lost to the Expedition.)

It was part of the conditions of the agreement under which I had joined the Expedition that the results of my work should become my own property after two years, and that I should have world-wide lecturing rights thereto immediately on our return to England. Also, I had agreed that Dr Wilson should have rights to my photographs for lecturing before educational and scientific bodies. This matter now became of considerable interest, as our lectures in the Hut had brought the matter into prominence, and Scott and Wilson had several discussions with me about the possibilities of the future. Captain Scott at once disclaimed any intention or desire to give more than perhaps half-a-dozen public lectures for the benefit of the Expedition funds. He told us it was his wish to get back to his work in the Navy again, as soon as possible after his return home. In this I thought he showed a fine spirit and devotion to his profession. Scott's ambitions were concerned only with the glory of his country, and he desired to serve it with every hour of his life.

After returning to London, Lady Scott told me that her husband had written her to the same effect. Captain Scott was, however, none the less cognisant of the great potential educational and moral value of the kinematograph films of the adventure; and he pointed out that, so far as Wilson and I were concerned, it was different matter. Wilson could not only tell about the zoology of the Far South, but, by means of photographs and films he would be able to show the nature of the animal life there. Also, he hoped that I would adhere to my intention of lecturing about the Expedition, as, in his opinion, 'such lectures would help to foster a fine and manly spirit in the rising generation.'

With the return of the sun, I was brought, during the next two months, into continual close association with Captain Scott. He came to my room one day and told me he realised that it would largely devolve upon himself to illustrate the Polar journey. Then, in that nice way in which he always asked a favour of anyone, he said that I should render a very great service to the Expedition if I would take him, and a few others in hand, and coach them in photography. I replied that nothing would give me greater pleasure than to do anything in my power to help him and any of my comrades – and from that time my dark-room became a very busy place indeed.

It had, from the outset, seemed strange to me that among so many brilliant men no one had more than a superficial knowledge of photography. Indeed, the Western Journey of the previous summer had suffered badly from lack of adequate illustration in consequence. I felt that the results attained in the past could be easily improved upon in the future; so, as there was no lack of cameras, I began to coach Bowers, Debenham, Gran, and Wright, as well as Captain Scott. Both Scott and Debenham had some knowledge of photography, but it was too elementary to cope successfully with the difficult problems that would now have to be faced.

Debenham at once exhibited a capacity for taking pains that was soon productive of the most encouraging results. His retentive memory – aided by a genuine affection for photography, and the recognition that it could be of much value to him in his science – rapidly absorbed all that I was able to impart as to the primary principles, and ere summer came he was fairly expert with his camera; he produced beautiful photographs of really difficult subjects.

Captain Scott and Bowers applied themselves to the work with extraordinary enthusiasm. Indeed, Scott's zeal outran his capability; he craved to be initiated into the uses of colour-filters and telephoto lenses before he had mastered an exposure-meter. I had to express my disapproval of such haste, and firmly decline to discuss these things until he could repeatedly show me half-a-dozen correctly exposed negatives from as many plates. When he had achieved this result under my guidance, he would sally forth alone with his camera.

He would come back as pleased as a boy, telling me quite excitedly he had got some splendid things, and together we would begin to develop his plates – six in a dish. When five minutes or more had elapsed and no sign of a latent image appeared on any of them, I knew something was wrong, and a conversation would follow, something in this wise:

'Are you quite sure you did everything correctly?'
'My dear fellow' (a great expression this of Scott's), 'I'm absolutely certain I did. I'm sure I made no mistake.'
'Did you put in the plateholder?' 'Yes.'
'Did you draw the slide?' 'Yes.'
'Did you set the shutter?' 'Yes.'
'Did you release the shutter?' 'Yes.'
'Did you take the cap off the lens?' 'Yes.'

Then he would rub his head, in that way he had, and admit: 'No! Good heavens! I forgot. I could have sworn I had forgotten nothing.'

He would then fill up his holders again, and be off once more. He fell repeatedly into every pitfall in his haste – with unfamiliar apparatus. One day he would forget to set the shutter, another time he would forget to release it, and each time he would vow not to make the same error again – and then go out and make some other. But I liked him all the more for his human impatience and his mistakes. How often have I not made them all myself, in my own early days with the camera!

Knowing the importance of the Polar and other journeys being thoroughly illustrated, I spared no effort to communicate every short cut to efficiency that I knew. With such exceptional 'pupils,' remarkably fine results were soon being produced by all. When Scott was able at length to secure good results with colour-filters, orthochromatic plates and telephoto lenses, his pleasure was very real indeed; for then he knew he was capable of dealing with any subjects he would meet with on the Beardmore Glacier. Finally, he and Bowers were shown how to release the shutter by means of a long thread, so that all who reached the Pole might appear in the group to be made at the goal.

More than once when I was out with Scott I was surprised to find that he seemed to feel the cold much more than I did. Standing waiting for an hour or more in zero temperatures is not altogether a pleasant experience; but when photographing it often has to be done, as the clouds are frequently troublesome, or the sun does not properly light the subject. Under such conditions Scott would vigorously stamp his feet to stimulate the circulation, when I was experiencing no discomfort. This was probably due to his not having taken such precautions as the nature of my work necessitated.

I took every care to guard against cold myself. In zero weather I wore four pairs of thick woollen socks, and one pair of heavy goat-hair ski-socks; I wrapped dried saenne grass round these, and over all wore a pair of finnesko, or Norwegian moccasins, made from the leg fur of reindeer. I wore two suits of thick 'Wolsey' woollen underwear; thick corduroy breeches and puttees; a heavy woollen guernsey, a thick woollen coat and a flannel-lined leather coat; a woollen wrapper and a seal-skin fur helmet. On my hands I wore a pair of woollen gloves, a pair of thick woollen mits, and thick dog-fur mits reaching almost to the elbows. All of this clothing was absolutely necessary when standing about; but when pulling my sledge, one or other, and sometimes both of the coats were discarded. When working the camera, I would remove both pairs of mits until my hands began to chill in the woollen gloves; then bury them again in the warm fur, and beat them together until they glowed again. But my fingers often became so numbed that I had to nurse them back to life by thrusting my hands inside my clothing, in contact with the warm flesh. Scott one day told me: 'This photographing is the coldest job I have ever struck, as well as the most risky'

– the latter because it so often happened that the best subjects were only to be secured in the most dangerous places.

In summer it was, of course, not necessary to wear so much clothing.

Photographing in such extremely low zero temperatures necessitates a great deal of care; there are many pitfalls, into all of which I plunged headlong. I had to pay dearly for some of the experience I gained. Perhaps a few of the troubles I learned to avoid may be of interest. I found that it was advisable always to leave cameras in their cases outside the Hut. There was sometimes a difference of more than one hundred degrees between the exterior and interior temperature. To bring cameras inside was to subject them to such condensation that they became dripping wet as they came into the warm air. If for any reason it was necessary to bring a camera indoors, all this moisture had to be carefully wiped away; and the greatest care had to be taken to see that none got inside a lens. To so much as breathe upon a lens in the open air was to render that lens useless, for it instantly became covered with a film of ice which could not be removed. It had to be brought into warm air and thawed off; then wiped dry. Every trace of oil had to be removed from all working parts of kinematograph cameras and focal-plane shutters, as even some 'non-freezing' oil (which I had bought in Switzerland) froze.

Lubricating had to be done with graphite. Several of my colour-filters became uncemented from the expansion and contraction caused by changes of temperature, and were useless; and some of my shutters became so unreliable that I had to discard them and make all exposures by makeshift expedients.

Great care was required to prevent plates being ruined before use. There was not sufficient room in the Hut to store my entire stock, so the supply in the dark-room was replenished, from time to time, from the stores outside in the snow. Plates had to be brought indoors gradually, in order to prevent unsightly markings. This took two days. I placed them for a day in the vestibule; then left them at least another day in my room, to accustom them to the temperature before opening. No such care was necessary when taking plates into the open air. After exposure, plates could be brought indoors at once, if they were to be developed immediately. The first batch of English plates that I brought indoors and left in a warm place – before learning by experience that care was necessary – were completely ruined by wave-like markings. Even with all possible care markings would frequently appear; but a brand of American plates – to which I am much attached, having found them very reliable, in every conceivable climate, during my travels – remained practically unaffected so long as they received reasonable care. Greater precautions had always to be taken with orthochromatic than with ordinary plates.

Roll-films and film-packs stood every test magnificently, and yielded splendid results. There can be no question that, taking into consideration the great saving in weight, reliability and extreme convenience, films are pre-eminently suited for travel and exploration photography. Eastman kinematograph film never failed to yield the finest possible results.

Every film and plate exposed in the South, as well as many thousands of feet of kinematograph film, were developed in the Hut, with the maximum of convenience, by means of 'Tabloid Rytol,' which I had chosen because of its proved excellence.

To 'thread' a film into a kinematograph camera, in low temperatures, was an unpleasant job, for it was necessary to use bare fingers whilst doing so. Often when my fingers touched metal they became frostbitten. Such a frostbite feels exactly like a burn. Once, thoughtlessly, I held a camera screw for a moment in my mouth. It froze instantly to my lips, and took the skin off them when I removed it. On another occasion, my tongue came into contact with a metal part of one of my cameras, whilst moistening my lips as I was focussing. It froze fast instantaneously; and to release myself I had to jerk it away, leaving the skin of the end of my tongue sticking to the camera, and my mouth bled so profusely that I had to gag it with a handkerchief.

Shortly after the welcome daylight had come back, Captain Scott, with Lieut. Bowers, Dr Simpson and Petty Officer Evans, departed on a two weeks' reconnaissance of the western side of the Sound, to get his hand in for sledging after the long winter's rest, and to give our meteorologist an opportunity of experiencing the more strenuous side of Polar life.

As soon as possible after the sun returned I made some photographs of the Castle Berg, which had so entranced me since its arrival off our cape the previous autumn. The weathering process, to which it had been subjected by the winter storms, had but added to its wonder. During the long months of darkness, I had often stood beneath its crystal bastions and marvelled at the skill with which the hand of Nature had built and chiselled the frozen walls into the semblance of a Norman tower. In the brilliant Polar moonlight, with the soft beams silvering each curve and ridge and angle of its structure, it had seemed a veritable fairy-tale in ice – a fitting palace for King Jack Frost, whose home I never doubted this to be.

Now, as the sun flooded it with his light, the berg became of such gleaming beauty that even the most unimpressionable members of our community felt the influence of its spell. There was but one opinion concerning it amongst us – that it was the most wonderful iceberg ever reported in the

The Castle berg

Polar regions; and, for my part, I never wearied of searching for some fresh picture in its ever-changing aspects.

On one of the earliest of the sunny spring days, I went out, accompanied by Clissold, to do some work round about others of the stranded bergs. Now, in the ordinary course of things no one would want to climb an iceberg; but fine views can sometimes be obtained from such an unstable elevation. After visiting one of these vantage-points, we proceeded to another berg, which I had named The Matterhorn, because of its resemblance to the 'Lion of the Alps' when viewed in profile. It had a long sloping back, which was easy to ascend, and by no means slippery, as it was well crusted with *nevé*.

Noticing that Clissold was inclined to be incautious, I admonished him – after the manner of Alpine guides with new climbers – that over confidence when on ice was but bravado, and only shown by those who fear nothing because they know nothing: that all experienced climbers recognise danger and respect it. I exhorted him not for a moment to be off his guard, and never to minimise risks. As I wanted him to pose in several views, to take no chances I made him put on my steel crampons (spiked climbing-irons which are fastened to the feet), and I lent him my ice-axe. There should be no danger whatever of slipping when so outfitted.

After taking several photographs on this berg, I descended to the sea-ice to secure a final plate or two of Clissold standing at the top of the slope. When this was done, I shouted to him to come down, and then packed my apparatus on to the sledge, and pulled off a short distance to wait for him. The day was very calm and sunny, and as I sat on the sledge, bathed in the grateful sunshine, I heard a light thud, but thought nothing of it, as fragments often fall from icebergs. Clissold, however, neither appeared nor answered my shouts, and I began to get uneasy; then I recalled the thud of a few minutes earlier with a chill of apprehension. I ran back to the berg, now thoroughly alarmed; and when I saw my ice-axe at the foot, sticking upright in the snow, I realised the worst. Ten yards further lay Clissold on his back. From the position of the ice-axe, so far from him, he must have slid thirty or forty feet down a steep slope, and then fallen sheer, about eighteen feet, on to the hard ice.

He exhibited not the slightest sign of life. I held him in my arms, calling him frantically by name and imploring him to speak to me; but his head fell back lifelessly, whilst his half-open eyes showed only the white. No breath came from his lips, and his heart seemed to have ceased to beat. I felt his neck, his limbs, his back and body, but could detect no broken bones. Almost distracted at such a dreadful ending to our interesting afternoon, I knew not what to do. I was nearly two miles from the Hut, with poor Clissold apparently dead.

For some time – I don't know how long; it may have been minutes only, though it seemed an hour – I tried to revive him by chafing his neck and hands and constantly speaking to him; but in vain. There was no symptom of life. I dared not apply known methods of restoring animation, for fear that, if he still lived, his ribs might be broken and might thereby injure his lungs. And I could not leave him to seek help, for it was twenty below zero, and if he were alive he would inevitably freeze to death. As I was deliberating what to do in this dilemma, a great bubble came slowly from his lips, and burst. Overjoyed at this evidence of life, feeble as it was, I carefully dragged him to a soft place in the snow, stripped myself of my coats and muffler, and wrapped them about him; then I ran for help.

As I rounded the corner of the berg, I saw Nelson at his 'hole' about half a mile away. I ran towards him, gesticulating wildly, and shouting to him for help. But he only waved to me, and retired behind his snow wall to get on with his work. (He told me, afterwards, he thought I was joking, because of my unusual antics in the effort to make him understand.) As I drew nearer, he appeared again; and now realising I was in real distress, he ran to meet me. Greatly agitated and out of breath, I briefly explained what had happened. Then he raced back to his shelter, and telephoned (fortunately a telephone had been installed there a few days previously) to the Hut for a rescue party immediately to be sent to the scene.

We both ran back to the berg, where Clissold lay apparently lifeless; but when we raised his head and called him, he faintly moaned, and uttered the words 'My back! My back!' Then he became unconscious again. We were thankful, however, to know he still lived.

Captain Scott, who had taken a short cut across the cape, was the first on the scene from the Hut. He was greatly distressed to find Clissold in such a plight; by that time, however, the poor man was breathing feebly, but regularly. Soon, the rescue party came up with a sledge, and a sleeping-bag, which they cut open and wrapped round the injured man; then they took him home as rapidly as possible.

That evening was an anxious one, as for a time it could not be ascertained if Clissold had been hurt internally. He came to his senses for a few minutes, but he was suffering so acutely that Dr Wilson injected morphia. Then he relapsed into unconsciousness. A careful examination proved that no bones were broken; but there were bad contusions of the back and head, and severe concussion. For many days the poor man lay in pain, and it was a great relief to all when he was out of danger: perhaps especially so to me, for though I had taken every precaution to avoid any mishap, I felt very keenly my responsibility in the matter.

It was nearly six weeks ere Clissold was himself again. He was never able to recall anything about his accident, beyond remembering that he slipped. The rest was blank, until he came-to in the Hut. There were some jagged lumps of ice near-by where he lay. Had he fallen on to those he must inevitably have been killed, so, all things considered, the accident had a very fortunate ending. To Clissold's lasting regret, however, he had not recovered in time to accompany the Motor Party on the Pole journey, to which, for his mechanical knowledge, he had been appointed.

CHAPTER XVI

The Start for the Pole

The return of the sun had been a bracing stimulant to all. The vicinity of the Hut was now a hive of industry, and everyone went about his work with buoyant spirit and confidence in the future. Much had been accomplished during the winter; but the daily increasing altitude of the sun reminded us how much yet remained to be done before all was ready for that tremendous journey which was to plant the Union Jack at the South Pole.

When the Leader had completed all his plans, and had figured out all requirements for man and beast, these were checked and counter-checked, and finally submitted to the examination of Bowers. Scott wrote: 'In the transport department, in spite of all the care I have taken to make the details of my plan clear by lucid explanation, I find that Bowers is the only man on whom I can thoroughly rely to carry out the work without mistake, with its array of figures.'

Then innumerable linen bags were filled with rations – pemmican, butter, sugar and cocoa – and put up with biscuits, into packages sufficient to last four men for one week. Pemmican is a preparation of the finest dried lean beef, ground to powder and mixed with 60 per cent of beef fat. It is the mainstay for the support of life in all Polar exploration. It is eaten as a thick soup, stiffened with biscuit, and, whenever possible, with chopped seal meat. This is called 'Hoosh.'

Sledges and tents and Primus stoves were then overhauled, and footgear and clothing carefully examined. Nothing was left to chance.

The ponies were now exercised for longer hours, to harden them: and, for the same object, the dogs made several trips to Hut Point with advance loads of stores. The dogs were strange beasts. They harked back to a wild ancestry – wolves. Some of them even now were more like wolves than dogs; others seemed nearer akin to coyotes – with their sharp snouts and foxy-looking eyes. Only in their massive forelegs did they resemble the heavier North American 'husky'; but they made no bones about undertaking a husky's work. Though the biggest of them turned the scale at under 80 lbs., a team of eleven would sometimes pull a load of 1,000 lbs. to Hut Point, fifteen miles away, in four hours; whilst with lighter loads they would make the journey in ninety minutes. They were always ready for work; indeed, they seemed to regard work as the only sort of fun to be had in these regions – and they were not far wrong.

If anyone appeared at the door of the Hut with dog-harness in his hand – or anything that looked at all like harness – every dog would yelp and whine and howl with delight, in the hope of being the first to be harnessed up. Loafing was abhorrent to them – to judge from the joy they manifested when work was in sight. Sometimes, however, a dog would become sluggish and fail to pull his weight in the team. Whenever this occurred – either from unwillingness or fatigue – as soon as a dog saw his team-mate's efforts slackening, he would jump over the main trace and give him a sharp nip, just to remind him of his duty, and then drop back into his place without losing his stride.

The dogs were driven tandem fashion – each pair pulling from opposite sides of the long main trace. It was not the business of the leading dog to do much pulling, however; he was there to use his head, and was chosen for his sagacity and reasoning powers. His duty was to see that the commands of the driver were obeyed, and to set the example to the others by immediately obeying them. Independently of such directions, the leader was expected to use his own judgment – to select the best ground for travelling over, and to avoid the rough patches and *sastrugi*.

The best work can be got out of a dog-team by driving in rapid bursts, with frequent stops for a brief rest. After cleverly negotiating a piece of bad ground, at the next stop the leader would look round for the approval of his driver and team-mates. If, however, he failed to obey with alacrity and

Chris, one of the sled dogs.

to exercise good judgment, he was reduced to the ranks, and another of the team exalted in his stead. A dog so degraded would show by his demeanour that he felt the disgrace much more than the labour entailed – which he undertook willingly enough. The promoted dog would immediately adapt himself to his new duties, knowing that he was now expected to use his brain rather than his strength.

The leader was instructed entirely by shouts, delivered in Russian – the only language the dogs understood. He was simply told whether to go to the right, or to the left, or straight on, or to stop. A good leader obeyed instantly.

Well-trained, reliable leaders seldom showed any lack of initiative; but it encouraged the team to have an occasional change, as it inspired other dogs with the hope that some day they might be promoted to the post of honour. Such changes were advisable, too, to make provision against possible accident to the leaders. Most of the dogs, however, were more fitted for pulling than for leadership.

Harnessing up a team, when fresh, was a job which required clever management. Unless the sledge was securely 'anchored,' the dogs would assuredly bolt in their excitement; then there would be the very dickens to pay. The sight of penguins on the ice would send them mad with the lust for blood. When these extraordinary creatures were about, the obedience to command, reliability and self-restraint of the leading dog were put as much to the test as the driver's skill and control over his team. The leader would studiously avert his eyes from temptation, and exert his utmost strength to pull the team away from the squawking sirens; whilst the driver would have to put forth equal strength to 'brake' the sledge with his 'chui-stick' – an indispensable part of his equipment without which the team would be quite unmanageable.

Both Meares and Dimitri were fine drivers, and brought their teams safely through many a dangerous predicament. Once Meares' team got completely out of hand at the unprecedented sight, to the dogs, of a whale 'breaching' in a near-by lead. Maddened by the sight, they made for the whale, and it looked as though the whole team would dash into the sea; but Meares' fine management of his animals saved them from disaster.

Whenever a dog managed to break loose from his kennel, as sometimes happened, he would invariably go off baiting a seal, and harry the unfortunate creature to death if it could not find safety by slipping into the water.

During the winter, one of the dogs, Julick, disappeared. A month later, when a comrade and I were taking a walk round the icebergs about 10 o'clock one night, we talked about the dog, wondering what had become of him. Just then we noticed a dog running towards us from the west. He came up with every evidence of unrestrained delight, and to our astonishment we recognised the lost Julick. Where had he been all that time? We never knew; but it was not difficult to deduce what he had been up to, for his coat was matted with blood. He was very thin, and seemed pleased enough to be taken home again.

Osman was the head dog of the pack; and, unlike many of his subordinates – some of which would snarl at everyone except their drivers, and were ever ready to sink their teeth in anyone they took a dislike to – he was gentle and good-natured. Osman was the dog that had been washed overboard in the gale in the Sixties, and saved by one of the seamen when carried aboard again on the crest of the next wave. He had been the fiercest dog of all, when in New Zealand; but that adventure seemed to have a sobering effect on him. Henceforth he regarded us all as friends. He was now a sociable, docile animal, and exhibited obvious pleasure when anyone exchanged a few friendly words with him. With his massive build and magnificent head, he looked every inch the chief he was; and his great strength and wonderful reasoning powers qualified him for the important part he took in our adventure.

Vida, the leader of the second team, was another superb dog, with a head suggestive of a parentage of Chow and St Bernard. He was equally as strong as Osman, but, though as fine of appearance, he had none of Osman's amiable characteristics; he distrusted everyone, except those with whom he was brought into constant contact. Vida was a proud, uncondescending creature, seemingly fully conscious of his own strength and fitness for his work; and conscious, too, of his ability to hold his own in combat with any of his associates.

Stareek was another leading dog, used alternately with Vida. His head was almost as fine as Osman's, but with more of the Eskimo about him. He was gentle as a lamb to those whom he regarded as friends, and had a lovable habit of licking his lips and wagging his tail wildly whenever anyone talked to him; and then he would lie on his back with his tongue out, and paw his face with pleasure.

Tresor was perhaps the handsomest of all the dogs. With his beautiful fluffy coat and black ears, he was more like an Eskimo than any of the others. But with so many good-looking animals in the pack, opinions differed as to which was our Adonis. Meares considered that Krisarovitsa took the palm for looks, and he certainly appeared to be purer to a type than the rest. 'Kris' was undoubtedly a beautiful creature, and so was Volk – who regarded me with contempt while I was taking his portrait. Then there was the sturdy, black Lappy – playful as a puppy – who didn't realise the sharpness of his teeth in the ardour and impetuousness of his hefty caresses. Hohol was another handsome animal, and so was Koomagai. Brodiaga made friends with no one, but had an angry snarl for all; he would wrinkle his nose, curl his lip, and show his great canine teeth threateningly whenever anyone drew near. And I must not omit to mention Kesoi the one-eyed, and Bieleglas, and Biele-Noogis, and the wolfish Ostrenos – and of them all Ostrenos was nearest to a wolf, with his long, treacherous head and narrow eyes.

There were a dozen or more others, and each of the wild creatures had his own peculiar appearance, individuality and characteristics. No two were alike, except in their eagerness for work, their thirst for the blood of seals and penguins, and their readiness to fly at each other's throats on the slightest provocation – or even without any pretext whatever.

When Scott and Meares had almost miraculously escaped with their lives from the crevasse adventure on the Great Ice Barrier, in February, two dogs had even fought fiercely whenever they swung within biting distance of each other, whilst suspended by their harness in the abyss. The other dogs, on being rescued from their dangerous plight, immediately made for the second team, standing by, and engaged in furious conflict with them – so that rescue work had to be stopped for a time until the combatants were separated.

Of the nineteen ponies with which we had left New Zealand, ten had survived the perils and hardships of the past year. Of these ten, two are deserving of special mention – Nobby and Christopher. Nobby, the prettiest of all, was the pony that had such a narrow escape from the jaws of the Killer whales in March. He was Dr Wilson's special protégé, and invariably presented a better-groomed appearance than the others; for, as becomes a lover of animals and an artist, Nobby's owner usually kept his mane and forelock nicely combed and plaited.

Christopher was the strongest and worst tempered. Captain Oates always looked after this pony himself. He would let no one else take the risk – for Christopher was vicious and dangerous. It usually took three or four men to harness him, and he always had to be thrown, and his head held down, before he could be 'hitched-up' to a sledge. Only a born horseman could manage such a wicked little brute; and that is what Titus was – a born master of horses. His patience and imperturbability were inexhaustible. He never got angry or excited; but always talked to Christopher in calm, reassuring tones – no matter how wildly the sinful animal reared and plunged and lashed out with his hoofs. Titus certainly took his life in his hands every time he harnessed Christopher, and owed his immunity from harm to his own skill, agility and fearlessness.

Man had to be hardened as well as beast; so to get fit we played football for an hour, two or three times a week. We always played 'Soccer,' and were able to put two full elevens into the field – the field being the frozen sea, and the goalposts bamboo poles. The teams were well-matched, and, as the full-backs on each side were well up to their work, the goalkeepers usually had a chilly time of it – with the temperature thirty or forty degrees below zero, and often a crisp breeze blowing.

The hard crusted snow which covered the ice gave a good footing; but falls were apt to occur just as they do in football matches anywhere else. It was unfortunate that the most serious fall happened the day I was taking moving-pictures of a game. Debenham fell headlong, and badly strained his knee. This was something in the nature of a disaster, for he was to have started, two days later, with a party, led by Taylor, on a second geological journey to the western side of the Sound. The accident delayed the start three weeks, during most of which time Debenham lay on his back, to give his knee complete rest. It transpired that Debenham had had trouble with his knee before, and he should not have taken any risks with it.

This was the third mishap that had occurred when I was photographing – first Gran's fall when ski-ing; then Clissold's fall from the iceberg, and now Debenham was hors de combat. Also, I had had several narrow escapes myself, since my adventure with the Killer whales. The whale incident had, of course, inspired numerous quips about Jonah; and Taylor had invented a new verb, consisting of the first syllable of my name – 'to pont,' meaning 'to pose, until nearly frozen, in all sorts of uncomfortable positions' for my photographs. This latest mishap revived all the former quizzing about the evil-eye propensities of my camera, and I was once again the butt for no end of twitting about 'the peril of 'ponting' for Ponko' – the latter being my nickname. The more I protested – that I had kinematographed Gran's feat at his own special request; that I had taken every possible precaution to ensure safety when out with Clissold; that Debenham had fallen twenty minutes after I had taken my film, and instanced the scores of occasions on which nothing had occurred to mar the success of my pictures – the more persistently these crimes were fastened on to me.

But such railleries were always good-natured, and everyone in the Hut was subjected to them whenever the slightest occasion presented. No opportunity was missed of poking fun at one another, and everyone hastened to give as good as he received whenever he had a chance of 'getting his own back.' The saving grace of humour served us in good stead always.

Day and Lashly, who had been busy giving the motor tractors a final overhaul during the past few days, now proceeded to bring their machines from their winter shelter for a trial spin on the ice. It really seemed that things were beginning to move, in every sense, when once again we heard the roar of their open exhausts – that always reminded me so of the Brooklands race-track. I got my kinematograph bearing on the scene, as the first of the weird-looking things rolled, in an unearthly manner, out of its snow-walled retreat, and lolloped clumsily over the uneven ground towards the frozen sea. It crept over a rise, and then headed downhill towards the tide-crack. There was some rough and lumpy ice at this point, and as the tractor slumped into it and over it, the rear end came down with a nasty jar, and the engine stopped. Oil poured out of the back-axle, and on examination the aluminium casing was found to have cracked. Dismay entered the hearts of the onlookers – of whom I was one – at the obvious serious nature of this fresh mishap; but for some unaccountable reason this stroke of bad luck was not laid to the charge of the evil influence of my camera – much to my relief. The axle was immediately dismantled, and our motor-engineer and mechanic at once set to work on it. When, two days later, the axle-casing – repaired in a remarkably neat and workmanlike manner, and better and stronger than ever – was once more in place, I realised that Day and Lashly were men whom nothing could daunt, and whose resource and skill were equal to any emergency.

The time was now drawing nigh for the start of the great journey that was the primary object of the Expedition, and a week before the day set for the departure of the Southern Party, the motor contingent set out. One of the tractors was driven by Day, the other by Lashly; Lieut. Evans and Hooper accompanying them – their duty being to walk ahead of the machines and steer them by a short length of rope attached to a pole in front. Evans was the navigator of the party. As the speed of the motors usually did not exceed three miles per hour, their conductors were not hard pressed to keep ahead of them.

In these regions steering gear would be an unnecessary complication. Whenever the steersman desired to change the course of his machine, he simply pulled it round by the rope.

Each tractor hauled three large sledges. Three were laden with stores to be depôted on the Barrier for the use of the Southern Party; two with petrol and lubricating oils, and the sixth with the Motor Party's own rations and camping equipment. But the party didn't get far the first day, as further mechanical adjustments were found necessary before they had rounded the cape. This delayed them until the following morning, October 24th, when the motors got well away, and provided fine subjects for the kinematograph, as they wallowed leisurely towards the southern horizon.

A few days before the start of the Southern Party, Captain Scott had informed us about his instructions to Lieut. Pennell, now commanding the *Terra Nova*. There was small likelihood of the Polar Party being back at Hut Point ere it would be necessary for the ship to return to New Zealand again. The ship was therefore to leave McMurdo Sound not later than the end of the first week in March, or earlier if in danger of being frozen in. If by chance the party were back, some of the Expedition would return home; but, if all went well, it was Scott's desire to remain, with the majority of the members, in the South for another year, to continue other important exploration work. Five of our number would, in any case, be going home – Simpson, whose leave of absence from the Indian Meteorological Office at Simla would have expired; Taylor, who had to return to his work in Australia; Day and Meares, who could not remain another year; and myself, as my work would be finished by the end of the summer, all my kinematograph supplies exhausted, and I should require many months in which to superintend the finishing of my results for publication.

The evening before the start of the main party, Uncle Bill handed me a parcel which contained all his sketches. He asked me to take charge of it, and to deliver it to his wife, telling me it was his earnest hope that we might have a joint exhibition of our work – his sketches and my photographs. He gave me carte blanche to arrange this as I liked – not to wait for the return of the remainder of the Expedition, if I considered it expedient to exhibit the pictures earlier. I was much pleased at this expression of friendship; but I told Uncle Bill that under no circumstances would I arrange for anything of the kind before the Expedition had returned, and that I could ask for no greater honour than to be associated with him in such an exhibition. I preferred, however, not to take the responsibility of being the bearer of the valuable parcel, and arranged to hand it to Lieut. Pennell, to be placed in the *Terra Nova*'s safe, and thence forwarded home by registered parcels post.[1]

I was anxious to accompany the Polar Party as far as possible; but Captain Scott explained that it would be quite impossible to transport my heavy apparatus. Every ounce that could be carried on the sledges, other than camping equipment, would be food. 'Everything must give way to food' he said. After the party had reached the Great Ice Barrier, there would be nothing to photograph but the level plain of boundless, featureless ice, with the long caravan stringing out towards the horizon. Besides, too, work of more importance awaited me elsewhere – in recording the seal and bird life, which he regarded as of the highest value to zoology. I realised the sound reason of this, but at my earnest request it was arranged that I should drive by dog-team to Hut Point to record the start from the Discovery hut; and thence on to the Great Ice Barrier to secure some final films. Beyond that, it would be impossible for me to go. I rejoiced, however, that I was to have an opportunity of accompanying the party, if only for twenty-five miles.

October 31st, 1911, the long awaited day, came at last. The first of the ponies got off in the morning; then, at 4 o'clock, I took my place behind Meares on a dog-sledge, and we were soon skimming swiftly over the frozen sea, to the soft pattering of many dogs' paws on the crusted snow.

To drive by dog-team over the frozen sea, in the crisp Polar air, is one of the most exhilarating experiences imaginable. The yelping of the excited creatures as they are harnessed up; the whining and howling in pleasurable anticipation as they strain at the traces, impatient to be off; the mad stampede with which they get away, when the driver gives the word to go; the rush of the keen air into one's face; the swish of the sledge-runners, and the sound of forty paws pat-a-pat-a-patting on the crackling snow, is something that cannot be described. It must be experienced.

As we rounded the cape and made for the west end of Razorback Island, the whole great mass of Erebus was on our left, with its ten miles of seracs and crevassed glaciers tumbling down to the sea in the wildest confusion. And on our right the beautiful Lister massif, seventy miles away, heaved from below the western horizon far up into the skies. We sped past the imprisoned icebergs, and, as we neared Razorback, we saw many seals lying about under the lee of the land. The sight filled me with hopeful anticipation, for it was my intention to spend much time there during the next few weeks. With occasional stops to give the willing dogs a breather, we pressed on past what remained of Glacier Tongue since the break-up of the phenomenon in March; past the Turk's Head, Hutton Cliffs and Castle Rock, until Hut Point loomed before us.

The snow-clad promontory is a most impressive sight. On its summit stands a great white wooden cross, erected to the memory of George T. Vince, one of the men of the *Discovery* Expedition, who lost his way in a blizzard, and his life by falling over the near-by ice-cliffs. This farmost symbol of the Christian faith on earth, gleaming golden in the evening sunlight against the leaden southern sky, seemed like some guardian angel at the threshold of the Forbidden Land beyond – reminding those who would venture further that in the midst of life they are in death, yet holding out the hope of Life Eternal.

I saw nothing more inspiring in – nor have I seen in all the world besides – than that simplest and most sacred of emblems on that snow-clad hill, raised in honour of a seaman of the British Navy, who, in this remote corner of the world, died in the performance of his duty.

We reached the Discovery hut at 6.45, having made the journey in well under three hours, and soon had a hot meal sizzling on the fine blubber stove that Meares had built of bricks and a sheet of boiler-iron during his previous visits. Three hours later, the vanguard of the Southern Party arrived – Dr Atkinson and P.O. Keohane, with the ponies Jehu and Jimmy Pig. The rest of the party, who started a day later, drifted in during the following afternoon – in order, P.O. Evans with Snatcher; P.O. Crean with Bones; Bowers with Victor; Oates with Christopher; Wright with Chinaman; Scott and Anton with Snippets; Cherry-Garrard with Michael; Wilson with Nobby, and Dimitri with his dog team. All were housed by 5.15 – fourteen men and four ponies in the hut, and six ponies in the stable – the dogs, of course, being berthed outside, as usual.

Though we were early astir the next morning, the ponies did not begin to get off until 8 p.m., as it was intended to march by night, in order to give the animals the benefit of the warmest hours of the twenty-four for resting. I secured kinematograph records of the various units, and at midnight started by dog-team with Dimitri, for Safety Camp, on the Great Ice Barrier.

Captain Scott had counselled me to be very careful not to permit the dogs to get too near the ponies, as he was concerned lest the animals should take fright and bolt. When we approached the Barrier I had some difficulty in making the Russian, Dimitri, understand about not getting too near the ponies; he objected to keeping too far out on account of bad crevasses near

Dog team resting by an iceberg

White Island. However, he drove carefully up the slope from the frozen sea on to the greatest ice-sheet on earth, and we saw the whole party, about a mile ahead – the foremost units preparing to move on, after a short rest. Dimitri anchored his team a hundred yards away, and all was well. I was in time to have a final meal with them before kinematographing the start of the first Barrier march of the whole cavalcade, by the light of the cloud-hidden midnight sun.

At last came that never-to-be-forgotten moment when I must part from Scott and Wilson, who formed the rearguard. It was very cold, and a biting wind was blowing; and ice and sky mingled in the South, into which the foremost units of the caravan were rapidly disappearing. On the bosom of that vast wilderness of ice, I could think only of the unknown perils and hardships that lay ahead of them; and when I tried to speak, I could not voice the words I wished to say. I could only look into Scott's eyes and grip his hand, as he wished me 'Good-bye and good luck!' with my work. But I felt he understood.

And then mutely I turned to Uncle Bill, who was smiling as he always smiled. I think he was a little touched himself, as reassuringly he laid a hand upon my shoulder, and said: 'Cheer-up, Ponko! Good luck!' They were the last words the splendid fellow ever spoke to me, and I shall always remember him with that smile upon his fine, strong face.

As they plodded beside their ponies away into 'the stark and sullen solitudes that sentinel the Pole,' I recorded the scene in moving-pictures, and Uncle Bill looked back and waved to me. I stood, with a feeling of depression and loneliness at heart, until they shrank into the distance, half wondering if ever I should see them again.

But I had gazed for the last time on the faces of my fearless Chief and friend. They were destined never to return from the heart of the Great Alone.

Death met them on their homeward way.

Midnight sun.

CHAPTER XVII

The Polar Summer

With a final lingering look at the rearguard of the Southern Party shrivelling into that desolate wild, Dimitri and I got on to our sledge and headed back for Hut Point. It was 2 a.m. with a cold, keen wind blowing; and long ere we had reached the Discovery hut our faces wore heavy masks of ice.

On the morning of the third day after the departure of the pony units, Meares and Dimitri harnessed the excited dogs, mounted their heavily-laden sledges, and started off for the Barrier – expecting to catch up with the main Southern Party two days later.

Soon after seeing them off, Anton and I started at 10.30 a.m. for Cape Evans – man-hauling our sledge. The day was clear and sunny, but heavy drift during the preceding twenty-four hours had made the surface of the sea-ice very bad. Moreover, it was but 10° below freezing and the weather calm, so that the heat of the sun became quite oppressive and the snow soft and sticky. Before we had gone a quarter of a mile, we found our work cut out in places to so much as move the heavy twelve-foot sledge with its 400 lbs. load of photographic gear and camping equipment – and we hoped to cover over fifteen miles that day! Sometimes we came to welcome runs of clean ice, and sped along at a merry pace – the sledge seeming a mere featherweight. Then we would run into a great, sticky snowfield again, and the sledge immediately became like a deadweight mass of lead. Warm weather like this certainly has its disadvantages when sledging in these regions, and we should have been glad if the 'mercury' had dropped ten degrees nearer the zero mark.

That was the most strenuous day's work Anton or I ever did in our lives. After struggling on until 10.30 p.m., we had covered eleven miles; but it became obvious that we could not get home that night. When about half-a-mile south of Razorback Island, Anton told me he could pull no further. I was not sorry to hear it, for I was done myself with the labour of the past twelve hours; I therefore decided to camp. After we had pitched the tent and had some cocoa and food, I was preparing to turn-in in my sleeping-bag, when Anton gave me to understand, in his broken English, that he did not like the idea of sleeping out on the ice, as the weather looked threatening in the south. He asked me if I would permit him to walk on to the Hut – about three miles away.

I tried to laugh away his fears; but, knowing his highly superstitious nature, and seeing that he really dreaded the idea of sleeping on the ice – though the night was light as day – I consented to his making his way home, telling him to come back to help me in the morning. I watched him through my glass until he reached the land; then, weary with the effort of the day, I crept into my warm reindeer bag, and slept.

I was awakened a couple of hours later by the drumming of the wind against the tent, and, on looking out, saw that heavy drift was blowing. It was a soothing sound, however, and lulled me to sleep again. I dreamed about music and singing and the gramophone. The singing grew louder and louder, and the tune was strangely familiar. Then I distinctly heard and knew the words. The dream became so real that I woke up, and, emerging from my sleeping-bag, found Gran and Nelson sitting beside me, singing 'We All Walked Into The Shop.'

It was midday, and as the drift had died down they had come out to help me, and had considerately chosen this manner of rousing me pleasantly from my slumber. The weather was too overcast and threatening to do any photography at the Razorback seal rookery, so we packed my sledge and returned to Cape Evans.

I was now free to carry out as much of my programme for the summer as the weather and other circumstances would permit. Captain Scott had finally discussed this with me during our last evening at the *Discovery* hut. It would be advisable to secure the seal records as soon as possible, as it was now the calving season. Then several visits to the Adélie penguin colony at Cape Royds would be necessary, to record different stages of the incubating of the eggs and the brooding of the chicks. There was also a lot of scenic work yet to be done. After finishing this, if it should be possible to do so, I could take Clissold and Anton and make a journey to the Koettlitz Glacier – the great ice-river at the foot of Mt Discovery which was named after the surgeon and botanist of Scott's 1901–4 Expedition.

As matters turned out, I was unable to accomplish the entire programme. Owing to much delay by unusually bad weather; to the fact that it was found advisable to send a further party out to the Barrier with supplies; and to the early breaking up of the ice in the west of the Sound – to my lasting regret it was impossible to make the journey to the glacier in the Western Mountains.

I found the Antarctic a very disappointing region for photography. It was exasperating to find the weather so often thwart one when half-way to some goal – for a journey to a point even a few miles distant could not be undertaken lightly. My camera and kinematograph equipment weighed more than 200 lbs.; and when visiting a point a few miles away it was wise to take camping kit and food for several days, lest a blizzard should descend upon us. Pulling a load of 400 lbs. deadweight, two men could not maintain a greater pace than one mile per hour; and if the surface were bad their progress might be much slower. Because of the serious losses to our transport, there was seldom a man available to help me with the photographic work, whereas in fine weather I could have used the services of two constantly. However, notwithstanding the many impediments with which Nature sought to baulk one, it was surprising how much could be accomplished by persistent effort, and by grasping every opportunity she gave whilst in more amicable humour.

As soon as possible after my return from Hut Point, I proceeded with the illustrating of the life and habits of the seals, the Adélie penguins and the Skua-gulls – on which I had already made a good beginning the previous summer. Before the present season was over, this work was completed, and I offer some observations on these interesting creatures in subsequent chapters of this volume.

In the intervals of studying and recording impressions of the Nature life about me, I was ever mindful of the Polar scenes midst which these creatures found existence. There was no lack of subjects for the camera, and I might have made a hundred pictures from the door of our Hut without directing my lens elsewhere than into the heavens.

At one season or another there are wonderful scenes to be witnessed in the atmosphere from almost any land on earth. I have many a time marvelled at the beauty of the cloudscapes suspended over London – yet I seldom saw a face uplifted to behold them, except at sunset. How many ever look at the wonders of the heavens at noon?

The pageantry of the skies was no less beautiful here, at the end of the earth, than in temperate and tropical lands. The desolate tract of ice that swept from our door to the northern horizon was an inspiring foreground for many a glorious transformation scene. Sometimes great billows and bellying spinnakers of cumulus would roll over the glacier ridge between Erebus and Cape Barne, and pile high up into the ether in flowing convolutions of vapour that gleamed whiter than the snows below in the midday sunshine. At other times beautiful combinations of cirro-cumulus would fill the skies;

whilst often – too often – a canopy of stratus was suspended like a shroud above us. Sometimes, too, a great forbidding nimbus, heavily charged with snow, would sweep down over the ice, and race towards us with crested name above, and all blue and iron-grey below. It was well to waste no time in seeking shelter when these ominous confederates of death were unleashed, for a lost wayfarer's life would be of small account if caught unprepared in the raging blizzards that accompanied them.

The most beautiful clouds of all were cirrus. These feathery harbingers of the wind would radiate from some spot on the horizon, and spread in fanlike fashion towards the zenith, changing with kaleidoscopic rapidity in some tempest of the upper air, whilst below all, as yet, was peace. One such cirrus formation was the most remarkable cloud effect I have seen anywhere in the world. The sky was cobalt at the time, and the low-lying midnight sun stained each fibrous wisp and plume vermilion, so that the heavens seemed aflame from a furnace on Cape Barne. It was a gorgeous spectacle, and provided one of the most beautiful photographs of the scenery at the gates of heaven that I secured from the door of our winter-quarters Hut.

For a brief season, in the height of summer, the Antarctic is the most wonderful place on earth. When the temperature rose to anywhere near 'Freezing,' if the skies were clear and the wind at rest, one could sit on the rocks and bask in the sultry rays of the sun at any hour of the twenty-four. In such weather the door of our Hut was left open, to freshen the interior with the sweet pure air; whilst the joyous squealing and raucous laughter of the Skua-gulls never ceased about us.

Hauling a sledge in such weather could not be done without shedding garment after garment as one progressed, and the snow sparkled underfoot with a myriad brilliants. When one donned the indispensable non-actinic goggles to guard against snow-blindness, the brilliants immediately became gems of every conceivable hue. But such welcome conditions did not last for long. Even a zephyr astir made all the difference; and, except for those few brief weeks at the end of the year, the sky more often than not was overcast, whilst the 'mercury' level exhibited a strong affinity for the bulb.

Whilst this pleasurable season lasted, the stern countenance of Nature relaxed into smiles, and assumed such gentle aspects as seemed almost incredible after the frowns and passions that had marred it for so long. Even our sterile peninsula simulated a comeliness of mien of which I had not suspected it capable – with the laughing Skuas gambolling in its flashing lakelets, whilst the hills around were, as yet, shrouded with snow.

Everywhere beautiful contrasts of light and shadow played; and as the earth revolved around the sun the noonday highlights became the midnight shades, whilst the shadows of midnight were the highlights of noon. When the sun was in the east, the crenellated precipices of the glacier – inhabited by the echoes whose acquaintance I had made that evening in the winter night – threw long blue shelters from the glare. But when the sun passed round to the west, his glory was reflected by a thousand flashing mirrors in the gleaming walls.

It was wonderful, too, to watch the changing aspects of the polished icebergs, as the sun meandered round the sky. The warm rays, beating on their crystal turrets and parapets and gables, melted every particle of snow, so that white ice only remained, tinged with the delicate hues of aquamarine and tourmaline; whilst every crack was turquoise and each deeper fissure azure. The sunlit side of every berg would be all a-dripping from the heat; but from each cornice in the shade a fringe of icy stalactites depended, and the walls and slopes glistened with the lustre of cut-glass.

I spent many happy hours with my cameras amongst them – and the glaciers and islands and other lions of the vicinity. Cape Barne is the most remarkable feature of the region. It is a column of lava, 250 feet high, which solidified in the vent of some volcano that long ago disappeared, leaving this monolith as its cenotaph. One day, as we were returning from Cape Royds, I asked Nelson to stand near the foot of the column, to give scale to my photograph. But, as showers of fragments were occasionally falling from the tower – due to expansion of the mass by the heat of the summer sun, after its contraction in the winter – he exhibited a lack of joyfulness about accepting this invitation. However, as it was obvious that a figure was necessary to my picture, and as Nelson is a good fellow, he did as I bade him and 'made no bones.'

The evil-eye of my camera was blind on this occasion, and I secured an excellent photograph, without mishap.

When it had been found necessary to send further supplies to One Ton Camp, Day and Hooper of the Motor Party – who had returned safely from the Barrier with the news that all was well with the Southern Party – started out again five days later, accompanied by Clissold, he having now recovered from his accident. In the absence of our chef, those who knew anything about cooking now had an opportunity to distinguish (or extinguish) themselves. Simpson, at once, frankly admitted that if we were going to place any reliance in him, we should have to subsist on canned meats and 'hard-tack' as he had never so much as boiled an egg in his life. Fortunately, others had had a wider experience, and on the whole we did not fare so badly. In my California ranching days I had learned to cook from a man who was a real culinary artist. That was a long time ago, and I had seldom tried it since. I took my turn however, and soon got my hand in again.

One day, about a month later, we espied the party, five miles away, returning over the frozen sea from Hut Point. As it would take them about three hours to reach home, and with the return of the cook there would be no longer any necessity for my, or any other's efforts for the table, I decided, with the help of Anton, to have one final fling, and to prepare a welcome surprise for the party – to show them that we had not been altogether helpless. Hastening back to the galley and its pots and pans, we broached the stores for a banquet.

In due time the party arrived with true sledging appetites, thinking, as they afterwards admitted, they would have to dine on canned meat and biscuits. Instead, they found the ward-room table laid with a hot roast leg of mutton, an Irish stew, mashed potatoes and sprouts, hot custard with stewed pears, a large cold raspberry-jelly, pastry jam-tartlets and a 'three-decker' jam cake (two specialities of mine), bread, butter, jam, cheese, chocolates, and great jugs of hot cocoa.

For a moment they stood aghast, with incredulous gaze riveted on the table; then they rubbed their eyes. Having convinced themselves that they were awake, with a wild 'who-oop' they fell upon the feast – and never did food disappear with such extraordinary rapidity.

Away to the west, whenever the weather was unusually clear, there unfolded to our gaze a panorama such as I doubt the world can show the parallel. Since that memorable day when first we saw the Western Mountains across McMurdo Sound, we had seen the peaks under every phase of light and shadow. We had seen them freshen to the morning; basking at noonday, and dozing in the evening – in those sunny, summer days; and we had watched them sleeping with wide open eyes under the mellow midnight sun. We had seen them lashed and tormented by the autumn tempests, until obliterated from view. We had seen them suffused with gory afterglows, and shrink like spectres into the Polar night. We had seen them 'bare their fangs unto the moon,' and had watched them wake from their long winter slumber, and blush to the kiss of the returning sun.

'No words of mine can convey the impressiveness of the wonderful panorama displayed to our eyes,' wrote Captain Scott.

For my part, I have felt the spell of the rugged beauty of the Alps, and the enchantment of the varying moods of the sacred Fujiyama. I have seen morning gild the mighty Everest; and evening stain the snows of Kangchengjunga. I have viewed the Spanish Sierras from the towers of the Alhambra; and the Aiguilles of Haute Savoie from the summit of Mont Blanc. I have seen the rugged Rockies and the pine-clad Sierra Nevadas; the shapely Californian Shasta, and the exquisite Javanese Merapi. And in similar latitudes at the other end of the earth I have seen the midnight sun shine on the crags and table mountains of Spitsbergen.

Higher mountains I have seen – higher by far – but in all the world I know of none more serenely beautiful than those fifty miles of snowy heights in tempest-swept Victoria Land, as seen from Ross Island, across the frozen sea.

Scott told me that a panoramic telephotograph of the range would be of lasting value to geography. I knew it would also be a remarkable feat of photography. I had soon realised the difficult nature of the task, however, for in those first sunny summer days the radiation from the sea had been so great that the quivering air rendered telephotography of distant objects impossible. One day in the autumn I had, however, succeeded in telephotographing the Queen of the range, Mt Lister, over 13,000 feet high and seventy miles away, during a brief lull in the wind. But, for the coveted panorama I had to wait until the weather became colder; and when it did so, the few days on which the mountains appeared clearly were so windy that the feat was equally impracticable.

An equivalent focus of nearly six feet would have to be used – six magnifications of an eleven-inch lens, which took the extreme limit of the extension of my camera. A six-times colour filter would be necessary in conjunction with an orthochromatic plate, and a medium diaphragm. Photographic enthusiasts will understand that to attempt to use such a combination on a windy day would be to court certain failure. Moreover, it was necessary that the picture should be taken from as great height as possible; for the tendency of telephotography is to annihilate perspective, and from sea-level the intervening icebergs would appear to be close to the mountains, some of which were about ninety miles away. I should therefore have to get above the highest of them. This increased the difficulty, for the wind was invariably stronger on high ground. I selected a position on the Erebus moraine, above the Ramp, where, in the lee of a debris-cone, there would be, to some extent, shelter from the prevailing wind, if any, and an uninterrupted prospect from an altitude of about 250 feet.

To accomplish the feat had become for the time being the principal aim of my existence, and I had kept a watchful eye on the weather, in the hope that, if but for one single hour, the elements might prove propitious. But,

Ramparts of Mt Erebus

to my disappointment, the winter had crept upon us without any chance having occurred to attain the object of my desire. When, after those months of darkness, the welcome sun once more caressed the virgin peaks, the yearning to record the wonder was greater than ever; but week after week passed by, and still no opportunity occurred. On the rare occasions when the wind was at rest and the mountains visible, the radiation from the ice was now as bad as formerly it had been from the open water. It was impossible to focus. As it was now mid-summer again, I began to fear I might never get the coveted picture; for, once the ice broke up, the character of the scene would be completely changed. A frozen sea was essential.

But early in January there came a day when the visibility was perfect, and only a light breeze, sufficient to eliminate all radiation, was blowing. I decided that the chance of a lifetime had come; so 'packing' my things up to the Ramp, I set the camera on a heavy, rigid tripod in the shelter of my debris cone. All the peaks stood out distinctly in the marvellously clear air; but the sea edge of the glaciers – at the base of the foothills, forty miles across the Sound – was invisible, as it was below the horizon.

After carefully checking some calculations, I exposed a double series of 7 x 5 plates on the panorama, telephotographing the entire range from end to end; and I had the satisfaction of developing, an hour later, twelve beautiful negatives of one of the longest-distance panoramic telephotographs ever secured.

CHAPTER XVIII

Concerning Seals

Captain Scott, when at the point of death, in his last message to his wife, wrote: 'Make the boy interested in natural history if you can; it is better than games; they encourage it at some schools.' (Vide *Scott's Last Expedition*.)

Cape Evans was not an ideal location for the study of Antarctic zoology. There was a lack of variety of fauna, though of the few families that occur individuals were numerous enough.

Unlike its antipodes, on the Antarctic continent there are no Polar bears; neither are there wolves, foxes, nor any other fur-bearing creatures. In the Far South no land animals exist. The only living creatures are such as find subsistence in the sea, and sea-birds.

Though innumerable sea mammals frequent the islands some 1,500 miles further north, only three species visited us during our stay at Cape Evans. Of two of these three species we saw only a single specimen; they were a Sea-leopard, and a Crab-eater seal. I have already mentioned that we first saw Crab-eaters in the pack-ice.

The only Sea-leopard that had the misfortune to visit us, came during the winter. One moonlight day in May – which is one of the three months of darkness – I was out with Day, near a place known to us as the Big Crack, when I came upon a seal which I proceeded to stir up for fun. To my surprise I saw that what, in the darkness, I had taken for a complacent Weddell seal, was really a very different kind of beast – slim and clean-cut of form, with a well-defined neck, a long head, and an array of teeth that it showed in a most aggressive manner, as it first snarled, and then went for me. Day, who recognised it from his previous experience of seals on the Shackleton Expedition, shouted to me: 'Look out! It's a Sea-leopard! It'll bite your leg off!'

I did 'look out'; and put up the smartest bid of dodging and sprinting that I did the whole time I was in the South, with the beast wriggling and flapping after me, close at my heels. Day, who is longer of leg than I, ran up and diverted its attention, and then we lured it well towards the Hut, half a mile away, where we left it – as blown as ourselves – and called Uncle Bill,

Weddell seal and calf.

who came out with his club and dirk, and despatched it, for his collection. It was a young animal, about nine feet long: a full grown adult bull would be more than double the length.

The Sea-leopard, though a true seal, is an ocean carnivore that lives on warm-blooded creatures such as penguins; it also preys on the fish-eating seals. Sir Douglas Mawson relates how, during the Australian Antarctic Expedition, he saw one chasing a Crab-eater seal. It has a wicked-looking array of teeth – as terrible as a tiger's – and no doubt it would mangle a man badly should one be so unfortunate as to fall at its mercy. From the amazing speed at which this nine-foot specimen wriggled along, we realised in what an unpleasant dilemma one might find oneself if a twelve-footer were stirred up in mistake for a Weddell.

Of Weddell seals we saw any number; they were always with us during our stay in the South. Numerous specimens were eight, nine or ten feet long; and some of the big bulls that I observed on the floes – but could not get near to – must have been quite four yards from the tip of the snout to the end of the tail flippers. Weddell seals are fish-eating mammals – inoffensive creatures so far as man is concerned; but a big bull is a formidable looking beast as he lies slumbering in the lee of an iceberg – three-and-a-half yards of pulsating flesh, with appropriate girth.

They have beautiful coats, which vary so much in their markings that sometimes it seemed hardly possible that neighbours basking on the ice could be of the same species.

Most commonly, the upper part of the coat is a rich chocolate-brown, graduating to a lighter brown, or fawn, and streaked and spotted with white or dark brown under the belly. Other specimens are mottled all over, whilst others again have rich black markings, and some are streaked with grey and silver. The finest coats exhibit all these shades, from black to silver, and are exceedingly handsome. But they are not fur; the skin is covered with short hair, which, however beautiful in life, is little sought after by the furrier. If Weddell seals were fur-bearing creatures, their handsome coats would speedily prove a curse to them, and render them liable to the danger of extermination.

The Weddell seal in its native element is an agile, graceful creature; but it is a most ungainly animal when out of water. Unlike the Sea-leopard, which can travel so rapidly on the ice, or the Crab-eater, which wriggles along at a fairly quick pace too, the Weddell undulates its great bulk laboriously forward in a caterpillar-like manner, alternately humping up its back and straightening out – propelling itself thus with the assistance of its paddles and tail flippers.

In the Antarctic, seals seem to be quite devoid of fear when on the ice. This is because they have no enemies when out of the sea. When in it, they must ever be on the watch for their mortal enemy, the Killer whale. When the weather was fair and there was no wind, the great, fat creatures would bask and sleep in the sunshine for days together in the summertime. Often they seemed to be dreaming, for they would start in their sleep, and snort and gnash their teeth, whilst a quiver ran all over their sleek, floppy forms. Their dreams always seemed to be of a pleasant nature, perhaps reminiscent of catching some fat fish that lurked amongst the rocks; I never saw them exhibit any symptoms indicative that their encounters with the Killer whales were troubling them.

We used to get much fun out of teasing fat old Weddell bulls, whose blubber was so thick that prodding them with a stick at first failed to wake them. When at last they did awake, their astonishment was most comical; they would stare and blink at us, as though trying to make sure that they really were awake, and not having some horrible nightmare. Our vertical habits seemed to puzzle them greatly. Their range of vision is very limited when they are out of water; how far they can see when in it is, of course, unknown. Judging from their demeanour, we seemed to loom suddenly upon them when we drew near. Becoming aware of our presence, they would stare at us in blank amazement with their great soft eyes, and roll over and regard us sideways, first on one side and then on the other; then they would lie on their backs and scrutinise us upside-down, in the vain endeavour to see us horizontally and make us into seals. Finally, presumably coming to the conclusion that we must be merely well-developed penguins, if left alone they would resume their interrupted slumbers and bother no more about us.

If we approached near and provoked them, they would chatter their teeth rapidly, and, opening their mouths wide, they would snort and bellow in a blustering sort of way, in the effort to frighten us. As this invariably failed to have the desired effect, and we stood our ground, they would then exhibit real symptoms of fear, and remove themselves out of the way as quickly as their ponderous bulk permitted, looking at us, with head upraised, furtively along the backbone as they did so. A few yards seemed to eliminate us from their vision, and having thus shaken off the nightmare, they would roll over and snooze again.

Though, as a natural protection against the cold, they have a substantial lining of blubber, or fat – two to three inches thick – between the hide and the flesh, they do not like zero temperatures. If a keen wind arose, and they were unable to find any shelter from it, they speedily retired into the sea for warmth. Even in the coldest months of the year the water was always of a uniform temperature of three degrees below the freezing-point, though the air temperature might be eighty degrees lower. During the winter, though they kept their blow-holes open, they only came on to the ice to sleep when the weather was calm. We found that holes, which we made in the ice for fishing purposes, froze eighteen inches or more in twenty-four hours; so the seals must have to be continually on the alert to keep alive. For the three winter months – from the middle of May till mid-August – there is, save for the periods of moonlight, darkness day and night. They must, therefore, have some instinct that amounts to a separate sense, other than sight, to guide them to the blow-holes on which their lives depend; and in low zero temperatures they must find it necessary to visit these holes frequently to keep them from freezing solid. Sometimes a seal would arrive at a hole in such distress that the vehemence of the first expiration of its too-long pent-up breath was almost like the blowing of a whale; and the rapid breathing that followed showed plainly that it had remained submerged almost to the point of exhaustion. I do not think it unlikely that some are drowned under such circumstances. Several times I saw dead seals in the sea when the ice was breaking up in the spring, and thought it not unlikely that they had met their end by drowning, for they exhibited no injuries.

It was a weird experience to stand beside one of their blow-holes on a calm, moonlight winter night. The thin film of ice over the water indicated that the breathing-place was in frequent use. Suddenly, a tremor would ripple through the film; then a seal's head would break it and shoot out of the hole, all glistening in the moonlight, and, loudly snorting, its owner would draw in long draughts of the keen, biting air. I have often stood ten or fifteen minutes beside a hole, waiting for a seal's appearance; and have even felt its hot, fishy breath in my face, as, furiously panting, it gazed at me with its great soft eyes in blank amazement, obviously wondering what manner of creature I might be.

Once, in the winter, when the keen air seemed almost effervescing with the intensity of the cold, and my breath solidified the moment that it left mouth and nostrils, and rapidly accumulated into a mass of frost-rime about my warm fur-helmet, I proceeded to a favourite hole and waited. Before I had been there five minutes, a seal emerged, its beautiful head all blazing with phosphorescence; and, as the water trickled down its neck, for a few moments it seemed to be covered with little streaks of flame, whilst a ghostly glimmer shone in the hole. After half-a-dozen healthy blows, it shut its dilated nostrils, almost with a snap, ducked quickly below the surface, and disappeared – perhaps feeling somewhat uneasy in mind at seeing me there.

As the weather grew colder still, the seals would scarcely show their heads at all; they merely poked their nostrils an inch or two above water, and filled their lungs with a fresh supply of air.

When the sun came back again, these breathing-places were fine observation holes through which to watch what went on in the depths below. At one place there was such a hole, with a much larger one nearby, through which, when the sun shone brightly, a great ray of light penetrated deep down into the sea. One day I was lying prone at the smaller hole, watching the passing marine life revealed by this light from the larger one, when a big bull seal made for my peep-hole, with the intention of shooting out on to the ice. He appeared so suddenly, and with such a burst of speed, that I only saw him coming just in time to avoid being bowled over. Even so, I got a punch on the nose from his muzzle; his prickly whiskers brushed my cheek, and I received the full blast of his fishy breath in the face. As I sat back, rubbing my nose ruefully, the seal treaded water, regarding me for a full half-minute in bewilderment, obviously undecided whether I was friend or foe; then, deciding to take no chances, he abandoned his idea of emerging, and subsided whence he came.

Once – through one of these windows in the ice, where the water below was about three fathoms deep – I watched a seal catching fish. The bed of McMurdo Sound swarms with a genus, to which I have before referred, somewhat resembling a small rock-cod, called *Notothenia*. They have large heads, with bodies that taper off rapidly to the tail, and large wing-like fins. These fish lurk amongst the rocks, sometimes lying for many minutes motionless – as gudgeon lie on the pebbles of a river-bed. One day when I was watching them, a seal came gliding along within a yard of the ocean floor, prospecting for its dinner. Its curious tail-flippers, undulating almost imperceptibly, were the only method of propulsion; but they sent it along swiftly and phantom-like, without any commotion to disturb its prey. I saw it pick up several fish, which made no effort to escape; they seemed to be terrorised into a fear that paralysed them, rendering escape impossible. Fixing its victim with its great eyes – which must look goblin-like when under water – the silent apparition simply glided up and sucked them in.

It is of course well known that certain mammals, reptiles and fishes possess the power of fascination, or mesmerism, to a remarkable degree – some even depending upon it as a means of procuring their food. I have personally observed several interesting instances. Once, in my California ranching days, I came upon a large lizard transfixed, as though carved by some clever Japanese sculptor in bronze. On looking in the direction of its intent gaze, I saw a rattle-snake, a yard long, slowly – almost imperceptibly – gliding towards the lizard, with fire blazing in its eyes. So absorbed was the snake with its mesmerising, and so completely was the lizard under its spell, that neither seemed to be aware of my presence, though I stood watching within ten feet of the pair of them. There was almost human terror in the eyes of the lizard, as, riveted to the spot by the awful spell of the fiery eyeballs, it stood as though turned to stone, whilst the flickering forked tongue drew every moment nearer. When within a yard of its victim, the snake drew itself up to strike. The moment it did so, my gun – along the barrel-rib of which I had watched the drama – spoke, and as the 'rattler' writhed out its last spasmodic moments, the terrified lizard, none the worse for its adventure, was scuttling half-a-mile away – judging by the way it scampered off the moment the spell was broken.

When I saw a seal catching fish in McMurdo Sound, I came to the conclusion that these *notothenia* – which can move with lightning-like rapidity when they like, and probably could easily avoid the seal's capacious maw – fall an easy prey, because they become paralysed with fear and are powerless to escape.

When the sea ice became ten feet thick or more – so that there was a good bank of it above water – the seals found it a difficult matter to get out to sleep. If at the first rush they could project themselves far enough out of water to get their side-flippers on to the ice, they could usually work themselves out, after much floundering about. But if these efforts failed, they would proceed to overcome the obstacle by cutting away the ice with their teeth, using both upper and lower incisors and canines in the process. They do not bite the ice, but, opening their jaws wide and using the shoulders as a pivot, they swing their heads from side to side, and saw, or scrape the ice away. Thus, they scoop out an inclined trough, equal to their own width, up which, with a tremendous expenditure of effort, they laboriously drag themselves.

The value of the kinematograph in faithfully recording such animal habits was never better exemplified, during our Expedition, than in this case. Moving-picture films of this remarkable habit – which has been witnessed by only a few observers – were secured, conclusively proving that the process is as described above, and not, as Dr Wilson thought, and described in *The Voyage of the Discovery* by fixing the teeth of the lower jaw and revolving the upper jaw upon it. I watched many seals thus engaged, and the cutting away of the ice was invariably accomplished by swinging the head from side to side, as shown in the films.

They sometimes continued sawing long after any further cutting was necessary. Once, I saw a large female Weddell seal scraping at the flat surface of the ice when she was already well out of water; and on another occasion, I witnessed one sawing away assiduously just below water – for what object I could not imagine. Kinematograph films were secured of both these instances of unnecessary waste of effort. From my observations, I was led to believe that Weddell seals do not utilise all this energy solely for a useful purpose. I think some of them like doing it, and this conviction became the more certain when one day I saw a baby seal, not much over a month old, copying its mother, and sawing away with its little ivory pegs like anything – and seemingly enjoying it.

The young Weddell seals are born about the end of October, or early in November; but I was unable to get to the calving grounds at Razorback Island as early as I would have liked. When, towards the end of October, I started off with cameras and kinematograph, a blizzard threatened when I had proceeded about half way, and I had to return home. Then, owing to the start of the Southern Party on November 1st, and, later, more bad weather,

I was unable to begin the work of illustrating this interesting chapter in the life of the seals until ten days later, by which time practically all the calves were born.

On the second day after my return to Cape Evans from the Barrier, I went with Anton to the Razorback seal rookery. As we neared the lee of the land, the sounds reminded me of a sheep meadow in the lambing season; for the calves bleat very much like lambs, and the call of the mothers is half way between the baaing of a ewe and the lowing of a heifer. When we arrived, only a few belated mothers were yet to be delivered; but there were several calves a few hours old.

In the Arctic regions baby seals are white as the snow on which they lie – a provision of Nature to hide them from the searching eyes of Polar bears, until they are old enough to take care of themselves. But in the Antarctic there is no need for such protective colouration, for there are no Polar bears or other land creatures of any kind to prey upon them. The southern seals are pigmented by Nature for protection when in the water, not when safe on ice or land.

I do not think there can be a prettier creature than a baby seal. The little Weddells were about a yard long, and they had thick, soft, woolly coats of down, sometimes cream coloured all over, but more usually fawn, graduating to black at the tail flippers. They were very lively little creatures, with lovely dark eyes, full of wonder; and they looked infinitely more intelligent than their parents.

The mothers were lying about asleep on the ice, suckling their little ones, just as sows lie with a litter – for seals suckle their young like other mammals. Some of the mothers had twins, but this was unusual. If we approached too near, the mother would bellow at us in the endeavour to frighten us away; and occasionally one would 'lope' towards us in a threatening manner, not always bluffing either – sometimes we had to slip quickly aside to avoid her charge. The babies stared at us in open-eyed wonder. They would open their pretty, pink little mouths, if we teased them; and they had a queer way of bending the extremities towards us until head and tail almost met, and then suddenly roll over and flip them round to the other side. And sometimes they would lie on their backs, with tail towards us, and, with head uplifted, regard us along their 'tummies.'

When they were a week or so old, they loved to play pranks on their snoozing mothers; they would nose and romp about them, and bite them playfully – the mother sometimes waking up and joining in the game. When Mama went off hunting, she most certainly instructed her offspring, in some manner that it understood, not to move from the spot until she returned. Then she undulated off to her blow-hole and disappeared for an hour or so; meanwhile the baby curled itself up and lay open-eyed, but never budging from the spot. When the mother returned, she made a bee-line for her offspring, and fondled it with obvious affection.

There is nothing more beautiful on earth than the love of a mother for her child. And so with animals, too. One has only to observe a cow with her calf; a doe with her fawn; a tigress with her cub – to realise that it is something more than instinct which forms that inseparable tie between them. Animals love their young relatively as humans do, and are often ready to lay down life itself in their defence. Seals are no less devoted than the queens of the forest in this respect. To watch the mother seals playing with their little ones, was to realise that amidst the relentless struggle for existence that ever wages in those Antarctic waters, love – unselfish, self-sacrificing, mother love – warms the hearts of the creatures that find existence there.

Once I watched a mother seal with twin babies for an hour or more, and could have spent hours more observing them, if time had permitted. Sometimes the two little animated rolls of down would snuggle side by side and suckle together, while the mother dozed. Then the little imps played pranks upon her, brushing and tickling her face with their flippers, and nipping at her head and neck, as they frisked and teased around her. She dozed with one eye half-open – always keeping a watchful glance upon her offspring – and now and again she would lift her head to regard them, and to give a deep bay, which I could only interpret as an expression of unalloyed contentment with her happy lot. Occasionally she would caress her babies, sniffing at and nibbling them, and running her teeth all up and down their little fluffy forms. She never licked them as a cow licks her calf, for seals are short-tongued creatures, and that is foreign to their nature.

The habit of sniffing their young prompted me to make an experiment, to ascertain if they really did possess the sense of scent. One day, after a mother had left her baby, I teased the little one until I had got it by a circuitous route far away from where she had left it. In due course she returned; but, as the cub was not where she had exhorted it to remain, she exhibited great agitation, bellowing loudly, and rushing about excitedly. Not finding it, she hastened to several neighbouring mothers, frantically sniffing their cubs, but quickly rejecting them. She was received with hostility by the other cows, and there might have been bloodshed if she had not hurried away on her search. Still failing to find her little one, she returned to the spot where she had left it, and carefully smelt about until she had found the trail; then she went off on the scent, with her nose to the ice, until she had covered the whole of the course that her cub had taken. When at last she found her baby, her joy, and her affection for it were obvious. She seemed positively to purr with pleasure as, after caressing and sniffing the little one, she lay and suckled it.

By the time they are a month old the young seals have shed all their down; and in their beautiful new coats of silver-grey and black – sleek and glossy and suitable for rapid progress under water – they are ready for their first dip. I had only one case of this baptism under observation; but it was one of my most fascinating glimpses of the Nature life of the Antarctic when the baby seal lay bleating on the brink, whilst Mama in the water exhorted it in vain to take the plunge. The baby craned its neck over the edge, and, with dilated nostrils and great eyes full of fear, gazed into the pool, emitting plaintive bleats as its courage over and over again failed at the last moment. For a long time the mother coaxed and cajoled unavailingly, as she splashed and dipped and snorted to show how enjoyable it was; then she would disappear for a few minutes, leaving the cub gazing into the deep, that looked so terrifying by contrast with the brilliant sunlit ice. At last, however, the little fellow did make up his mind – whilst his mother was under the ice, too. Slowly and very cautiously he allowed himself to overbalance, and, closing his nostrils with a snap, slid head-first into the water and under the ice, no doubt to find Mama waiting there to act as guide. I stayed some time, but as they did not reappear I concluded that the little chap was finding the wonderful experience more pleasant than he expected, or that Mama had conducted him to some other, and easier, exit hole.

The mothers continue to suckle their cubs for some weeks after they have taken to the water; how long I cannot say, as we lacked opportunity to observe them continuously. The Razorback breeding-ground was too far away to visit except when the weather was fair, and we had a good deal of bad weather about that time. I saw many youngsters still suckling that were evidently well broken to the water. But as the ice, in some seasons, probably breaks up as far south as the island in December, I have no doubt that, in order to meet such a contingency, the young ones are all weaned long before the end of the year – or about a month, or less, after entering the sea.

Though Weddell seals are not gregarious creatures in the same sense that penguins are, yet their herding nature is indicated in the habit of frequenting certain favoured spots for bringing forth their young. Neighbouring females would lie in close proximity, together with their cubs, apparently oblivious of each other's presence. Once, however, I saw two females have a sparring match. Each seemingly suspected the other of designs upon her own offspring, as, in rolling over, they approached one another. With much bellowing they reared and squared up, and with open mouths made passes for each other's throats; but the defence on each side was as good as the offensive, and the bout soon ended without blood-shed. I never saw a fight between two large bulls, but Dr Wilson, during the *Discovery* Expedition, witnessed several desperate encounters for the possession of the females. Lieut. Campbell, of our Northern Party, also reported a fierce fight between two big bulls, in which they gashed each other through hide and blubber until they were bleeding badly. We seldom killed a bull seal that had not deep scars on its hide, and it was easy to distinguish those sustained in combat with their own kind; they were quite distinct from the terrible cicatrices, sometimes a yard or more in length, of wounds received in their adventures with the Killer whales.

If there is one thing seals love more than anything else, it is to lie at the edge of the shore and let the incoming waves roll them over. It seems to give them infinite pleasure. I have even seen a seal allowing itself to be rolled about by the waves amongst the rocks – and kenyte rocks are not the most pleasant for such a purpose, for they are jagged with points and spurs and covered with rasp-like crystals. Their bellies are sometimes lacerated in crawling over these rocks; and often, when they essay ashore in such a spot, their flippers leave a trail of blood behind.

Once, we saw a seal get itself into an extraordinary predicament through a bad error of judgment, which, though ludicrous to us onlookers, must have been anything but pleasant for the seal. In the ice-foot, which extended some ten yards from the land, there was a hole; but the ice was four feet thick and the bottom of it rested on the rocks. The seal, making for the water, plunged headlong into the hole, to which there was no exit below. Finding itself unable to get further in, it was also unable to get out again. For some minutes its nether portion squirmed about in a frantic manner, until, finally, the unhappy creature managed to wriggle its head back as well; and there for half an hour it lay, doubled up in the hole – with both head and tail protruding – before it succeeded with a supreme effort in freeing itself.

The vocal propensities of a bull Weddell seal are remarkable. Dr Wilson, in *The Voyage of the Discovery*, gave the following description of the performance:

> It was a constant source of amusement to us to stir up an old bull Weddell seal and make him sing; he would begin sometimes with a long musical moan at a high pitch, which gradually got louder and sounded like ice-

moans that are common on an extensive sheet of ice. This was followed
by a series of grunts and gurgles, and a string of plaintive piping notes
which ended up exactly on the call note of a bullfinch.

Though Weddell seals are harmless creatures, seldom showing fight except
in defence of their young, yet I discovered more than once that it was as
well to treat them with respect. A ten-foot bull is eight feet or more in girth,
and would weigh from 900 to 1,000 lbs. One day, I came across one of these
big fellows among the ice-blocks at West Beach – a sandy stretch of shore
at the end of our cape, much frequented by seals as a convenient sheltered
spot for a snooze. I tried to persuade him, by poking him with a stick, to
rear up his head into a favourable position for a portrait. Having worked
him into a fine pose – with head and shoulders well arched back, staring
at me open-mouthed, and flippers extended – I was focusing him on the
ground-glass, with my eyes in the hood of my reflex camera, when, just as I
was about to release the shutter, he suddenly evinced the most determined
objections to the proceedings. Lunging forward open-mouthed, with a loud
bellow, he seized me by the shin and sent me flying backwards.

With several hundredweight behind it, the blow might well have broken
my leg; but fortunately I was caught off my balance, and the fall saved
me. Having sent me sprawling, he retreated, apparently as scared as I was
– regarding me suspiciously along his backbone. I limped slowly back to the
Hut in a good deal of pain, and could feel the warm blood trickling down
my leg, until my foot seemed to slip about in my boot each time I stepped.
On arriving at the Hut, I unfastened my clothing as quickly as possible,
fully prepared to find my leg in a horrible state; but to my surprise there
was hardly any haemorrhage. There were four teeth cuts on my shin, a red
bruise, and a mere spot of blood; that was all. My thick clothing had no
doubt saved me from worse injury. It was a curious instance of the power
of imagination, for I had felt convinced the wound was bleeding freely.
These seals have clean, healthy mouths, and no trouble ensued from the
bite; I dressed it antiseptically and it healed up rapidly. After this adventure
I treated these big Weddell seals with more deference than hitherto; it was
obvious that one of them enraged might easily break a man's leg with its
jaws; they could also do so with a rapid blow of the heavy tail flippers, which
are no mean weapons either. In this case I had certainly invited, and, no
doubt, from the seal's point of view, deserved the punishment I received.

On another occasion, when I was kinematographing a large Weddell seal
amongst the rocks, some sudden impulse urged it to go for me. The unusual

manoeuvre was so unexpected, and the seal charged at such a rate that I had to pick up the camera and dodge aside; even so the 900 lb. beast very nearly knocked both me and my apparatus over.

One day when the *Terra Nova* was moored to the ice, off Hut Point, I witnessed – and had the good fortune to kinematograph a great part of – a stirring drama of Polar animal life. A school of Killer whales appeared, cruising along by the ice-foot, on the look-out for seals. There were about a dozen, and some of them must have been huge fellows, judging from the height of their dorsal fins, which projected five or six feet above the water. The sinister shapes rose and sank, and rose again, as the evil creatures moved along – a small forest of spouts preceding each appearance of the fins. Suddenly, a big cow Weddell seal shot out of the water ahead of the whales, and landed with a resounding smack on the ice. Instead of shuffling off to safety, the terrified animal immediately turned round and, bellowing loudly, hung over the ice edge, peering into the water. I wondered what such madness meant; but in a moment a baby seal appeared, and made frantic efforts to struggle out to join its mother. Frenzied with fear for the life of her little one, the mother rushed back and forth distractedly, as she saw the heaving fins drawing momentarily nearer; whilst the baby, piteously bleating, with its little paddles on the ice-edge, struggled in vain to get its body out of water. When the ill-omened rising, sinking, fins were within a dozen yards, the mother rushed and leapt into the water, almost on to the very top of them. I thought she had sprung to certain death; but, with one accord the rhythmical fins now moved outward from the ice, and then I knew that this was but a ruse on the part of the mother to lure the dreadful creatures from her baby. A minute later the cluster of fins turned again towards the ice, and almost simultaneously the mother reappeared and leapt out of the water again – twenty yards in front of them – close to the bleating, struggling baby. Bellowing loudly, she pushed her nose right into the little one's face, as though in a last despairing caress; then she seemed to try to pull it out of danger with her teeth. Again the devilish fins approached, and once again the mother sprang into the very jaws of death – risking her own life without a moment's hesitation to act as a decoy to save her little one. Again the stratagem succeeded, and the fins turned away once more; meanwhile the bleating baby vainly kept on straining to get out. The mother now appeared again, not, however, this time to leap on to the ice, but to try and heave the baby out upon her back. The dorsal fins had turned about again, and I held my breath for the tensity of my nerves, as the devoted mother lifted the baby clear out of the water, and had it within a single inch of safety, when the poor little chap, clawing madly with its flippers, rolled off her shoulders into the sea, and both mother and baby disappeared – not five yards ahead of the nearest of the Orcas, as they rose to sound and then followed their quarry under the ice-sheet.

I waited to see if they would reappear, but I saw neither seals nor whales again. I could only conjecture the tragedy that perhaps was being enacted below the ice on which the sun was shining so serenely – whilst fervently hoping that the devoted mother had devised some expedient to save her little one, without sacrificing herself. It was the most beautiful example I have ever known of devotion of an animal mother for her offspring, proving, as it did, that the love of some wild creatures for their young is not inferior to that of human beings.

This incident has a sequel that is perhaps worth telling. On my return from the Antarctic to Australia, I was pressed by a reporter of one of the leading Sydney daily papers to give a story for publication about the animal life of the South. I agreed, conditionally that the story should be printed word for word as I told it, without addition or alteration, and that a proof should be submitted to me for correction before it appeared. This, the reporter promised, and I related the above incident just as I have told it here. I did not receive the promised proof, however; and the next day an amazing article appeared in the columns of *The Sydney Morning Herald*. If I did not witness the end of the drama, that Sydney reporter did, and – as a finale to his, not my, garbled account of the most unheard-of habits of seals and penguins – he finished the story of the seal and the whales with the assertion, with which he credited me: 'This went on time and time again till the Killers finally reached her, their jaws snapping and tearing at her sides, till the sea was red with blood!'

CHAPTER XIX

The Buccaneers of the South

We saw comparatively little of Polar bird life at Cape Evans. There were only the amphibious penguins and Skua-gulls. McCormick's Antarctic Skua-gull – which was named after Mr McCormick, the naturalist of Sir James Ross's 1840 Expedition – was, so far as one could discover, the only flying-bird that breeds on Ross Island; it was certainly the only bird that bred at Cape Evans whilst we were there. A few Giant petrels visited our promontory occasionally, but though several were shot, nothing was learned of their nesting habits, for they breed many hundreds of miles further north. When in the air they were an imposing sight, for they have a spread of wing some six feet or more from tip to tip; but aground they were ugly, ungainly, disgusting creatures – with big beaks – that would gorge to repletion on the refuse of a freshly-killed seal, and then squat on the floes and doze for hours. They were very timid, and on the approach of anyone, first they vomited the contents of their stomachs to relieve themselves of the weight, and then ran with outstretched wings for twenty or thirty yards ere they could gather sufficient way to enable them to leave the ice – similarly as an aeroplane 'taxies' over the ground before developing sufficient speed to rise into the air.

But the Skua-gulls were with us for six months of the year, and nested within a hundred yards of our Hut. We did not find them altogether pleasant neighbours, for they were extremely noisy and of a most quarrelsome disposition; throughout the summer their raucous screaming never ceased, day or night, around us. They are great scavengers, and the spilling of blood always attracted them in numbers. We first became intimately acquainted with them when the ship moored alongside the icefoot at Cape Evans, to discharge her cargo. Immediately they evinced a lively interest in the scraps thrown overboard from the galley, and soon exhibited their carnivorous propensities. No sooner had the first penguin been killed by the dogs than Skuas flocked to the scene of the tragedy, and were quickly picking at the victim's remains.

These birds are greedy and selfish to the point of folly. After the cook had taken the titbits from a slaughtered seal, a dozen or so Skuas would instantly gather about the carcass, and quarrel so furiously over the remains that sometimes the flesh froze as they fought, and finally they would have to abandon what, but for their avidity, would have been sufficient to provide a feast for a hundred – as even their sharp beaks could no longer make any impression on the meat. We found that a good deal of work could be saved in the flensing of seal-skins by simply laying the pelts on the ice, hair-side downwards; the Skuas rapidly cleaned them of every particle of blubber.

Though numbers of these rapacious birds frequented our vicinity, we soon found that they had no kindred feeling whatever for each other. Each individual regarded its neighbours as its mortal enemies, as indeed they were, for Skuas – whose normal food consists of offal, small fish, *Crustacea* and anything else they can find in the sea – prey also on the eggs and chicks of penguins, and on each other's eggs and young. But, curiously enough, though a Skua will at once pounce down upon, carry off, and devour a neighbour's eggs or chicks, if left unguarded, yet I have never seen one touch a dead adult of its own species. Many gulls were shot around our Hut; but their bodies lay unmolested by their kind – this respect for the dead being one of the few pleasant characteristics of a fowl which I describe for lack of more agreeable creatures to write about.

The Skua-gull's only other virtues are its personal appearance and its love of cleanliness. It has a passion for fresh water, and whilst the snow lakes were open on our cape, scores would congregate in the largest of these to gambol and cleanse themselves in the waters for hours on end, squawking their harsh cries, meanwhile, in delight. I never saw them venture under the cascade during the few days that it rippled down the rocks; but there were always many in the pond above. Standing in the shallows, they would stretch and flap their wings, and scream at the heavens; then, ruffling their feathers, they would settle down, and, with much splashing, send the cold refreshing water all over their bodies, working it well into the skin with evident pleasure – judging by the chorus of shrill cries that accompanied the process. When this diversion was no longer possible, on account of the frost, occasionally they would cleanse themselves in the sea; but only on the sunniest of days, and in a desultory manner, as though it were a duty, and never with any of the visible signs of enjoyment that characterised their frolics in the lake.

Estimated by outward and visible signs, the Skua-gull is a gentleman, and his mate a dainty, well-dressed lady – appearances being thus deceptive, for, except for their looks and cleanliness, there is nothing refined about either male or female; both are scamps and malefactors. Full-grown Skuas are about four feet from tip to tip, and there is little apparent difference between the cock and hen. Their plumage is a symphony in browns, varying from a soft fawn-coloured breast, to rich, dark-brown wing and tail feathers, which are well graduated, with lighter edges; and often there is a golden tinge about the neck of the male. On the pinions there is a broad streak of white, which gives the birds a remarkably handsome appearance when on the wing; this white band is less marked on the upper side of the feathers.

Unlike the penguins – who greeted us as friends – the Skuas regarded us as enemies, and became exceedingly fierce if we approached their nests. They were nesting when we landed, and I spent much time endeavouring to illustrate their habits – a none-too-easy task, which was rendered more difficult by the fact that some of our party failed to comprehend that the gulls were but exhibiting a natural instinct in objecting to our presence near their nests, and in endeavouring to frighten us away by threatening manoeuvres and harsh cries. Finding themselves attacked by several of our number, the gulls quickly regarded us all as enemies, whereas some of us were friends, and anxious only to study their habits. I endeavoured to gain their confidence, and found that they would not molest me as long as they felt I had no evil intentions.

The Skuas began to manifest the desire to nest in December, and many sites were submitted to trial before the location where the eggs were destined to be laid was finally decided upon. The nest was merely a slight hollow scooped out in the kenyte covered ground, where there was fine gravel. The hen birds would try out one place after another, so that the cape was pitted with such 'scoops' that were never used. These unused nests puzzled me greatly, until I discovered the reason for their numbers. About the end of the year two eggs were laid, three inches long, of a greenish-brown colour with dark brown splotches. The eggs were incubated for three weeks.

During this period, if anyone appeared near the nest the hen bird would utter piercing screams and squawks of fear, and, leaving the eggs, would follow the invader with bitter cries, whereupon she was quickly joined by her mate. The pair would then swoop down upon the interloper, as though with intent to attack; but courage usually failed at the last moment, just as the blow seemed imminent, and they would rise again without striking. The menace, however, was sufficient to make one careful, and when one day I did get a blow on the head – and a good hard one too – I deemed it wise to hold a ski-stick above me for protection in future. This was a certain safeguard, as the birds then went for the stick, and not for me. One could not always be on the watch, however, and as time went on I received several sounding whacks. The Skuas never struck with their beaks or claws, but always with the joint of the wing, and the blow was usually delivered from behind.

At Cape Royds the gulls were even more savage than in our own vicinity, and the above expedient availed us nothing against the disgusting practice they there had of vomiting on intruders. They would fly towards us from the rear, and, carefully making allowance for speed and distance, discharge a nauseating shower of filth. Photography had to be done despite such discomforts, and though I protected myself with canvas and constant watchfulness, I was more than once the victim of this revolting habit – whilst the air was rent by what sounded to me very much like screams of sardonic laughter. The Skuas at Cape Evans, though exceedingly truculent, were altogether better-mannered, and never exhibited this unpleasant trait. We accounted for this by reasoning that probably the same birds return yearly to the same locality, and that those at Cape Royds had learnt to adopt such defensive measures during the sojourn there of the Shackleton Expedition.

Once, at Cape Royds, when the Skua chicks were hatching, I decided to kinematograph the process. Having selected a nest where the chicks were about due to appear, I set up the camera, focused it on the eggs, and then went away – so that the mother might return and become accustomed to the machine. Later, I went to the nest again, and, finding that one of the chicks had now pipped the shell, I exposed a few feet of film. The mother was then permitted to return for half-an-hour, when more film was used – and so on for several hours. More than one nest was used to complete the film of the hatching of the eggs, as, had I interrupted the process too frequently with the same clutch of eggs, they would have been chilled and the chicks killed.

When I was recording the final phase of one of the chick's kicking off the last bits of shell, the parents were swooping wildly around me, screaming with rage and fear as they heard the 'peeping' of the struggling little one. Just as I had finished the work and rose from my kneeling position, I received two blows in rapid succession, one on the back of the head and the other in the right eye. As I held both my arms close to my face for protection, two more blows were delivered, one just at the back of the ear, which almost bowled me over. Suffering acutely, I lay on the ground for an hour or more, my eye streaming with water, and I could see nothing with it.

I really thought the eye was done for – as it probably would have been, had I not been wearing a heavy tweed hat with a wide brim. The joint of the gull's wing struck the brim of the hat, and beat it down against the eye; but for that wide brim I should certainly have received the blow full in the eye, and probably have lost it.

The infuriated birds made no further attempt to molest me as I lay on the ground, nor did they attack the camera either – seemingly comprehending that it was an inanimate thing that could do them no injury. Had they not attacked me, no harm would have resulted to the chick, for I had just finished the picture; but by the time I had recovered sufficiently to take the camera away, the chick was frozen stiff, the parents had forsaken it and were nowhere to be seen. My eye was weak for many days afterwards; but fortunately it had suffered no permanent damage, and it ultimately got all right again.

Once, when I was photographing a clutch of eggs in the nest, and the owners were circling around, screaming loudly, another Skua swooped down, and, snatching up one of the unprotected eggs in its beak, made off with it – the lawful owners following in hot and clamorous pursuit. Before they had gone far, the robber dropped the egg, which broke on the rocks; but the owners continued the chase, bent, I assume, on administering summary justice; though I did not see the end of the incident. Later, I learned by witnessing repetitions of such offences, that any egg left unprotected for a moment was certain to be thus stolen.

Having discovered this thieving propensity of the Skuas, it was easy to understand why each nesting pair of the miscreants regarded their neighbours with apprehension and hatred.

Though two eggs were laid, and sometimes both were hatched, I noticed no instance where the mother had more than one chick after the first week. I do not know what became of the other: whether some cannibal neighbour made off with it, or whether the pangs of hunger had made the dainty morsel too tempting to one or other of the responsible pair, for – yes, I will state it, though it seems too horrible – I even suspect these unprincipled birds of the crime of eating their own young, for a dead chick was never to be seen. Whether my suspicions be well-founded or not, I must in common fairness state that the surviving youngster was always watched, protected and provided for with irreproachable care.

One day I came upon what I regarded as a real 'find.' Approaching a sitting mother, who flew away to give sufficient height and distance to swoop at me, I discovered that there were two eggs and a chick in the nest. Delighted with what I supposed was an unprecedented case, I photographed the happy family. On reporting my find at the Hut, I found that I'd been 'had.' One of our party, having been attacked by a gull, had killed it with a stick, and then had placed the orphan chick in a neighbouring nest. Extraordinary to relate, the returning gull had mothered the little stranger, instead of eating it – a departure from custom which could only be accounted for by the fact that the gull, being in a state of repletion, was hoarding the chick for the next meal. That any Skua would voluntarily foster a strange chick with good intentions, I could not believe. The next day the chick was not there! Further comment would be superfluous!

The chicks are beautiful little creatures. Their down is a lovely pearl-grey, and they have blue-tinted beaks and legs. They can walk almost as soon as hatched, and seem to inherit, from the egg, the hatred of their kind which is so characteristic of the adult. When but a day old, any movement on the part of one of a pair would cause them to look daggers at each other; and less than a week after they were hatched they would sometimes fight furiously without any provocation whatever, whilst the parent bird looked on approvingly. Several times I tried to kinematograph one of these 'scraps', without success. Whenever I appeared on the scene, the combatants forgot, for the time being, their dislike for each other, in their apprehension of what they regarded as a common foe. They glared fiercely at me, instead of at one another.

During the incubation of the eggs the cock relieved the hen periodically, whilst she went off to feed; and, later, when the chicks were hatched, he guarded them when she took a spell off for the same purpose. Returning to feed the little ones – or, perhaps I should say, little one; for, as I have already stated, there was never more than one after the first week – she would retch a few times, and then vomit forth a mass of half digested food on to the ground, which the chick would go for greedily. I spent many hours in trying to kinematograph this habit, but in vain. On each occasion when – after standing still and silent as a statue for long periods – I began to turn the handle, as the mother was about to regurgitate, the moment I stirred she was frightened and stopped at once. Though I tried every manner of ruse – including keeping my hand moving as though working the camera, until I was compelled to stop from fatigue – I never succeeded in recording this interesting trait by moving-pictures. It was the clicking of the camera that defeated me. I think, however, the coveted record would have been secured, but for an unfortunate incident. By dint of stalking one mother and her chick for nearly twenty consecutive hours, I had got them thoroughly accustomed to my presence and the camera; but whilst I went to take a few hours' sleep, someone killed the mother. When I returned to continue my vigil, she was lying dead on the ground, not twenty yards away; and another gull had doubtless carried off the unprotected chick, for it was no longer to be seen. Fortunately, however, I had already made a 'still' photograph of the mother disgorging for the chick; it was the only study of the kind I ever succeeded in getting. I vowed inwardly that when I returned home I would endeavour to have a noiseless kinematograph made, before I tried to secure moving-pictures of animals or birds at close quarters again.

One day I was watching a group of a dozen Giant petrels that were sitting on an ice-floe – gorged to lethargy on the offal of a dead seal – when the big ungainly creatures were suddenly harried by several Skua-gulls. I thought at first this was merely fun, or mischief, on the part of the gulls, and was not a little surprised – never having credited them with a sense of humour. I was soon undeceived, however, for it proved to be merely a cunning manoeuvre on the part of these crafty birds to get a meal on the cheap. Before the heavy petrels could rise on the wing and free themselves of their aggressors by flight, they had to disgorge the contents of their stomachs, and as soon as they did so the Skuas fell upon the feast. Really, each fresh insight that I gained into the habits of these unlovable birds increased my dislike for them; but I think the limit of repulsion was reached when I saw a couple of Skuas having a tug-of-war with a yard of a seal's intestines, which parted in the middle and sent the two ghouls sprawling – reminding me of a similar incident that I had seen several years before, on the banks of the Ganges near Benares, when a pair of vultures were all tangled with and tugging at the entrails of a corpse.

The one great redeeming feature of this Antarctic pariah is the excellence of its eggs. A Polar appetite is calculated to relieve one of any little prejudices in the matter of food, and once one's antipathy to the bird is overcome sufficiently to try its eggs, one finds they are fit for an epicure. After all, barnyard fowls are not over squeamish about their diet, and I doubt if anything that a Skua feeds on would be refused by them. Skuas' eggs, when boiled, are semi-transparent and jelly-like, and taste like the eggs of plovers – the only drawback in our case being that we could not get enough of them. The breast flesh of the Skua-gull is quite good eating too.

As the chicks grew older, they quickly lost the pretty appearance they exhibited when in the down. They became ugly, leggy creatures, bristling with stubbs, that ran away as fast as they could go – with backward, furtive looks – on the approach of man. As winter drew near; as the daylight waned away; as the weather became frigid, and the sea froze over again, the gulls gradually diminished in numbers on our cape, until only those were left that watched their unprepossessing fledglings until they were able to take care of themselves. As soon as these ill-favoured youngsters were full-grown and independent, they and the last of the adult stragglers departed too, and there was a peace around the Hut such as we had not known since our arrival in the South.

And, let me confess it, I missed them. When they had gone, I wished them back again, I even longed to have them back; for they had provided me with many interesting days of Study when there was little else to investigate. And their savage and revolting ways were, after all, but instincts well in keeping with the pitiless conditions under which Nature has decreed that these buccaneers of the South shall struggle for existence.

CHAPTER XX

The Real Inhabitants

Of all creatures within the Antarctic Circle penguins stand first and foremost in interest; and of the southern penguins there are more than half-a-dozen species – Adélie, Emperor, Gentoo, King, Ringed, Royal, and Victoria. Of only two of these can I write from personal knowledge – the Emperor and the Adélie – for we were many hundreds of miles south of the haunts of the others, and therefore I had no opportunity of observing them. We were unfortunately situated at Cape Evans for studying animals and birds, as, save for the Skua-gulls, no living creatures frequented this desolate and uninviting spur of the earth after the sea-ice had broken up. Occasionally Adélie penguins paid us a brief visit of inspection, or came to moult; and sometimes a seal landed to pass a few hours in slumber on our cape, but that was all. The locality that we had chosen for our base seemed to be in bad repute – an almost forbidden land to the denizens of the South. For almost all insight that I was able to gain into the habits and domestic life of Antarctic creatures I had to go miles away. Often I thought with longing of Cape Crozier and its zoological wonders; and envied those explorers who have had birds and animals swarming around their winter-quarters.

My chief regret, on leaving the South, was that, though a fairly complete history of the life of the Adélie penguin had been recorded by camera and kinematograph, I had been unable to secure any moving-pictures of its larger compatriot, the Emperor. The life and habits of these beautiful creatures still remains to be illustrated; and he who succeeds in securing a complete animated pictorial record of them will render a valuable service to science, and earn the lasting thanks of all zoologists. The difficulties before him will be many, and may prove insurmountable; for these extraordinary birds breed in the depths of the Antarctic winter – during the months of constant darkness – when the 'mercury' hovers between eighty and a hundred degrees below the freezing-point. Not only will intense cold have to be endured; but the lack of any light whatever will render kinematography impossible, unless sufficiently actinic flares can be devised for the purpose.

An heroic effort was made by Dr Wilson, Lieut. Bowers and Mr Cherry-Garrard, of the present Expedition, to increase our knowledge of the Emperor penguins. For five weeks in the winter these three were absent from our midst, on a journey to Cape Crozier, for the sole purpose of studying the breeding habits of these strange birds. Their journey was one of the most arduous ever made in the history of Polar exploration; and in one respect it was unparalleled, in that it was undertaken during the period of greatest darkness. The results of the adventure did not come up to their hopes, owing to the tremendous difficulties encountered and the extreme severity of the weather; but much valuable knowledge was gained.

Perhaps the most remarkable information that the party brought back was that these eccentric birds, not content with breeding in the coldest part of the earth in the coldest month of the year, do not even nest upon the land, but hatch their chicks on the ice that covers the sea. Obviously, eggs laid on the ice would chill quickly, so the birds incubate them standing – tucking the single egg that is laid into a deep crease in the soft, downy feathers of the lower abdomen, where it is held in place between the feet. So great is the desire of the Emperor to incubate a chick, and so foolish is the creature, that Dr Wilson averred he saw eggless birds thus brooding and endeavouring to hatch rounded lumps of ice; just as, during the *Discovery* Expedition, he found them incubate a dead and frozen chick if they were unable to secure a living one. 'Both Bowers and I, in the failing light, mistook these rounded dirty lumps of ice for eggs, and I picked them up before we realised what they were. One of them I distinctly saw dropped by a bird, and it was roughly egg-shaped and of the right size,' wrote Wilson in his diary.

He told us that when a party, during the *Discovery* Expedition, first visited this place, they found a large number of chicks; and such was the craving of the adults to possess the youngsters, that if one fell out of the downy abdominal crease in which it was being held by the parent, a rush was made for it by every chickless bird that witnessed the mishap, and in the common desire to secure and protect it, the little unfortunate was sometimes grabbed by half a dozen 'grown-ups,' and literally pulled to pieces.

It all sounds almost incredible; but surely one can believe anything of a bird that breeds in such a place, at such a season.

It is probable, however, that the Emperor penguins do not breed at the coldest period of the year from choice; but from the necessity of doing so thus early, so that their young may be old enough and big enough to fend for themselves at the end of the succeeding summer. It is not, however, so easy to understand why the birds do not migrate further north to reproduce their species.

The first of the three Emperor penguins that we saw at Cape Evans before the winter darkness fell, came when the sea had frozen over as far out as the bergs that had grounded in two hundred fathoms off our cape. When I was testing the new ice – which was six inches thick near the shore – I spied him about a quarter-of-a-mile away, standing perfectly still, either asleep, or lost in meditation. He looked a perfect giant; but, on getting my glass to bear, I found that this gigantic appearance was due to his image being reflected in the glassy ice on which he stood. Summoning two of the men, Anton and Clissold, who were near at hand, I went out to interview him. As we approached, he came forward and bowed his head in greeting, with 'a grace that a courtier might envy.' We clumsily returned this salutation; whereupon his majesty made several more genuflexions. After this ceremonial, he gazed at us; and then advancing to within two yards, delivered a short speech in penguin language, to which we endeavoured to make appropriate replies. It was obvious that the complaisant bird, never having seen our like before, took us for fellow creatures, and was extending to us a friendly greeting; but he appeared to be much puzzled at our speech and hilarious demeanour. Though he must have thought us a set of dull-witted churls, as we stood there like yokels, in comparison with his perfect self-possession and faultless manners, making silly attempts to imitate him; yet this polished gentleman of the eternal snows exhibited no annoyance. He graciously began the whole formality over again; uttering a further speech in soft, guttural accents, accompanied by more punctilious bowing.

Thinking he might at any moment take alarm at our stupidity – and strict injunctions having been given to every member of the Expedition to endeavour to capture any Emperors we might meet with – I treacherously took advantage of his trust, and slipped about his chest a noose which I had hastily made in the web of my camera shoulder-strap. The moment he felt the strap about him, he lost all confidence, and, becoming thoroughly alarmed, flopped down on to his breast and made off on 'all fours,' with a precipitancy that jerked the strap away. But Clissold managed to catch it, and the eighty-pound bird went scrambling off over the glassy ice, dragging the cook spread-eagled behind him. Anton joined in the chase; which now became a rough-and-tumble, with the great bird flapping and kicking, and the two men hanging on and trying to hold it. I have never seen a more absurd sight. With every semblance of dignity thrown to the winds, the now ridiculous creature was making prodigious efforts to reach the water, thirty yards away, and was gradually dragging Clissold and Anton with him. As the ice began to bend beneath their united weight, I shouted to them to let him go, for now I began to fear that comedy might end in tragedy. Just at that moment, they both got a firm hold of his legs; and the unhappy bird, blown with exertion, was caught securely. Much protesting, he was then led by the web and a ski-stick to our Hut, where, under the influence of an anaesthetic, he joined our zoological collection. We softened the qualms of conscience – for our perfidy in taking advantage of the trusting creature's confidence and friendliness – with the thought that science demanded the despicable act.

Our captive was a fine specimen, standing nearly four feet high; he was in beautiful plumage, with a snowy white breast, and grey-black back, and there was a collar of orange merging into yellow about his throat. The feet, head, and eyes were raven black, and the long curved beak was edged with violet. We found that he turned the scale at over eighty pounds. Some Emperors have been known to weigh as much as ninety.

No Antarctic creature has endeared itself to explorers so much as the Adélie, or Black-throated penguin. There is no memory that those who have penetrated into these Polar seas cherish so much as their meetings with these busy, lovable little people – for one cannot help thinking of the Adélies as fellow-creatures. Penguins are the real inhabitants of the South Land. The proud, stately Emperors – with their courtly, polished manners – are the upper classes, the aristocrats of the eternal snows; but the Adélies are the multitude, the bourgeoisie. It is said that when Anatole France first saw warm-water penguins he wept. One wonders what the famous *littérateur* would have done if he had seen Adélies. He might have wept still more – with laughter.

The Adélie penguin was so named by the French explorer, Admiral Dumont D'Urville, when he discovered – and named after his wife – Adélie Land, in 1840.

Neither Emperor nor Adélie penguins have ever been transplanted from the Antarctic regions – to which they are indigenous. The penguins to be seen in our own and continental zoological gardens are habitudes of temperate seas, and possess neither the beauty of the incomparable Emperor nor the captivating drollery of the Adélie.

From the first hour that we saw Adélie penguins in the pack-ice, we found their quaint ways and curiosity intensely interesting; and this feeling deepened to real affection as we got to know more of them. My great regret was that we did not see enough of them. We were just a few leagues too far south; for the furthest south penguin colony known was situated at Cape

Royds – some seven or eight miles north of our own cape. The occasional visitors that honoured us were always welcomed; and the interest we took in them was certainly mutual, for they regarded us with equal curiosity. Sometimes small roving parties would come and inspect our Hut, our stores, our sledging-gear, and the dogs. The dogs were a never-ending source of wonder to them, and inspired in them no fear whatever. In their desire to examine more closely these wild beasts – for the instinct of the dogs to kill was instantly aroused at the sight of any living creature – they sometimes lost their lives by the merciless teeth. The survivors of the party never learnt anything from such bloodshed; and, more than once, two or three of the little innocents shared the same fate one after the other.

This roving tendency of the penguins is characteristic. They wander for miles over the ice at times, seemingly aimlessly. They are also very fond of exploring the land; for no other object, so far as we were able to discover, than to see something of the world – for there is nothing ashore for them to eat, and therefore no incentive for such excursions, other than curiosity. They had little use for our sterile and featureless peninsula; but a considerable colony made their headquarters at Cape Royds – whereby they exhibited excellent judgment, for Cape Royds is quite an interesting and not unpicturesque locality. Practically all my observations of Adélie penguins were made there. Barring their occasional visits of inspection of our stores and dogs, the penguins only used our promontory as a convenient place to moult; during the two summers we were in the South, a few dozens took possession of the extreme end of the cape for that purpose.

This lack of interest in our cape was probably due to the fact that they found no part of it suitable for nesting purposes. In order to incubate and hatch their eggs with a minimum of risk, penguins require a situation as free as possible from snow; therefore they choose exposed ground, where the wind gives the snow little chance of settling. Though our cape was swept by storms, its conformation was such that snow accumulated on it almost everywhere, and it did not melt until the height of summer; the locality was therefore unattractive to the penguins.

Adélie penguins exhibit at times remarkable instincts and judgment; at other times their stupidity is almost incredible. Their pertinacity is exemplary, their curiosity ludicrous, and their bravery amazing. A full-grown adult stands about two feet high, and though it is one of the most grotesque of birds, it is certainly one of the most beautiful of Polar creatures. It would be difficult to imagine anything more handsome than the contrast of the raven-black and snow-white plumage of its new coat after moulting, unless it be that of the elegant and more highly-coloured Emperor. Though the feathers are short and stubbly, they combine into a smooth coat which exhibits a beautiful sheen; and the only touch of colour about the Adélie is the feet, which are pale salmon-colour. The back, head, neck, and upper side of the wings (or flippers) are black; the whole of the breast, underside of the flippers, and the legs are white; and the Adélie is the only known penguin with white eyelids and white rims round the eyes. It is these white rims and eyelids that give the Adelies such a quaint appearance; and which, combined with their droll habits, make them the comedians of the South.

One's first interview with Adelies leaves an impression something like this. You are out on the ice, when you meet a company of marionettes, dressed in swallow-tail coats with an excessive expanse of shirt-front. They are all standing at ease, muscles relaxed, clothes fitting atrociously – all loose and baggy, as though the owners were clad in 'reach-me-downs.' You become an object of interest. Each marionette suddenly stands to attention; and the floppy clothes immediately become the most beautifully-tailored and 'spic-and-span' of garments. A perfect little knut of a fellow then steps out from the crowd and approaches you with a 'Charlie Chaplin' gait.

He is evidently well-disposed and peaceably inclined; but somewhat wary, palpably wondering what manner of penguin you are. Your proportions perplex him; of that there can be no doubt, for he regards you first out of one eye, and then out of the other, with obvious suspicion. If you move ever so slightly, his head goes back, his beak up in the air, and he squints at you with both eyes; at the same time the poll feathers ruffle – a sure sign that he is alarmed, and perhaps a wee bit angry too. When within a couple of yards, still transfixing you with a squinty stare, he challenges you with a defiant and raucous 'squawk' – a demand that you declare your intentions. The squawk is not difficult to imitate, and, if you are wise, you attempt to do so. You find your effort has an appeasing effect, for it proclaims your kinship, though you are not understood, and are probably regarded as something of a fool. The whole party then advance to inspect you, squawking their opinions to each other.

It is well to 'get in' a few bows about this time, and to affect the air of an Emperor, muttering after the manner of their kind as you do so. You find that such efforts are well received, though doubtless considered loutish. If you remain motionless, all misgivings will be allayed, and the spokesman and his friends will relapse into a bunch of baggy misfits and bother no more about you. But if you have the misfortune to give offence in any way, the chances are that the little valiant will go for you; and if he does, look out! He will seize your nether garments above the knee in his beak, and lay about you with such a rapid rain of blows with his flippers – which are hard as bone and can hurt like anything – that unless you cry mercy and beat him off, you will find yourself bruised black and blue.

The procedure at these meetings varied a good deal. When the spokesman squawked in challenge, and we answered 'Quaawk!' he would usually repeat what he had said; then, finding it impossible to get any intelligent reply, he would go and apparently say to his companions: 'There's something wrong with this chap. I can't make out what he's talking about. You have a try!' Then several would come, and all start talking to us at once. Finding, however, that they could make no headway with us, they talked to each other about us. We hoped their comments were favourable; but from their expression and demeanour we felt somewhat inclined to doubt it.

But far away in the background of all this comedy, there is much of scientific interest about the penguins; and there is more than a touch of the pathetic too. It is well known that as conditions under which animals live change, the animals in course of time change too – limbs either developing or deteriorating, according to the use that is made of them. We know that the Polar regions have not always been desolate, ice-bound wastes. Ages ago, very different conditions prevailed. The climate was of a mild, if not tropical nature; and that either forests or peat-beds abounded is proved by the outcrops of coal-measures discovered in the very limited geological examination that has so far been possible. Exhaustive prospecting perhaps might prove the presence of vast deposits; though, even if discovered, it is unlikely they would ever be of any economic value, as the region is too inaccessible.

In those distant, temperate ages, the penguins possessed the power of flight, and lived either on the vegetable growth or insect and small animal life of the land. As the climate changed, and became so cold that all life and vegetation died, the penguins, like the seals – which were at one time land bears and roved through the forests – had to seek their living in the sea. As ages passed, their wings – like the legs of the seals – adapted themselves to the purpose of propulsion through the water, with consequent loss of power as a means of flight. The penguin, in short, is a creature that is not progressing; but in the course of ages it has retrograded.

As I got to know the Adélies better, close observation disclosed more than one indication that, hidden away in some corner of the brain, hazy instincts of powers, which ages ago they possessed, are still transmitted. At the Cape Royds colony several times I saw an Adélie, as a Skua-gull flew over head, closely watch the bird; then suddenly rise on its feet, stretch itself to its full height and flap its degenerate wings, as though in the effort to follow its inveterate enemy. The whole gesture was expressive of the desire that unquestionably animated it. It said as plainly as words: 'Oh, how I wish I could fly!'

And again, I have often seen penguins sleeping with their heads bent sideways, and their beaks buried well in the breast feathers, by the joint of the flipper. What else can prompt this habit but the rudimentary instinct that impels birds of many kinds to roost with the head tucked under the wing?

Should the climate in these regions, in future ages, once more become temperate or torrid, as vegetable growth and animal life again evolved on the land, the penguins would probably again develop as birds, and in time recover the powers they have lost. The Weddell seals would take to the land and revert to land bears; whilst the Sea-leopards might become terrors of the forest again – always provided that they found it easier to make a living on the earth than in the sea. Nature works by natural laws; she compels every wild creature to earn its living and to struggle for existence, and whilst all seek the line of least resistance, she watches the balance, and sees that supplies are equal to the demands that are made upon them.

On my return from the South, I spent my first Christmas on a holiday in the Alps. One evening, at one of the Swiss winter-sports hotels, I was invited by a number of ladies to tell them something of my Antarctic experiences. I had just imparted the above information about our Polar friends, when one charming member of my audience, who had been listening with every feature intent, and her eyes full of interest and sympathy, remarked – as I referred to the degeneration of the penguins, which has been going on for ages – with tender feeling in her voice: 'Oh, what a shame! Couldn't something be done to stop it?'

The delightful artlessness of that remark was worth all the discomforts entailed in gathering my experiences of penguins.

Penguins possess great speed in the water; and, so far as I was able to see, gain it entirely by means of their powerful nippers, letting their webbed feet drag behind them. I cannot be sure on this point, as they always swam so fast; but I believe it is established that penguins do not use the feet in swimming, except as accessory rudders to the tail. In the sea, the same natural law obtains that rules the forest – the strong prey upon the weak. As the penguins do not require this great speed for catching the small shrimps on which they feed, one knows that it has been provided by Nature as a means of avoiding their natural foes, the Sea-leopards and the Killer whales.

Adélie penguins have a habit of leaping along the surface, much as dolphins do, which we called 'porpoising.' This is a very rapid mode of progress, and they use it frequently, especially in sunny weather. I think they often do this purely for fun, as once I watched a number playing a game, which irresistibly reminded me of the song 'Follow the man from Cook's' in *The Runaway Girl.* They would string out in a line behind the leader and porpoise along the surface of the water; then double back on their tracks and strike off in another direction.

There were some ice-floes near, and the 'man from Cook's' made for them, leading his party under some floes and over others, sometimes porpoising along the water, then tobogganing over the ice. They followed in a line behind the leader, doing exactly as he did. The fun became fast and furious, and I suppose they got a bit winded; for, after a while, the courier gave them a rest. Following his lead, they all sprang on to an ice-raft; then, still imitating his example, they settled down on their breasts and basked awhile in the sunshine – prior to doing a few more laps. That they all thoroughly enjoyed the game there could be no possible doubt.

It was not until the third week of November, that I was able, accompanied by biologist Nelson, to make a second visit to Cape Royds, after illustrating the seal life at Razorback Island. As the weather was fair, we camped on the snow, instead of taking up quarters in Shackleton's hut.

Most of the penguins had by that time mated, and had begun to incubate their eggs. But, scattered about the rookery, there were many couples standing expectantly beside their nests, looking somewhat worried – no egg having as yet arrived. Either a dearth of males, or a lack of gallantry on their part, seemed to be indicated by the number of females who stood about the place, as yet unattached, looking very disconsolate in comparison with the businesslike air of the mated and sitting hens. There is no difference in appearance between males and females; but we assumed that these lonely individuals were hens. In each case the eligible one had either taken up her position beside an old nest site, or had scooped a little hollow in the ground. Here she stood and waited for a male bird to come along and pay court to her, making no attempt to build a nest on the selected spot.

Occasionally these lonesome females would indulge in an extraordinary practice. Standing upright in their excavations, they would gaze intently into the heavens, and, slowly waving their flippers, give throat to a soft, guttural, humming sound – as though abandoning themselves to a state of rapture.

This ecstatic condition never lasted more than about fifteen seconds, but it seemed to be exceedingly infectious. As soon as one bird started, others in the vicinity would at once follow suit, until sometimes a score or more might be seen in this state of beatitude, humming and flapping in unison. I first interpreted the performance to be a cry for a mate; but, later, I saw mated hens, with eggs, conducting themselves thus – and supposed they were calling for their husbands. Subsequently, as I saw both husbands and wives behaving so together, I had to 'give it up', and confess that I had no idea what the habit could mean; unless the birds were under the influence of some sensation that is common to both sexes, and peculiar to the breeding-season – for I never saw them perform thus except when nesting.

I was glad to note that all these lonely females found their vigil at last rewarded; during our stay they all became mated, and I witnessed several of these fateful meetings. I observed one bachelor land at Cape Royds almost immediately after our arrival. At that time there was no open water visible through my glass, though from a hill, 700 feet high, named High Peak, I could see ten miles beyond Cape Bird – which is thirty miles from Cape Royds. This penguin must therefore have tramped at least forty miles over the ice. Small wonder the pilgrim appeared fatigued!

He staggered up the slope leading from the sea to the breeding-ground, rolling about in an inebriated sort of way from sheer weariness of the flesh, and came to a halt within a short distance from where I had taken up my watch with a camera. Having reached his destination, and too exhausted to go another step, the trim little figure sank into a baggy misfit, all huffed up, vainly trying to keep open the eyelids that were obviously as heavy as the weary feet. Thus he stood, propping himself up with his stiff tail-feathers – which penguins always use as a sort of third leg to preserve balance when standing upright – tucked his head under one of his flippers, and fell asleep. In about ten minutes he suddenly became alert, and, jumping on to a stone near-by, proceeded to take stock of his surroundings. This, evidently, was no laggard in love who would permit a rival to surpass him in chivalry; for, jaded as he still was, after a few minutes' survey, he leapt off the stone and proceeded about his courting.

Advancing to the nearest of the eligible hens, he inspected her critically, from a distance of a yard – walking leisurely around her as he did so. During this scrutiny the lady took no notice of him whatever, merely looking coy. But, for some reason or other, she didn't seem to please him; he went off without a word, and she looked after him in the most comical manner, as though scarcely believing it possible she had been rejected. Two more hens were then inspected, and in turn passed by, after a careful estimate of their merits. But when this 'young Lochinvar' met the fourth of the eligibles, without inspecting her at all he stood vis-à-vis, and bestowed upon her an ardent glance which I can only describe as the 'glad eye.' Far from responding in the same spirit, the lady received this fond look with the most frosty of stony stares. This, however, did not dismay our friend; on the contrary he seemed to make up his mind to tame the little shrew.

Picking up a small stone in his beak, he advanced, and laid the offering at her feet. He then looked up into her face and said 'Quaawk!' – to which remark she deigned no reply, nor took any notice of him whatever. He then brought and offered another stone, with the same result, and yet another – each time looking into her eyes, and saying 'Quaawk!' On the tendering of the fourth or fifth stone, her disdain began to break down, and she regarded him critically; whereupon, he stretched himself to his full height for her inspection. He was obviously approved and accepted on the spot; for they both began squawking a raucous duet, stretching their necks and swaying their heads from side to side and gazing skywards as they did so.

Now it was quite plain what all this meant. Penguins make their nests of stones, and the offering of them was unmistakably in the way of a proposal of marriage. Later, I saw a hen receive her would-be suitor in a very different frame of mind. She seemed to be a shrew not only in looks, but in nature; for, each time the male bird tendered an offering, she would scold and peck him apparently savagely. But this did not discourage her suitor; and, as he valiantly persisted in his attentions, I concluded that this rough treatment was in the nature of caresses. His endearments, however, were of a gentler and altogether more humane character. After subduing the little scold by much coaxing and persuasion, he would nibble at her mouth, and take her beak into his own – the while she sat on the ground and trembled visibly.

All this love-making was very interesting to watch; but its course did not always run smoothly. Cock penguins are not only of a very amorous, but they are also of a very pugnacious disposition. As later arrivals reached the rookery, it was not unusual to see two cocks righting for the favours of a single hen, though there were unmated hens, near-by, to be had for the asking. Once I saw a swashbuckling bully deliberately make love to a hen – who cowered on the nest – under the very eyes of her mate. The husband loudly protested, in vigorous squawky accents; and then went for this Lothario. A battle royal ensued; and blood was soon flowing freely, for penguins fight with beaks and flippers and deliver savage pecks and cuts. When one of the combatants got a fair hold, he would hang on to his opponent and rain blows about him so rapidly that, whilst one could hear the whirr of them, the movement was too quick for the eye; or, he would hold one flipper at the guard and deliver cuts with the other, if for a moment his opponent was unwary. The snowy breasts of both contestants were soon streaked with blood, and their heads swollen from the pecks that reached their mark as each aimed for the other's beak and eyes. I ran to get my kinematograph bearing on the battle; but before I could do so it was over; the defeated bully was beating a wobbly retreat, leaving the rightful protector blood-bespattered, but without a stain upon the honour for which he had fought.

Such scenes were common among the community about this time, and became more frequent later; for, after all the hens had met their affinities, belated cock penguins caused much trouble. Unable to find mates, they became shameless profligates, and seemed to make it their business to break up the domestic happiness of the more fortunate earlier arrivals.

To the Adélies we were, of course, just as incomprehensible as we were to the Emperors and the seals. If we didn't bother them, they didn't bother us. They made no objection to our presence on the breeding-ground, so long as we did not intrude too near their nests. I found it advisable to keep absolutely motionless when observing them. To move about, was only to disturb their thoughts; with the result that they immediately ceased any particular habit in which they might be engaged. One day, whilst standing thus, a penguin waddled up to me and placed a pebble at my feet, saying 'Quaawk!' as he did so. I made no movement, and he presented me with another stone, and still another – each time squawking loudly. Thinking to encourage him as he said 'Ouaawk!' after depositing the fourth stone, I replied with as near an imitation as I could – with the immediate result that he fled on all fours as fast as legs and flippers would enable him.

Day told me that a similar incident occurred to him, during the Shackleton Expedition, and he looked upon it as a demonstration of friendliness. I endorsed this theory: modesty forbidding me to entertain the only alternative explanation – that my admirer took me for an exceptionally well-developed female penguin, and was making love to me.

After the birds had mated, they busied themselves with the building of the nest, whilst waiting for the arrival of the eggs. Now, the building of a penguin's nest is an almost interminable affair. It is made of stones; and as the demand for stones for this purpose is greater than the supply in the immediate vicinity, petty larceny is a common offence. Penguins are habitual thieves, and cannot resist the temptation to pilfer a stone from a neighbour's nest whenever a chance occurs. Constant vigilance is necessary to prevent this robbery. It was the duty of the male bird to collect the stones; which he brought, one by one, in his beak to his mate, who arranged them in order about her. There was no building in the true sense of the word; the stones were merely laid on the ground, and incessantly re-arranged.

The stealing that attends the making of the nests is one of the characteristics of a penguin colony; it was a source of constant amusement to us, for it continued during the entire period of incubation. As the colony filled up, all the available stones on the breeding-ground were used; so that unless late comers searched further afield, their only chance of securing any was by robbing earlier arrivals. New stones, that had not been previously used for nesting, were not in much demand; preference was always given to those which had been used for years for a similar purpose – well-rounded stones, with all interstices well clogged up from much service, being most appreciated. But when the available supply on the breeding-ground was exhausted, hitherto unused stones from the adjacent hills were occasionally brought into circulation.

It was a common sight to see a cock sally out, and, stealthily creeping up behind a sitting hen, snatch a stone from her collection; then, with conscious guilt stamped all over him, make off with it – a chorus of protesting squawks and pecks being aimed at him by every penguin that he passed on his homeward way. After delivering the prize to his mate, he would repeat the raid in some other direction. It was the duty of the hen to protect the hoard thus feloniously accumulated. Neighbouring nests sometimes plainly showed the result of vigilance, or of lack of vigilance on the part of the hens; or of lack of courage or deftness on the part of their mates. Some nests were full of stones; whilst others, near-by, were almost devoid of them. A poorly-furnished nest was usually due either to stupidity on the part of the hen, or to ignorance of the wicked ways of her kind. Once, I watched a husband diligently working away, stealing, and bringing stone after stone to his wife; but as soon as his back was turned, another thief would edge up – seemingly interested in anything else in the world except the stone he was after – and suddenly make a dart for it and be off, whilst the hen appeared incapable of understanding what was going on almost under her eyes.

The hens thieve too, but in a different way. There was one little group of nests in circular formation, situated so close to each other that each was within reach of its neighbours. Never-ceasing robbery went on here, for as frequently as one hen stretched out her neck to steal from the nest in front, her neighbour behind seized the opportunity, whilst she was off her guard, to abstract a stone in her rear; and each back-door neighbour round the circle did the same. Thus, four or five were sometimes simultaneously being robbed, whilst themselves engaged in robbery – the net result being that the balance remained even, as the stones merely circulated round the ring.

I will not go so far as to charge all penguins with being instinctively dishonest; I believe young birds may be honest enough at first, but they speedily become corrupted by the evil example of their elders. If they begin life with equitable instincts, they soon find that honesty is a poor policy; and the upright fall easy victims to the unscrupulous.

One day I watched a young newly-mated pair who were obviously inexperienced in the ways of the world, and trustful of their fellow-creatures to the point of folly. After the stone-offering preliminaries had been gone through, and they had abandoned themselves for a time to a state of rapture, they began to set about the building of the nest. The male bird went in search of stones; and as each fresh one was added, the hen casually adjusted them about her, in the customary manner, by wriggling, and with her feet. When about twenty stones had been accumulated, a knavish-looking fellow – one of a pair of older newly-mateds who were settling in the vicinity – spotted the treasures. Sneaking up behind the young hen, he quietly made off with one of them, without being noticed. Then, as fast as the young and honest husband added a fresh stone and departed to continue his search, the thief crept up again, and stole another; and sometimes he managed to purloin two or three stones whilst the honest husband was finding one. This went on for an hour or more; and as the thief's wife had extraordinary ability in arranging the stones, the nest of the dishonest ones became a little castle, whilst the virtuous pair were gradually deprived of everything they had. After a time, the honest husband took a rest, to inspect the fruit of his labours, and was obviously troubled to find no visible result. A good deal of discussion ensued between the pair, neither of whom seemed capable of comprehending the trick that had been played upon them.

There was something very human in all this. How often is it not the case that honest workers are defrauded of the results of their labours, through simplicity, or through over confidence in those whom, in their simple faith, they had believed to be their friends?

Most penguins, however, are filled with suspicion of their neighbours, and constantly dart distrustful glances to the rear and sideways; these are not easy victims. If a thief were detected in the act, he would usually brazen it out and dash off with the prize. But sometimes he would drop the stone as though it were red-hot – pretending to be interested in the weather, or else his toe-nails, or anything on earth except the stone he coveted – with an assumed expression of innocence that was too funny for words.

Suspicion of their neighbours engenders in the hen penguins violent hatred, and is the cause of constant brawling and dissension. It was quite common to see hens, on adjacent nests, with outstretched necks pecking savagely at one another. Sometimes their beaks would be interlocked for minutes, and the heads of many were swollen and bleeding from such conflicts. During these squabbles, the neighbours in the rear of the brawlers would regard the opportunity as favourable to purloin stones from the nests of the quarrelsome ones – and embrace it.

The period of incubation of the eggs of the Adélie penguin is about five weeks; and both male and female brood them in turn. The formality of relieving guard was accompanied by a good deal of ceremony. The returning cock, spotlessly clean and glossy from immersion in the sea, would, on reaching his nest, bow several times to his partner – making a soft, gurgling sound in his throat, as he did so. He would describe circles in the air with his head, still gurgling; and the hen would raise her head, stretch her neck, and describe circles and gurgle too. This would continue for some time, before she would permit him to have a look at the precious eggs; then, after much coaxing, she would stand up, and both would examine them with evident pleasure. It appeared to be a source of much satisfaction to the returning bird to find that the eggs were all right, and he was anxious to take charge of the treasures at once; but invariably the hen exhibited great reluctance to abandon them. Much wheedling had to be gone through before she could be persuaded to transfer the guardianship to her mate; consequently, relieving guard was a ceremony that usually took a good deal of time.

In the end, she would submit under protest, and sidle reluctantly away from the eggs; the cock would then quickly cover them, and, adjusting them with his beak, carefully subside on to them – whilst his 'better-half' took a spell off for feeding and relaxation.

Adélie penguins' eggs are about the size of a goose's; they are either white, or of the same shade as a duck's, but have much coarser shells. They are excellent to eat; the white being semi-transparent and gelatinous, and the yolk delicate of flavour. Two eggs are laid, with an interval of three or four days between. They are laid on the bare stones which form the nest, and are kept warm during the process of incubation by being enveloped in a deep crease in the thick, downy feathers of the lower abdomen. This crease permits of the eggs coming into close contact with the skin. The eggs are frequently turned, so that warmth can be applied equally. They are also aired from time to time; meanwhile the sitter takes the opportunity to stretch and flap his, or her, flippers, and occasionally to indulge in a few ecstatic exercises.

The operation of airing the eggs is always attended by a certain amount of risk. The Skua-gull is the relentless enemy of the penguin, and, from the moment the birds began to nest, numbers of these corsairs haunted the vicinity, to prey upon their eggs. They would stand about on the adjacent rocks, or soar in circles overhead – always on the watch to catch a penguin off its guard, when they would immediately swoop down and snatch up an egg. This pillaging was done with wonderful rapidity. A penguin would be unsuspectingly airing its eggs – the while stretching its flippers or perhaps indulging in ecstatics – when there would be a rush of wings, and, before the victim realised what was happening, the marauder had snatched up one of the exposed eggs in its beak, and was gone. I saw many eggs thus stolen; but I never saw the thief miss an egg, nor drop it. The victim of the outrage would raise a squawky 'hullaballoo' for a few moments, and then settle down with an air of resignation, and worry no more about it.

Between witnessing a Skua-gull plundering a penguin's nest, and photographing the act, there is a great gulf fixed; but I succeeded in bridging it, after vainly watching for hours, motionless, with my kinematograph levelled on some nest – in the hope that the tenant would air its eggs, and a gull seize the opportunity to steal one. I finally decided that the incident would have to be 'produced' – just as any drama film is produced – and the various characters concerned would have to be made to play their parts.

Accordingly, the instrument was focused on a certain nest, and the owner, much protesting, was removed and tied up out of the way; then I stood by and waited. In a few minutes a gull hovered around, and swooped down at the eggs; but as soon as I began to turn the handle of the camera, it took fright and flew off. Again and again it returned; but each time with the same result – the bird was frightened. So I adopted the expedient of keeping my hand moving; thus, when I did turn the handle I was merely continuing the motion. This had the desired effect. The pirate, becoming bolder, at last pounced upon an egg and carried it off; and I had the incident recorded on the film. It soon returned for the other; and again the theft was filmed. The owner then was released, and its return to its pillaged home was also recorded; also, its concern over the loss, and its final 'it can't be helped' attitude and expression, as it settled down on the bare stones with resignation.

The unwilling heroine of the tragedy was disturbed again for a moment, to be compensated with two fresh eggs – taken from two other nests. Her amazement was quite droll when she found the eggs were now restored. She accepted at once the substituted ones, and flopped down on to them; but she rose to inspect them several times, to make sure she hadn't deceived herself. Then, seemingly casting the whole recollection aside as some horrid dream, she settled down to business, and went on with her incubation duties.

The day was a memorable one, for remarkable success attended my efforts. The gulls had now become so accustomed to my presence, that they ignored it; and the next raider was so contemptuous of me – though the camera and I were not ten feet from the nest – that, instead of flying hastily off with the egg which it had snatched up, it stood there, facing me, with the egg held in its beak. Subsequently, it, or another gull – as I could not distinguish individuals – repeated the manoeuvre twice; and each time stood truculently facing the camera, holding an egg. Both these incidents were also kinematographed. This remarkable habit was thus not only proved by the indisputable evidence of the camera; but the resulting films show clearly the manner in which the gull holds the egg in its beak – not impaled on it, as reported by some observers.

The filibusters did not always wait for the eggs to be exposed. Several times I saw a gull fly down and attack a penguin from the rear, snatching up an egg as the bird rose and turned round to resist. On such an occasion, the victim would raucously squawk her rage at the thief; and, rising on tip-toe, would vainly stretch and wave her flippers, as though to say: 'Oh! If only I could fly, wouldn't I thrash you!'

The gulls never attempted to engage in conflict with the penguins, as they are no match for them, and took good care to keep out of reach of their beaks and hard-hitting flippers. But the poor Adélie is at a great disadvantage in being unable to fly, or even to jump off the ground; only by constant watchfulness against its inveterate enemy can it hope to hatch its eggs and rear a family.

On one of my visits to the Cape Royds colony during the breeding season, the temperature, in the few hours about noon, rose nearly to the freezing-point; consequently, the melting snows caused the waters of a small, near-by lake to rise to such an extent that some of the nests became flooded, and were deserted by their owners. Others, more resourceful, rearranged the stones as the water rose, in the endeavour to save the eggs from harm. All the nests in this ill-chosen place were finally forsaken, however, as the gulls took advantage of the general commotion to steal the eggs.

Although it was more sheltered than the higher ground, only a few birds had built in this low-lying locality. This was probably due to the fact that the place was known by the older inhabitants to be subject to this danger. I assumed that the flooded-out unfortunates were some of the younger and less experienced members of the colony.

As I got to know more about penguins, I realised that the more wind-swept the ground, the better it was for breeding purposes. Snow was apt to drift in the low-lying places, and those that settled there had a miserable time of it.

Occasionally, I noticed that almost every penguin in the colony, whether sitting or standing, was facing in the same direction; whilst at other times they would be facing every point of the compass. I was for a while puzzled by this unanimity of front; until I remembered that Lafcadio Hearn had once asked his Japanese ricksha runner why it was that a number of birds sitting on a telegraph-wire all faced the same way. The literal translation of the reply of the kurumaya was: 'Little birds always wind-to facing sit.'

There lay the explanation. Surely enough, when all the penguins faced in a certain direction, it was from that quarter the breeze was blowing; and as often as they were facing haphazard, it invariably happened that there was either no wind at all, or none worth mentioning.

When the *Terra Nova* passed the Cape Crozier rookery on the night we entered McMurdo Sound, we had seen, through our glasses, penguins performing the most astounding athletic feats – leaping from the sea on to an ice-foot six feet high, or more; but no such performance was to be seen at Cape Royds. The formation of the cape was such that they always came ashore leisurely, at the place known as Dead Horse Bay.

It is remarkable that any penguins should take the trouble to go all the way to Cape Royds, when they could breed at the Cape Crozier nesting ground – which, though about the same latitude, is on the Ross Sea coast, and is, therefore, in most seasons, at least thirty miles nearer open water as the summer commences. Except in years when an unusually stormy winter and spring prevents the sea from freezing thickly, McMurdo Sound remains frozen for weeks after the ice in the open sea has broken up. One can only account for the Cape Royds penguins taking all this trouble, by the supposition that, having been bred here themselves, instinct constrains them to return to their native place to reproduce their species. Even so, one would scarcely suppose that their forbears would have been so foolish as to travel such a distance in the mere hope of finding a suitable breeding-place. Probably, the original pioneers of the colony landed at Cape Royds in some unusually stormy season, which either prevented the ice from forming in the Sound, or else broke it up early in the spring. This, of course, is mere conjecture, as it is impossible satisfactorily to account for much that penguins do. For instance, at Cape Adare, where our Northern Party wintered, Adélies were known laboriously to climb the hills to a height of a thousand feet or more – which took them hours – and to make their nests there in preference to the shore below, where there was ample room for them. Also, when we passed Cape Crozier we saw numbers of Adélies nesting hundreds of feet up the mountain slopes – for apparently no other object than to command a better view, which was only gained at the expense of infinite labour.

Foolish as the Adélie penguin appears to be in such incomprehensible habits, it seems, however, a Confucian sage in comparison with the pompous Emperor. The little Adélie chooses the warmest months of the year to rear its young, when constant daylight prevails; whereas the preposterous Emperor breeds in the coldest part of the Antarctic at the coldest time of the year, the period of perpetual night – surely the limit of eccentricity if, indeed, it be not the penalty of necessity.

At the beginning of December, the weather being fine and apparently settled, I started off alone from our Hut for Cape Royds. But a recent slight fall of snow had made the surface very heavy, and, after almost exhausting myself by dragging the sledge for two miles, I had to give it up and return for assistance. Anton, the Russian groom, then came with me; and, as I expected to be absent not more than twenty-four hours, I announced my intention of returning the next evening. As events turned out, it was fortunate I had not been able to make the journey single-handed, and had found it necessary to return for help; otherwise I should have had a lonely time of it during the next ten days. We found the surface worse as we proceeded, and the going became harder each successive mile; so that we had to strip to our under-shirts, because of the terrific exertion – though there was about 10° of frost. As we drew near to Cape Royds, the snow was so thick that it became almost impossible to move the sledge. Not having expected anything like this – and knowing there were ample supplies in Shackleton's hut – we had brought nothing to eat; consequently, we both became weak from lack of sustenance and the great muscular effort. Our empty stomachs finally compelled us to leave the sledge, and go on to the hut for food. We soon had a fire blazing in the stove, and prepared a meal of canned chicken, peas, biscuits and cocoa, from the abundant stores left by our predecessors of the 1907 Expedition. Never did food taste so delicious. After thus restoring our tissues, and our trembling muscles with rest, our sinews became as wire. Feeling like giants refreshed, we went out to the sledge and made light work of hauling it up to the hut; then we turned-in in our sleeping-bags.

As meteorologist Simpson had not notified me of any indication of a possible change of weather, I was surprised to find it dull and stormy when we woke up; later, a blizzard broke which lasted for three days. After the wind abated, the snow continued to fall; not of the usual powdery kind to which we were accustomed, but in great flakes. When it ceased, the drifts were five or six feet deep around the hut. During the storm we had been 'hard put to it' to find and excavate supplies from the stores, and we had to search waist deep for broken packing-cases for fuel; so we did not lack for exercise to keep ourselves warm.

When the weather finally cleared, looking towards the penguinry we could see nothing but snow, where formerly had been many hundreds of birds. Not knowing what had become of them, or whether they had deserted the place – as there was not a single individual to be seen – I determined to investigate. Anton and I arduously made our way for a couple of hundred yards to the breeding-ground, but there was no sign of a penguin anywhere. The snow was more than knee-deep; and, as I was floundering about, wondering whether my penguin investigations had come to an abrupt end, I was almost 'scared out of my life' by a muffled squawk, and felt something wriggling under my foot. I had stepped on the back of a sitting penguin – buried nearly two feet deep in the snow!

As the victim struggled out, loudly protesting its wrath at this outrage, we were convulsed with laughter; then, roused by our noisy mirth, scores of black heads, with 'gollywog' eyes, suddenly protruded from the snow – to see what all the row was about. That was how we discovered them! They had not deserted the place; but were attending to their domestic duties under the snow – patiently waiting for it to blow away. There were penguins everywhere; it was impossible to walk without stepping on them. All had their necks craned upwards, and in most cases their breath had melted an airway in the snow; others, however, were completely snowed in, even the airway being covered by a thin film – but that in nowise discouraged the persistent creatures.

After the snow had ceased to fall, it was remarkable how quickly it flattened down under the ablating influence of the wind and the sun; even an hour made a visible difference. As quickly as possible, we laboriously got the kinematograph and a camera on the spot; but by that time the points of numerous beaks were beginning to appear above the surface. A little later, many of the more deeply snowed-up birds had been compelled to forsake their nests and had made their way out; they were soon tramping all over the place, helping out the levelling process of Nature.

It was obvious that the sitting birds must be suffering great misery; for the heat of their bodies melted the snow about them, so that their once neat, clean nests were now but bogs of slush, in which the eggs lay wet, and, as I then thought, chilled beyond all hopes of hatching. Occasionally an individual seemed to realise this, and forsook its nest; but the majority refused to abandon hope of rearing a family, and stuck to their swamped and bemired homes with a tenacity that was pathetic. But whatever commiseration I felt for the penguins, their tribulations were met, on their part, by the same 'It can't be helped' unconcern with which they always faced trouble. Truly the more I learned about Adélies, the deeper it was impressed upon me that mankind might learn from them some salutary lessons.

After two days of fine weather and comparative peace, another and much fiercer blizzard broke, and the hut creaked and groaned with the force of the wind. When gusts of almost hurricane force struck it, it shook and rattled on its temporary foundations, so that at times we almost feared it might collapse – as it probably would have done, had it not been well stayed on the windward side with wire ropes. It was bitterly cold; but the deep snow prevented us from finding packing-cases to break up for firewood, and we had not collected a sufficient supply to keep the fire alight. We had to conserve carefully the few sticks we had, for cooking purposes. Unable to go outside the hut, and with nothing to do inside it; as Anton's conversational powers were limited to a few sentences in broken English, we spent the greater part of the next three days in silence in our sleeping-bags.

On the evening of the third day the blizzard ceased, and the weather became gloriously bright and sunny. Once more we toiled – waist deep in snow – to the penguinry, and I used some additional hundreds of feet of film recording the manner in which the undaunted creatures were conducting their domestic affairs under truly dismaying difficulties.

Though the fine weather continued, I was unable to take further advantage of it, as there was nothing else to illustrate. It was exasperating to be thus helpless in these sunny days, and I was impatient to get back to winter-quarters, and proceed with other work.

On the tenth day after our arrival, I plodded through the snow to the sea-ice, to find if the surface was settling down and hardening sufficiently for us to end this enforced inaction, and return to Cape Evans. But the snow was still half-a-yard thick, and much too soft to travel on without ski, which we had not brought with us. Then I struggled to a hill-top, in order to reconnoitre the northward horizon with my glass, to see if open water was yet in sight. But though it was now December 10th, there was nothing but ice to be seen. On looking towards the south, I espied two black specks on the snow off Cape Barne, about three miles distant, which I took to be Emperor penguins. Examination showed that they were not penguins, but two men making for Cape Royds. I could not identify them at that distance; but surmising that they were coming to render assistance, and that, whoever they might be, they would arrive with robust Polar appetites, I made my way back to the hut, and instructed Anton to prepare a hot meal. When they came up, they proved to be meteorologist Simpson and Clissold. Knowing we had come away unprepared for so long a stay, they had come over on ski, as soon as the surface permitted, to help us to return home. We gave them a warm welcome, and they did not manifest any tardiness about accepting our invitation to the feast we had prepared.

Our thoughtful comrades had brought two spare pairs of ski, which they had dragged behind them; so we were now free to return with them. After they had rested for a couple of hours, we all buckled on this footgear, harnessed ourselves to my sledge, and returned to Cape Evans.

Owing to the frequent periods of bad weather that followed; and as there was so much work for all at Headquarters; and a party of three had to leave with further supplies to be depôted on the Great Ice Barrier, I was unable to visit Cape Royds again until four weeks later. On January 7th, once more I proceeded to the penguin colony, accompanied by Meares and Dimitri, who had recently returned from their journey to the Beardmore Glacier.

Almost all the chicks were by that time hatched, though even then there were still a few belated eggs to be found. This was fortunate, as I was thus able to secure moving-picture films of chicks just emerged from the shell, as well as of youngsters more advanced in the first stages of a perilous existence. Luckily, the weather kept fine; and I spent some exceedingly interesting days in recording the habits of the penguins and their chicks on hundreds of feet of film and many dozens of photographic plates.

The chicks were little dusky fellows, thickly covered with coats of smoke-grey down; but, unlike the little Skuas – which can run about almost as soon as hatched – the young penguins were quite helpless for the first few days. After that, they grew with incredible rapidity – as I could tell from neighbouring chicks which I knew could only be a few days older. As scores of nests had been wet and slushy after the snowstorm of my previous visit, I had then supposed the eggs must be chilled beyond redemption, and that there was no possible hope of their hatching. Yet, wonderful to relate, in hundreds of those selfsame nests there were now two lusty chicks. Perseverance and determination to 'stick it out' had accomplished miracles. The Adélie penguin has, from that time, been to me the emblem of persistent effort. I know of no other creature from which man may learn a finer lesson of how resolution and steadfastness of purpose may overcome every difficulty, than from the Adélie penguin.

The colony, which on my first visits in the present season had presented a somewhat indolent appearance – as almost all the birds had been incubating their eggs – had now taken on an aspect of bustling activity. There were many hundreds of little stomachs to be kept filled, and this necessitated ceaseless effort on the part of those responsible for their filling. The parent birds went about the work with a most business-like air. An intermittent stream of individuals proceeded sea-wards for food; whilst another stream, swollen with the loads they bore, flowed landwards.

At this time, the open water was quite twelve miles distant; and though a line of birds straggled out towards it, some few went no further than a crack in the ice, two feet wide, which was less than a mile away. There were *Euphausia* to be seen in the water at this place, but either the *Crustacea* were not in sufficient numbers, or else the birds suspected danger – perhaps fearing the crack might close up and imprison them hopelessly – as most of them jumped over it, and tramped miles beyond; but whether to the open water or some other wider crack, I could not say.

On reaching Cape Royds, the returning birds made anxiously for their nests, and proceeded at once to feed their youngsters. This they did by bringing the food up into the gullet; when the chick put its head into the parent's mouth and partook of it. At first the little ones had to be coaxed and taught to feed – which was done by holding a morsel at the end of the beak and tempting the chick – but they soon learned to insert their heads into the parent's mouth and eat. From a week old they had voracious appetites, and clamoured continuously for more, until they became distended almost, it seemed, to the bursting point. Their paunches swelled visibly as they gobbled away greedily, and one half expected to hear them go off – pop! The parent became slimmer inversely as the chick expanded, and rapidly shrank from a bulging food-bag into a trim and elegant marionette again.

As the chicks grew, they became a constant source of anxiety to their parents, who were hard put to it to feed and protect them from harm; for the ever-watchful Skuas were always on the alert to pounce down upon the progeny of the unwary. The chicks were brooded by each parent in turn for the first few weeks; but after that they increased in bulk so rapidly that to cover them was no longer possible. By this time, however, their thick coats of down made them impervious to the cold. As they gained in size and strength, they began to wander away from the nests, exposing themselves to danger from the gulls. This was a source of great anxiety to their elders, and it was a common sight to see a mother loudly squawking to a chick that was straying from the nest: 'Come back, you naughty boy!'

The tendency of the chicks to wander; and the fact that it now became impossible for one parent to provide the huge quantities of food required by the two youngsters, brought about a curious state of affairs, indicating that the Adélie is not lacking in organising ability. Little bunches of half-a-dozen or so chicks were to be seen in charge of several attendants. Either these chicks had wandered away from their homes, and, becoming lost, had gravitated together as companions in misfortune, and were being cared for by some of the kinder-hearted members of the community; or their respective parents had deputed certain of their number to protect the chicks whilst they themselves went off to forage for them. Dr Wilson, during the *Discovery* Expedition, was of the latter opinion – that the chicks were thus herded together by the adults so that they could more easily be defended from the attacks of Skua-gulls, whilst the parents were absent getting food supplies.

As each food-laden adult returned, it was pounced upon and chased by half-a-dozen or more wandering youngsters, each making a piteous appeal about its hunger – for any parent is good enough for any chick so long as it is food-laden. But every parent was not prepared to stand and deliver to just any chick that challenged him; the besieged was almost invariably obdurate, and, turning a deaf ear to all appeals and blandishments, kept on his way to his own family crèche.

So numerous were the chicks thus meandering about, that I imagine many of these hungry little wanderers never found their way back to their own units again, and became hopelessly lost. Yet, as, somehow or other, they all managed to get fed, I took it that the lost – being 'thrown on the parish,' so to speak – eventually came under the protection of some system, by which strays were taken in hand by charitably-disposed individuals. It is my belief that many of the chickless penguins – having perhaps failed to hatch any offspring, or having lost them through misfortune – devote themselves to the praise-worthy object of supporting and protecting these lost youngsters.

But the Skuas were ever on the watch for them. Having become detached from their legitimate food and protection base, and being dependent on charity, they had to struggle with scores of others for such bounty as there was to be dispensed. Dr Wilson wrote: 'In this race for life the weakest goes to the wall. A chick that cannot run down the old bird and its rivals in the race goes supperless. Needless to point out, the next race is still less likely to be successful, and the chick is soon marked down by a roving Skua, who quickly brings an end to its unsuccessful life.'

When about four weeks old, the chicks begin to shed their down, and there is no longer any necessity for guardianship. By that time they are almost as big as their parents, and are able to take care of themselves from the menace of the Skuas. By then, too, the services of every available adult are required for procuring food supplies. So much confusion now prevails because of the fledglings running about, that it must be almost impossible for any parents to find their own offspring. It is probable that a communal system exists for providing for and rationing the entire mob of hungry youngsters, and that at this stage of their growth it comes into practice.

During the two weeks that the chicks are shedding their down they are extraordinary-looking objects, as they stand about with their glossy new coats showing through patches where the thick, fluffy covering has fallen off. But clad in their new white-and-black suits, with a few obstinate patches of the old raiment still sticking to their backs, their chests or the crests of their heads, they are a still more comical sight. A little tuft on the poll is usually the last to go, and as soon as it disappears the youngsters are ready for the water. They never attempt to enter the sea whilst any down remains.

Before receiving their baptism in the element in which they must henceforth seek their living, the youngsters spent their last days ashore in fasting. They left the higher ground, and stood about in groups on the slope leading to the sea, or on the ice-foot overlooking it. When the wind blew the last patches of fluff from their polls, they looked exactly like their parents in all save bulk; and except that they had no white rims round their eyes. This white ring forms after the young Adélie is a year old, and is an easy means of distinguishing adults from chicks. Having lost the last remnants of their baby-clothes, the chicks made for the sea, and after some hesitation plunged headlong into it.

Once I saw some old birds porpoising about amongst a bevy of the newly-baptised youngsters, obviously coaching them in swimming and various tricks. The chicks seemed to be enjoying the new experience, but, from the snorting sounds they were making, I imagined they were not finding it altogether easy to keep the water out of their nostrils.

When I left Cape Royds on February 21st, after my first visit in 1911, there was not a single young penguin to be seen; for, once they had taken to the sea, they speedily adapted themselves to the new conditions of life, and returned to the scene of their infancy no more that year. It is believed that Adélie penguins spend the winter in the pack-ice; and that the young birds do not return to land to breed until they are two years old. The only remaining members of the former multitude, on the above date, were a score or so of old birds that had gone into the moult as soon as their family responsibilities ceased. These unfortunates stood about in such poor shelter as they could find – the picture of misery, with their moth-eaten-looking garments hanging in rags about them.

On returning to our winter-quarters, I found a number of moulting penguins at the end of our own cape, and I had them under observation for two weeks, during which time they fasted. As they never enter the water when in the moult, they are unable to procure food; consequently, what with lack of sustenance, and exposure to the awful storms and extreme cold, the unhappy creatures became so weak that they could hardly stand, and some of them died. When finally the survivors had got their beautiful new coats of raven black and snowy white, they were hardly recognisable as the fat and prosperous-looking 'people' of a month ago, for they had shrunk to half their former ample proportions.

Similarly as with the chicks and their down, just as soon as the last rags of their old coats had fallen from their emaciated bodies, they staggered to the edge of the sea, and fell rather than dived into it – where, with good food and plenty of it, we hoped they were able to recover their strength before they encountered the perils that there awaited them.

Long ere the great night had fallen on the Antarctic solitudes, they were doubtless far on their way northwards – on that migratory trek that all Adélie penguins make as the approach of winter begins to darken the midday heavens. Our hope was that they might overtake, on the way, the offspring they had so conscientiously raised; our earnest wish, that we might see them all again, when once more the triumphant sun had vanquished the legions of Jack Frost.

CHAPTER XXI

The Return of the *Terra Nova*

We might now hope to see the ship again as soon as the ice broke up and drifted out to sea. The previous summer the *Terra Nova* had moored to the ice-foot off Cape Evans on January 4th; yet now, a week later in the season, nothing but ice could be seen in the Sound, from High Peak, Cape Royds – eight miles north of our Hut. There was, however a 'water sky' in the distance, from which I estimated that there was open sea at Cape Bird, about thirty miles away; and out in the Sound to the west the ice had appeared to be in a rotten condition for some time past.

Each day, from Wind Vane Hill, I scanned the horizon with my Zeiss 12 X, to see if the *Terra Nova* were in sight. I could tell from the appearance of the clouds that the open water was daily drawing nearer; but the pack was very heavy, and there were many icebergs on the northern horizon.

About noon on January 17th, I was leisurely sweeping the north with die glass, when suddenly the masts of a ship came into the field of view. For a moment I could scarcely believe my eyes; but there could be no doubt about it. They were the masts of a barque; but presenting an extraordinary appearance, for they towered unnaturally high above the sky-line. Then I saw that what I was looking at was but a mirage. The real ship was hull-down below the horizon, and only the masts were visible. Above them, a wonderful mirage of the entire vessel, hull and all, appeared inverted; and over this first reflection there was a second image of the ship, upright. It was the upper image that I had at first seen.

Though we had observed many mirages of distant objects, nothing like this had been seen before. It was a most remarkable illusion; but the *Terra Nova* was undoubtedly there – about thirty miles away.

I ran towards the Hut, shouting excitedly, 'The Ship! The Ship!' Simpson and Nelson came running out immediately, and dashed up the hill. I handed them my glass as they reached me, and when they had convinced themselves that the ship was really there, we all cheered for joy. As, however, neither Simpson nor Nelson made any remark about the mirage, I took the glass to have another look myself; but to my surprise it was no longer visible. I told

Simpson about what I had seen, but he was quite incredulous, and seemed to think I must have imagined it. He said such phenomena had been reported before – as I knew – but that there was no instance on record of such a double mirage ever having been seen by a scientist.

But I had certainly seen the marvel, whether authentic instances were known to science or not – and emphatically told Simpson so. It was equally certain, however, that it was not now to be seen. It was very strange that it should have disappeared. Simpson asked me where I had seen it from, so I pointed out the place – about ten feet lower than where we stood. We went to the spot, and, on looking again with the glass, there it was, surely enough – a double mirage, one inverted and the other upright. I handed the glass to Simpson, who could not doubt the evidence of his eyes, and was greatly delighted that he, a scientist, could henceforth affirm that he had seen the phenomenon himself, and he carefully sketched it. It was certainly remarkable that so slight a variation in elevation as ten feet should make so much difference at a distance of thirty miles.

We were all very happy to know that news of home was so near once more; but, as events transpired, it was to be several weeks before the ship's party would be able to communicate with us, owing to the heavy nature of the pack-ice.

The First Supporting Party, as it was called – Atkinson, Wright, Cherry-Garrard and P.O. Keohane – brought the first news from the Polar Plateau on January 28th. We were glad to learn that all was well, and that the rest of the caravan were 'going strong' at the summit of the Beardmore Glacier, where this reinforcement had left them. They brought back a number of plates and films which Scott and Bowers had exposed. I developed these with great care, and was delighted to find that many of them yielded excellent negatives.

We watched daily, and the ship drew nearer from time to time as the ice in the Sound broke away. In stormy weather she would put out to sea for safety, and reappear a few days later, nearer than before. It was not until February 3rd, however, that she came near enough for Meares – who, with Dimitri, had returned from the Barrier a month ago – to drive out with a dog-team and communicate with those on board. He returned an hour later with two great bags of letters and papers; so we all spent the next few hours reading the news from home, and learning something of the events that had occurred in the great crowded world from which we had been absent for so long.

Two days later, the sea being open within two miles of the cape, the ship ran alongside the ice-foot and moored to it half-a-mile from the end of the

Barne Glacier. It was good to see our friends again, and to hear all they had to tell us of their own doings, and of the winter cruise of the *Terra Nova* in New Zealand waters.

When we had unloaded the stores she had brought, I lost no time in getting my gear aboard, and the old dark-room into order once more; for, as the ship would be cruising to various points during the next few weeks, I decided to take up my quarters on board without delay. I knew that a storm might necessitate her getting under way at short notice; and, as it happened, the next day a blizzard compelled her to seek safety out in the Sound.

When the storm ceased, the ship proceeded to the glacier at the foot of the Western Mountains, to pick up the Geological Party. It was only when we approached the far side of the Sound that we fully realised the height of those fine peaks, for their crests sank behind the foothills ere we approximated within a dozen miles of the ice-foot. After steaming for some time along the coast, we found and embarked Taylor's party. For three months they had explored and examined the valleys with searching eyes, and had gained volumes of information for the enrichment of their special branch of science.

We 'watered ship' at the glacier's edge, and then headed out of the Sound; thence northwards, to embark Lieut. Campbell's party at Terra Nova Bay, in South Victoria Land – some 150 miles north of Ross Island. The ship had picked up the Northern Party at Cape Adare on her way south, and had landed them at that place for Priestley to do a few weeks' geological work at the foot of Mount Melbourne.

We were not, however, able to get within forty miles of the place where Lieut. Pennell had arranged to meet the party, owing to the heavy pack-ice inshore. A south-west gale rising, we rode the storm for two days, keeping a vigilant watch for drifting icebergs; and when the wind moderated a further attempt was made. But the ship entered such heavy ice that it took more than thirty hours to extricate her from the newly-formed pancake floes, which were heaped up many layers deep on the surface of the sea for miles. It was a hard fight to get out of this bad ice; and when at last we were free of it, the *Terra Nova* steamed back to Cape Evans – to embark the other members who would be returning home – prior to making a further attempt later.

On reaching our cape, we heard that Lieut. Evans had been brought back from the Barrier to the Discovery hut, seriously ill with scurvy; and that Surgeon Atkinson was there in attendance on him. This bad news had been brought by Dimitri and his dog-team, five days before. The ship therefore immediately steamed for Hut Point, where Evans was brought aboard in his sleeping-bag. Surgeon Atkinson and mechanic Lashly and Petty Officer Crean also came aboard.

The story of how these two brave men saved Lieut. Evans' life, and delivered their officer into the hands of the surgeon, is told briefly herein, in the chapter 'The South Pole.'

It was now necessary to make another immediate effort to reach Lieut. Campbell; so the ship once more headed for Terra Nova Bay. The ice conditions had not improved, however, and it was impossible to get any nearer than on the previous attempt.

Again the ship fought her way back to Cape Evans, where Simpson, Taylor, Meares and Day were embarked. Petty Officer Forde, and Clissold also came aboard, to exchange places with Petty Officer Williamson, and Archer, the ship's cook, who were landed. The *Terra Nova* then steamed again to Hut Point, to land Surgeon Atkinson and Keohane, who would there await the return of Mr Cherry-Garrard and Dimitri – these two having gone by dog-team to One Ton Camp on the Barrier, in the hope of meeting Captain Scott and the other members of the returning Polar Party. Lieut. Evans, who was steadily recovering, now that a fresh meat and vegetable diet was available, remained aboard to be invalided home.

Henceforth, the party at Cape Evans were under the command of Surgeon Atkinson, who, throughout the difficult situations and events that followed, bore this position of responsibility most ably.

Every hour was now of importance, owing to the known bad ice conditions up the coast. The *Terra Nova* therefore left McMurdo Sound on March 5th, 1912, in a final effort to reach the Northern Party, before heading north for New Zealand.

From Cape Royds onwards we found the ice had thickened materially in the Sound; and soon the incoming floes became so heavy that it seemed doubtful whether the ship could force a way through them. Between Beaufort Island and Cape Bird she became fast, and all hands were summoned on deck to make a united effort to roll her loose. The entire ship's company, except the engine-room staff, assembled amidships, and, at the word of command from Lieut. Bruce, ran from side to side of the deck periodically, in the endeavour to sway the ship slightly, to keep her from freezing in. We had to continue this strenuous work for several hours, with occasional spells for rest, whilst simultaneously the engine backed and filled. It was an anxious time, for should the *Terra Nova* freeze into the pack at this place, she might be crushed in the pressure of the incoming ice, if it should begin to heap up from the resistance of the land. Slowly we battered our way, fighting hard for every yard, until at last the united effort of steam and human endurance told. We crashed through the remaining buttresses of the threatening prison walls, and were out in the ice-scattered, but open sea.

Once more the ship was headed for Terra Nova Bay; but the ice there was worse than ever. We could not get within ten miles of where we had been turned back at the last attempt. As the season was now far advanced, and ice conditions had become established that might remain for the winter, Lieut. Pennell was reluctantly compelled to give up further efforts to relieve the party, and the ship's course was laid for New Zealand.

The story of the adventures of the Northern Party is an almost incredible one. By the middle of March they realised that all hope of being picked up by the ship was at an end; they even feared the ship herself had met with some disaster. Their plight was, indeed, perilous. Marooned in the Antarctic, in the face of winter, and short of food and clothing and every other necessity – for they had landed with only a few weeks' supplies – only consummate leadership and resource could save them. And it did! In this unprecedented predicament, they burrowed into a glacier with their ice-axes, and lived in that icy dungeon for six months, subsisting on the flesh of seals and penguins. Their life was one of the most extreme hardship; indeed, it almost surpasses belief that human beings could survive a Polar winter under such primitive conditions of existence, in such temperatures as were endured. Yet, thanks to the splendid leadership of that sterling officer, Lieut. Victor Campbell; and to the magnificent spirit and bravery and resource of all, they passed through that terrible ordeal not only safely, but with hopeful, if not joyous hearts.

With the return of daylight, on October 1st, 1912, they abandoned their ice-cave, and started for Cape Evans, with two sledges and camping-outfits. After an adventurous journey down the coast and round the west side of the Sound, they reached the Hut, all well, on November 7th. The remarkable story of the Northern Party's adventures is briefly told in the second volume of *Scott's Last Expedition*; and fully in Raymond Priestley's *Antarctic Adventure*.

The day after we steamed away for New Zealand, a Sooty albatross circled round the ship. This was a good omen, for these birds are never seen south of the pack. The portent proved to be a true one, and we encountered no more ice.

Except for the gales we met with, the homeward voyage was uneventful. The climax of the bad weather was reached in 55° 51' S., when, to quote the words of the *Terra Nova*'s commander, Lieut. Pennell: 'The most severe storm raged that was encountered by the ship during her whole commission.'

The ship was now in ballast, and light; and it was magnificent to watch her fighting the mountainous seas which seemed, at times, as though inevitably they must engulf her. One minute she would be in an ocean valley, with waves ahead and astern higher than her maintop; the next she would be on the summit of one of these watery peaks. The storm provided a thrilling subject for the last phase of our adventure that I recorded in moving-pictures.

When a day's steam from land, we sighted a school of Sperm whales lazily spouting in the sunlit waves. They excited immense interest aboard, for these now rarely seen leviathans of the ocean are quite different from any other whales. Their heads, which are enormous, are shaped like the bow of a battleship. They spout diagonally forward, not vertically as do other whales, and the spiracle is in the front, instead of in the middle of the head. For some time the ship was manoeuvred in the hope that we might get near enough for me to secure some kinematograph records; but the great creatures were too wary, and kept a good quarter-of-a-mile out of range.

On the morning of April 1st, 1912, the *Terra Nova* steamed into the harbour of Akaroa, New Zealand. Words fail me to describe my feelings as once more I saw that lovely land. Indeed, I doubt if it is possible for anyone to appreciate the glorious beauty of leafy trees and pasture-clad hills, bathed in the warm rays of the sun, as could those who had just returned from a year's existence in the barren, blizzard-swept ice and lava wildernesses of the Antarctic. It all seemed like some wonderful dream. The Promised Land could not have appeared fairer to the Children of Israel, than did the green hills of New Zealand to me that day.

A boat came out to greet us; and we heard that the Norwegians had reached the South Pole on December 14th, 1911, and that their expedition had returned home.

We had always known that if all went well with the rival expedition the chances were all in favour of their being the first at the goal, as their base of operations was so much nearer than ours, and they had more rapid means of transport. Though we all felt much disappointed at this news, we were proud to know that the greatest of the earth's remaining geographical problems had been solved, and that the South Pole was a mystery no more.

And we, who had spent more than a year in the Great White South, could, perhaps better than anyone else, realise the magnitude of Amundsen's achievement.

CHAPTER XXII

The South Pole

Wild and wide are my borders, stern as death is my sway,
And I wait for the men who will win me, and I will not be won in a day;
And I will not be won by weaklings, subtle, suave, and mild,
But by men with the hearts of vikings, and the simple faith of a child.
Send me best of your breeding, lend me your chosen ones;
Them will I take to my bosom, them will I call my sons.

Robert W. Service.

With some trepidation I realise that it is now incumbent upon me – having related my personal experiences of this great adventure – to give some account, in conclusion, of the attainment of the primary object of the Expedition – the reaching of the South Pole. I will endeavour therefore to do so, as briefly as is possible consistent with giving a clear idea of what that colossal task entailed.

Though much bad weather was encountered, all went fairly well with the various members of the Southern Party for the first month after leaving Hut Point, except for the breakdown of the motor tractors. These machines gave constant trouble from the outset; the predominant complaint from which they suffered being overheating – due to their low gearing and slow progress. This necessitated frequent stops, to cool them; and invariably it happened that by the time the engine had cooled the carburettor and induction pipes were so cold that they had to be heated with a blow-lamp before the petrol would vaporise. To start the engines under such conditions was not easy. Consequent on these frequent stoppages, the rate of the southward advance of the motors did not exceed seven miles per day. But worse troubles were soon to come; two connecting-rods of Lashly's engine broke, and one of Day's, so that both tractors finally had to be abandoned, having accomplished a total combined distance of about 140 miles.

No praise could be too great for the persistence with which Day and Lashly struggled with these motors. Once, they worked all night – in a temperature of 25° Faht below zero, in a stiff wind – and, regardless of frostbites and chills, they dismantled one of the engines, and substituted for a broken connecting-rod the only spare they had with them. Under the frigid conditions in which the work was carried out, this was a wonderful feat. It was rivalled by the manner in which these two toiled and laboured to urge and coax the refractory machines to render all possible service for the great end in view.

Though the tractors did not realise the hopes that had been entertained of them, it should be understood that they were employed by Captain Scott purely as an experiment. He made all his calculations dependent on the likelihood of their breaking down; so, when they did, his plans were not in any way upset.

Knowing in what respects Scott's motors failed, and why, it would now be possible to build machines that would work satisfactorily in the Antarctic. To the memory of Scott must therefore be given the honour due to a pioneer of motor traction in the Polar Regions, for he used it with a certain measure of success.

When their machines finally had been abandoned, the four members of the motor party formed themselves into a single man-hauling unit; and pushed forward with as much of the former loads as they could haul, until, later, the pony units overtook them.

The fodder depôts, laid the previous summer, were located without difficulty, and as each fresh depôt was laid it was marked by the erection of a high snow cairn; smaller cairns were also raised at intervals of a mile or two between, so that any returning party might be able to find the way back in clear weather, without knowledge of navigation.

Though it was now summer and the period of continuous daylight, it was still very cold – the temperature remaining many degrees below zero. The marches were made at night; and each morning breast-high snow walls were erected to shelter the ponies from the wind. Snugly clothed in their rugs, they rested in comparative comfort behind these barricades.

Each day brought its problems and its difficulties; but perusal of the Leader's diary shows that problems and difficulties were always met with the same buoyant hope and unflinching determination to solve and overcome them. Even when others were at times inclined to take a pessimistic view of things, Scott refused to be influenced by any adverse happenings, and confidently hoped and expected that all would be well.

On November 7th, C. Meares and Dimitri – who had left Hut Point three days later than the main party – arrived with the dog-teams; and, from now on, the dogs with their loads easily followed the less mobile pony party each day.

The main caravan overtook the (now man-hauling) Motor Party on November 21st; three days later, B. Day and Hooper set out on the return journey to Cape Evans – which they reached safely on December 21st, having travelled about 250 miles en route. Lieut. Evans and Lashly then joined the main party, and harnessed up with Surgeon Atkinson – whose pony had broken down and been shot – man-hauling the sledge.

Atkinson's pony was the first to meet its predestined end. Each of the others would have to face the sacrifice which such work demands, as its load was depôted. Their mission in life fulfilled, the ponies in death rendered a further service to the enterprise, for their flesh was food for the men and dogs who carried on the work.

All units now being united, the Southern Party was complete. From the time they struck out on the Great Ice Barrier, a few miles from Hut Point, the caravan had been travelling over the surface of the greatest known ice-sheet on earth. On December 5th, they had covered nearly four hundred miles, and were about twelve miles from the foot of the Beardmore Glacier. Here, 'a raging, howling blizzard broke,' the worst of the many storms that had been encountered since leaving Hut Point. It lasted four days; during which time the party were compelled to camp. In this storm the temperature rose to a degree above freezing, causing intense discomfort from the melting snow, which was several feet deep.

The delay, consequent on the blizzard, was a most serious matter; and on the evening of December 8th, as the pony fodder was nearly exhausted, it was resolved to kill the remaining animals the next day. But the storm had ceased by the morning, and the march was resumed under appalling conditions in the deep snow. Only a few miles could be made, however; and in the evening the ponies, exhausted by half rations and the great strain on their strength, were shot. The place was called Shambles Camp – the 31st camp since leaving Hut Point. 'Poor beasts! they have done wonderfully well considering the terrible circumstances under which they have worked, but it is hard to have to kill them so early,' wrote Captain Scott.

The ponies' loads averaged something under 500 lbs.; and a minimum of 15 statute miles had been considered a necessary day's march. The journey from Hut Point to Shambles Camp had been made in 34 days, which, taking all delays into account, was an average of about 12 miles per day. On December 9th, the Southern Party were, therefore, about a week behind their schedule time – or nearly 100 miles north of the point Scott had hoped to have reached by that date.

On December 11th, at the foot of the Beardmore Glacier, C. H. Meares and Dimitri handed over their loads, and started back with their dog-teams for winter-quarters. The dogs had done excellent work. They had come over 400 miles; transported their drivers and their rations; 200 lbs. of stores were depôted, and 600 lbs. of food was turned over to the man-hauling parties that now went forward. Meares and Dimitri accomplished the return journey safely in 25 days, reaching Cape Evans on January 5th, 1912, after having made a short stop at Hut Point.

The Beardmore Glacier is a pass in the Queen Alexandra Mountains, which border the Polar Plateau; the Southern Party here left the Barrier, and had to make their way up this icy defile for more than 100 miles, and ascend some 10,000 feet. The caravan now consisted of three sledges, manned as follows:

Sledge 1. Captain Scott, Dr Wilson, Captain Oates and Petty Officer Evans.

Sledge 2. Lieut. Evans, Surgeon Atkinson, Mr Wright and Mechanic Lashly.

Sledge 3. Lieut. Bowers, Mr Cherry-Garrard, Petty Officers Crean and Keohane.

The passage of the Glacier was beset with dangers, and with difficulties which at times were sufficient to dismay the stoutest hearts; but difficulties are 'part of the game' in Polar exploration, and to overcome them is one of the lures of the South. Repeatedly both sledges and men were bogged in heavy snow, and the loads had to be transported piecemeal by relays; rough broken ice and pressure-ridges formed almost insuperable barriers at times; crevasses were frequent sources of peril; and snow-blindness, produced by the glare, caused agony to several members of the party. But, scorning every discomfort, difficulty and danger with which hostile Nature barred the way, these intrepid souls pushed onward to success.

Precipitous mountains flanked them on the west: mountains which only four human beings had previously beheld – Shackleton, Marshall, Wild and Adams. There was little leisure for studying scenery, yet Captain Scott and Lieut. Bowers took some excellent photographs of the principal peaks of the range – photographs which are proof of the care they devoted to this important work.

The ascent of the Beardmore Glacier had been a tremendous task; and on December 21st, when near the summit, Captain Scott told off four more of the party to depôt their surplus and return. His decision fell upon Atkinson,

Wright, Cherry-Garrard and P.O. Keohane. The Leader wrote in his Journal: 'All are disappointed – poor Wright rather bitterly I fear. I dreaded the necessity of choosing – nothing could be more heart-rending. ... We said an affecting farewell to the returning party, who have taken things very well, dear good fellows as they are.'

This, the First Supporting Party, as it was called, safely reached Cape Evans on January 28th, 1912, having covered the 500 miles in 37 days.

By Christmas Day, the Southern Party were well clear of the Glacier, and out on the plain of ice which Sir Ernest Shackleton had named, in 1908, King Edward VII Plateau – having ascended 8,250 feet since leaving the Great Ice Barrier. Lashly celebrated the day by dropping through the snow lid of a crevasse, and almost dragging the rest of the party after him. With some trouble he was pulled back to safety.

On January 4th, when about 150 miles from the Pole, height 10,200 feet above the Barrier, Lieut. Evans, Lashly and Petty Officer Crean were told off to return, and depôted their surplus.

The story of the adventures of this Second Supporting Party on their homeward way is a stirring one. Briefly, it is as follows. Before they had reached the foot of the Beardmore Glacier, Lieut. Evans became ill, and was found to be suffering from the Nemesis that dogs the heels of all Polar explorers, scurvy. He became gradually worse; but, with life at stake, struggled on until within a hundred miles of Hut Point, when he could go no further. His companions, Lashly and Crean, then pulled him on the sledge for four days; then a heavy snowfall made such transport any further impossible. Evans owes his life to the strength, courage and devotion of these two men, and to their resource in this dilemma. Whilst Lashly stayed to nurse him, Crean set out, in threatening weather, to march the thirty-five miles to Hut Point, for help. It was a forlorn hope; but he accomplished the feat in eighteen hours, reaching the *Discovery* hut in a state of exhaustion. Tom Crean's lone march that day was one of the finest feats in an adventure that is an epic of splendid episodes.

Fortunately, he found Dr Atkinson and Dimitri there, with dog teams. They immediately set out to the rescue, and brought Lieut. Evans and Lashly to safety. Evans rapidly recovered under Atkinson's care, and the effects of fresh provisions, and was invalided home in the *Terra Nova* on her second voyage.

For this gallant deed, on their return to England Lashly and Crean were each awarded the Albert Medal.

The Polar Party now consisted of Captain Scott, Dr Wilson, Captain Oates, Lieut. Bowers and Petty Officer Evans. They proceeded south with one sledge, laden with camping equipment and provisions for over a month.

Ever ready in appreciation and recognition of the qualities of his comrades, the Leader wrote:

Each is invaluable. It is quite impossible to speak too highly of my companions. ... Wilson, first as doctor, ever on the look out to alleviate the small pains and troubles incidental to the work; now as cook, quick, careful and dexterous, ever thinking of some expedient to help the camp life; tough as steel on the traces, never wavering from start to finish.

Evans, a great worker with a really remarkable head-piece. It is only now I realise how much has been due to him ... what an invaluable assistant he has been.

Little Bowers remains a marvel – he is thoroughly enjoying himself ... Nothing comes amiss to him, and no work is too hard. It is difficult to get him into the tent; he seems quite oblivious to the cold, and he lies coiled in his bag writing and working out sights long after the others are asleep.

Oates had his invaluable period with the ponies; now he is a foot-slogger and goes hard the whole time, does his share of the camp work, and stands the hardship as well as any of us. I would not like to be without him either.

With confident hearts and buoyant spirits they pressed on. 'What lots of things we think of on these monotonous marches! What castles one builds now hopefully that the Pole is ours,' wrote the Leader, as he reached Shackleton's 'Furthest South' on January 6th, 1912, Lat. 88° 23— ninety-seven geographical miles from the goal. The next day the maximum height of the Plateau was reached – 10,570 feet above the Great Ice Barrier. Henceforward, there was a gradual decline of one thousand feet; but, owing to the bad surfaces and bad weather encountered, it took ten days to cover the remaining distance to the Pole.

Up till now, no sign had been seen of the Norwegians; but Scott had not altogether banished the possibility that Amundsen might have preceded him. On January 15th he wrote: 'It is wonderful to think that two long marches would land us at the Pole ... It ought to be a certain thing now, and the only appalling possibility the sight of the Norwegian flag forestalling ours.'

The next day, January 16th, Scott wrote:

The worst has happened, or nearly the worst. We marched well in the morning, and covered 7½ miles. Noon sight showed us in Lat. 89° 42 S., and we started off in high spirits in the afternoon, feeling that to-morrow would see us at our destination. About the second hour of the march Bowers' sharp eyes detected what he thought was a cairn; he was uneasy about it, but argued that it must be a *sastrugus*.[1] Half an hour later he detected a black speck ahead. Soon we knew that this could not be a natural snow feature. We marched on, found that it was a black flag tied to a sledge bearer; near-by the remains of a camp; sledge tracks and ski tracks going and coming and the clear trace of dogs' paws – many dogs. This told us the whole story. The Norwegians have forestalled us and are first at the Pole. It is a terrible disappointment, and I am very sorry for my loyal companions. Many thoughts come and much discussion have we had. To-morrow we must march on to the Pole, and then hasten home with all the speed we can compass. All the day-dreams must go; it will be a wearisome return.

The Leader's simple words tell a story that should be perpetuated for England in the National Gallery. Few painters had ever a more dramatic theme. The setting, a vast and featureless plain of ice; the centre of interest an ominous black flag, contemplating which are five men in Polar clothing, dismayed but not disheartened; and the title of the picture 'Forestalled.' That is all; yet it would tell an epic tale.

It is a terrible disappointment, and I am very sorry for my loyal companions.

The greatness of the Leader shines out in that immortal sentence. In that tragic hour it was for his companions that he felt, not for himself and the blighting of his own hopes.

On January 17th Scott wrote:

The Pole. Yes, but under very different circumstances from those we expected. We have had a horrible day – add to our disappointment a head wind, with a temperature of – 22°, and companions labouring on with cold feet and cold hands ...

We started at 7.30, none of us having slept much after the shock of our discovery ... To-night little Bowers is laying himself out to get sights in terrible difficult circumstances; the wind is blowing hard, and there is a curious damp, cold feeling in the air which chills one to the bone in no time ... Great God! this is an awful place and terrible enough for us to have laboured to it without the reward of priority.

All the tremendous effort of those eleven weeks that had passed is felt in that one momentary, bitter cry to the Almighty.

It is the cry of a strong man out of whose heart hope is crushed. But in such a heart as Scott's it was human endeavour that mattered, not mere ambition to achieve. The crushing of a hope could not long depress such dauntless spirit as his; and the next day found him full of appreciation for his rival's successful work.

On January 18th, he wrote:

Decided, after summing up all observations, that we were 3.5 miles away from the Pole – one mile beyond it and 3 to the right. More or less in this direction Bowers saw a cairn or tent.

We have just arrived at this tent, 2 miles from our camp, therefore about 1½ miles from the Pole. In the tent we find a record of five Norwegians having been here, as follows:

Roald Amundsen
Olav Olavson Bjaaland
Hilmer Hanssen
Sverre H. Hassel
Oscar Wisting

16 Dec. 1911.

The tent is fine – a small compact affair supported by a single bamboo. A note from Amundsen, which I keep, asks me to forward a letter to King Haakon!

Left a note to say I had visited the tent with companions. Bowers photographing and Wilson sketching ...

We built a cairn, put up our slighted Union Jack, and photographed ourselves – mighty cold work all of it ...

There is no doubt that our predecessors have made thoroughly sure of their mark and fully carried out their programme ...

We carried the Union Jack about three-quarters of a mile north with us and left it on a piece of stick as near as we could fix it.[2]

In the photographs which they took that day, it is magnificently eloquent of the manner in which the explorers took the frustrating of their hopes, that one of the films shows four of the party laughing – obviously at

Camp at the South Pole.

some mishap to Bowers, just as he released the shutter, for the negative is blurred.

As Scott now thought of the tremendous journey that lay before them, he wrote:

> Well, we have turned our backs now on the goal of our ambition and must face our 800 miles of solid dragging – and good-bye to most of the day-dreams ... Now for the run home and a desperate struggle. I wonder if we can do it!

With such a colossal task before them; in the face of weather which he knew must inevitably become daily more severe, and without the incentive of being first at the Pole to cheer them, the Leader may well have feared that, though he knew their spirit would never fail them, their strength might be unequal to the call.

The pages of Captain Scott's diary, which follow, contain an account of the most heroic and self-sacrificing struggle in the history of Polar exploration.

By kind permission of the publishers of *Scott's Last Expedition* I am privileged to make a number of extracts from my late Chief's Journal; and I would here beg my readers to bear in mind that notwithstanding the infinite striving of each day – striving for dear life itself – and the gradual weakening of the party, the Leader yet found time each night to record the day's doings fully. Knowing, as we do, that this was only accomplished under appalling conditions of hardship, and after unprecedented putting forth of long-continued effort, Captain Scott's Journal must be regarded as one of the most remarkable attestations of devotion to purpose and duty in the history of our race. It is all the more remarkable, when we consider the simple beauty of the language used; and yet still more so, when we remember that, after all, this was only a diary – mere notes from which the Leader had intended, later, to write his book in comfort at home. Taking all the circumstances under which it was produced into consideration, and the literary quality of the result, it is doubtful if in all the world there is any more moving human document that this stirring and inspiring record of a brave but hopeless fight against over-whelming odds.

From the time of leaving the Pole, Scott seems to have been oppressed with a feeling of anxiety: It will be an anxious time, until Three Degree Depôt is reached (over 150 miles away). I'm afraid the return journey is going to be dreadfully tiring and monotonous,' he wrote.

Bad weather, bad travelling surfaces, and low zero temperatures with icy winds were encountered from the outset of the return journey.

'Oates is feeling the cold and fatigue more than most of us' wrote Scott on January 21st; and on the 23rd:

> Wilson suddenly discovered that Evans' nose was frost-bitten – it was white and hard. There is no doubt Evans is a good deal run down – his fingers are badly blistered and his nose rather seriously congested with frequent frostbites. He is very much annoyed with himself, which is not a good sign.
>
> I think Wilson, Bowers and I are as fit as possible under the circumstances. Oates gets cold feet.

On January 24th, the first note of serious apprehension was struck. Scott wrote: 'This is the second full gale since we left the Pole. I don't like the look of it. Is the weather breaking up? If so, God help us, with the tremendous journey and scanty food.' It is as though the Leader heard the approaching foot-falls of Death – and Death was not far distant.

Oates now began to suffer much with his feet, and Evans' fingers and nose were in a very bad state. Wilson suffered tortures from snow-blindness. He had the misfortune also to strain a tendon in his leg a few days later; and Evans 'dislodged two fingers-nails' the same evening. On February 1st, they were very bad, and the blisters burst; the next day Scott had a bad fall. He wrote:

Captain Scott writing in his diary from which he later hoped to write a book about the expedition.

All went well till ... on a very slippery surface I came an awful 'purler' on my shoulder. It is horribly sore to-night and another sick person added to our tent – three out of five injured, and the most troublesome surfaces to come. We shall be lucky if we get through without serious injury. Wilson's leg is better; but might easily get bad again, and Evans' fingers.

Petty Officer Evans had a bad fall on February 4th, and became 'dull and incapable' from the effects of concussion. The next day Scott wrote:

Evans is our chief anxiety now; his cuts and wounds suppurate, his nose looks very bad, and altogether he shows considerable signs of being played out. ... He is going steadily downhill.

Since leaving the Pole, the party had, up to now, been traversing the Plateau. On February 7th, the descent of the Beardmore Glacier was commenced.

To the lasting glory of his name, notwithstanding the plight of the party, Dr Wilson kept a steady look-out for geological specimens and fossils in the morainic matter passed, and collected many. In all 35 lbs. of specimens were gathered, and these they carried to the last. This devotion to science may well have meant the difference between life and death to them.

On February 11th, they got into a terrible place, the ice being broken up by pressure, and badly crevassed. In the uncertain light they were utterly at a loss which way to steer. Scott wrote:

There were times when it seemed almost impossible to find a way out of the awful turmoil in which we found ourselves. At length, arguing that there must be a way out on our left, we plunged in that direction. It got worse, harder, more icy and crevassed ... We had grown desperate. We won through at 10 p.m. and I write after 12 hours on the march.

February 12th:

... By a fatal chance we kept too far to the left, and then we struck uphill and, tired and despondent, arrived in a horrid maze of crevasses and fissures. Divided counsels caused our course to be erratic after this, and finally, at 9 p.m. we landed in the worst place of all. After discussion we decided to camp, and here we are, after a very short supper, and one meal only remaining in the food bag; the depôt is doubtful in locality. We must get there to-morrow. Meanwhile we are cheerful with an effort. It's a tight place, but luckily we've been well fed up to the present. Pray God we have fine weather to-morrow.

February 13th:

Evans raised our hopes with a shout of 'depôt ahead,' but it proved to be a shadow on the ice. Then suddenly Wilson saw the actual depôt flag. It was an immense relief, and we were soon in possession of our 3 ½ days' food. The relief to all is inexpressible; needless to say, we camped and had a meal. ... Yesterday was the worst experience of the trip and gave a horrid feeling of insecurity. In future food must be worked so that we do not run so short if the weather fails us. We mustn't get into a hole like this again ... Bowers has had a very bad attack of snow-blindness, and Wilson another almost as bad. Evans has no power to assist with camping work.

February 14th:

Wilson's leg still troubles him and he doesn't like to trust himself on ski; but the worst case is Evans, who is giving us serious anxiety. This morning he suddenly disclosed a huge blister on his foot ... Sometimes I fear he is going from bad to worse.

February 16th:

Evans has nearly broken down in brain, we think. He is absolutely changed from his normal self-reliant self.

February 17th, Scott wrote:

A very terrible day. Evans looked a little better after a good sleep, and declared, as he always did, that he was quite well. He started in his place on the traces, but half-an-hour later worked his ski shoes adrift, and had to leave the sledge ... I cautioned him to come on as quickly as he could, and he answered cheerfully as I thought. We had to push on, and the remainder of us were forced to pull very hard, sweating heavily ...

After lunch, and Evans still not appearing, we looked out, to see him still afar off. By this time we were alarmed, and all four started back on ski. I was first to reach the poor man, and shocked at his appearance; he was on his knees with clothing disarranged, hands uncovered and frostbitten, and a wild look in his eyes. Asked what was the matter, he replied with a slow speech that he didn't know, but thought he must have fainted. We got him on his feet, but after two or three steps he sank down again. He showed every sign of complete collapse. Wilson, Bowers and I went back for the sledge, whilst Oates remained with him. When we returned he was practically unconscious, and when we got him into the tent quite comatose. He died quietly at 12.30 a.m. ... It is a terrible thing to lose a companion in this way, but calm reflection shows that there could not have been a better ending to the terrible anxieties of the past week. Discussion of the situation at lunch yesterday shows us what a desperate pass we were in with a sick man on our hands at such a distance from home ... Providence mercifully removed him at this critical moment ... We did not leave him until two hours after his death.

'Taff' Evans had been regarded as the 'Strong Man' of the party; but the blasting of his beloved Chief's ambition, to be the first to reach the South Pole, was a blow from which the devoted man never recovered. His downfall began to date from that time: but he served his country with all his strength to the last hour of his life.

At Shambles Camp, renewed strength was imparted to the surviving members of the party by a plentiful meal of the horse-flesh depôted there; and supplies of the fresh meat were carried forward.

The grim footfalls, which had overtaken them, had now fallen to the rear again; but the Leader seemed ever to hear them. On February 20th he wrote: 'Pray God, we get better travelling as we are not so fit as we were.'

And on February 27th: 'Pray God, we have no further set-backs, but there is a horrid element of doubt.'

The cold continued intense, ranging from sixty to eighty degrees of frost, and the surface bad beyond their worst fears.

These things delayed them woefully, and the daily marches did not average more than five or six miles; whereas a minimum of nine had been allowed for – whilst it had been hoped that a minimum of thirteen miles per day might be accomplished. Delay meant further shortage of food and oil fuel.

The anxiety and terrific strain on their strength was beginning too surely to tell. On March 3rd Captain Scott wrote: 'God help us, we can't keep up this pulling, that is certain. Amongst ourselves we are unendingly cheerful, but what each feels in his heart I can only guess.'

March 4th: 'We are in a very tight place indeed, but none of us feels despondent *yet* or at least we preserve every semblance of good cheer, but one's heart sinks as the sledge stops dead at some *sastrugi* ... I don't know what I should do if Wilson and Bowers weren't so determinedly cheerful over things.'

We can but surmise what sufferings and misgivings lay behind the masks with which they concealed their feelings.

On March 5th, Scott wrote:

Oates' feet are in a wretched condition. One swelled up tremendously last night and he is very lame this morning ... Marched for five hours this morning, covering about 5½ miles ... The poor Soldier nearly done. It is pathetic enough because we can do nothing for him; more hot food might do a little, but only a little, I fear. We none of us expected these terribly low temperatures ... Wilson is feeling them most; mainly, I fear, from his self-sacrificing devotion in doctoring Oates' feet.

March 6th:

Things have been awful ... Poor Oates is unable to pull ... He is wonderfully plucky, as his feet must be giving him great pain. He makes no complaint. If we were all fit, I should have hopes of getting through; but the poor Soldier has become a terrible hindrance, though he does his utmost and suffers much ... One of his feet very bad this morning; he is wonderfully brave. We still talk of what we will do together at home.

The grim shadow was fast drawing near once more. Scott saw it, and wrote on March 7th: 'One feels that for poor Oates the crisis is near.'

March 8th: 'Wilson's feet giving trouble now, but mainly because he gives so much help to others. ... God help us indeed.'

On March 10th, the Leader wrote:

Oates' foot worse. He has rare pluck and must know that he can never get through. He asked Wilson if he had a chance this morning, and of course Bill had to say he didn't know. In point of fact he has none. Apart from him, if he went under now, I doubt whether we could get through. With great care we might have a dog's chance, but no more. The weather conditions are awful. At the same time of course poor Titus is the greatest handicap. Poor chap! it is too pathetic to watch him; one cannot but try to cheer him up.

March 11th: 'Oates is very near the end. What he will do, God only knows. He is a brave, fine fellow, and understands the situation. He asked us for advice. Nothing could be done but to urge him to march as long as he could.'

March 12th: 'The surface remains awful, the cold intense, and our physical condition running down. God help us! Not a breath of favourable wind for more than a week.'

March 14th: 'It must be near the end, but a pretty merciful end. Poor Oates again got it in the foot. I shudder to think what it will be like to-morrow. It is only with greatest pains rest of us keep off frostbites. Truly awful outside the tent. Must fight it out to the last biscuit, but can't reduce rations.'

On March 16th, Oates could go no further, and Scott wrote:

> At lunch, the day before yesterday, poor Titus Oates said he couldn't go on; he proposed we should leave him in his sleeping-bag. That we could not do, and we induced him to come on, on the afternoon march. In spite of its awful nature for him, he struggled on and we made a few miles. At night he was worse, and we knew that the end had come. He did not – would not – give up hope to the very end. He slept through the night, hoping not to wake, but he woke in the morning. It was blowing a blizzard. He said: 'I am just going outside, and may be some time.' He went out into the blizzard, and we have not seen him since ... We knew that poor Oates was walking to his death, but though we tried to dissuade him, we knew that it was the act of a brave man and an English gentleman. We all hope to meet the end with a similar spirit, and assuredly the end is not far.

I recall very clearly a memorable conversation that Oates had with Nelson and me one evening in my dark-room, during the winter of 1911. The point was raised as to what a man should do if he were to break down on the Polar journey, thereby becoming a burden to others. Oates unhesitatingly and emphatically expressed the opinion that there was only one possible course – self-sacrifice. He thought that a pistol should be carried, and that 'If anyone breaks down he should have the privilege of using it.'

We both agreed with this; but little did we think that within six months, one of us, and that one Oates himself, would be put to the test. Though no pistol was carried, when the time came for Oates to live up to his words, he was not found wanting. But his was not the act of one goaded by suffering into a last distracted, frenzied impulse. It was the deliberate act of a man who had thought out his duty to his companions beforehand, and in cold blood. There can be no question about the quality of Oates' sacrifice. It was sublime.

They pitched their 60th camp from the Pole on March 19th, eleven miles from a depôt of food and fuel. That day a blizzard began, which, as the meteorological records at winter-quarters show, lasted for ten days. For those three dauntless souls who had stuck to their sick companions to the last, the end had come.

Scott wrote:

March 19th:

We camped with difficulty last night and were dreadfully cold till after our supper of cold pemmican and biscuit, and half a pannikin of cocoa cooked over the spirit. Then, contrary to expectation, we got warm and all slept well. To-day we started in the usual dragging manner. Sledge dreadfully heavy. We are 15 ½ miles from the depôt and ought to get there in three days. What progress! We have two days' food but barely a day's fuel. All our feet are getting bad – Wilson's best, my right foot worst, left all right. There is no chance to nurse one's feet till we can get hot food into us. Amputation is the least I can hope for now, but will the trouble spread? That is the serious question. The weather doesn't give us a chance – the wind from N. to N.W. and -40° temp, to-day.

March 21st (Wednesday): 'Got within 11 miles of depôt Monday night; had to lay up all yesterday in severe blizzard. To-day forlorn hope, Wilson and Bowers going to depôt for fuel.'

March 22nd: 'Blizzard bad as ever – Wilson and Bowers unable to start – to-morrow last chance – no fuel and only one or two rations of food left— must be near the end. Have decided it shall be natural – we shall march for the depôt with or without our effects and die in our tracks.'

On Thursday, March 29th, the Leader made the final entry in his Journal:

Since the 21st, we have had a continuous gale from W.S.W. and S.W. We had fuel to make two cups of tea apiece and bare food for two days on the 20th. Every day we have been ready to start for our depôt 11 miles away, but outside the door of the tent it remains a scene of whirling drift. I do not think we can hope for any better things now. We shall stick it out to the end, but we are getting weaker, of course, and the end cannot be far.

It seems a pity, but I do not think I can write more.

R. Scott.

For God's sake look after our people.

Owing to the terrific weather, and the fall of winter and consequent darkness, it was not until the following spring (October 29th, 1912), that a Search Party, in command of Surgeon Atkinson, was able to set out, under the guidance of Mr C. S. Wright, who was a skilful navigator. By the evening of November 11th, they had covered the 140 miles to One Ton Depôt; and the next day, having travelled 11 miles further, they discovered the tent.

Wilson and Bowers were found in the attitude of sleep, their sleeping-bags closed over their heads as they would naturally close them. Scott died later. He had thrown back the flaps of his sleeping-bag and opened his coat. The little wallet containing the three note-books was under his shoulders and his arm thrown across Wilson. So, they were found – eight months later.

Beside the note-books were the little camera, and two rolls of film. In these films there were latent, amongst others, the three photographs reproduced herein which show the explorers at the South Pole – probably the most tragically interesting photographs in the world.

They were taken with a quarter-plate film camera; and, in the case of the groups, the shutter was released by a long thread, so that all might appear in the picture. Dr Wilson can be seen pulling this thread in one of the groups, and Lieut. Bowers in the other. The films were nearly two years old at the time they were exposed at the South Pole. For eight months those two rolls of film lay on the snow – beside the dead bodies of three of the five explorers whose images were hidden therein – until they were found by the Search Party. Later, they were developed by Debenham in the Hut at Cape Evans. It seems almost incredible that they should have yielded excellent negatives.

In one of the note-books, Captain Scott had written these lines:

MESSAGE TO PUBLIC

The causes of the disaster are not due to faulty organisation, but to misfortune in all risks which had to be undertaken.

1. The loss of Pony transport in March 1911 obliged us to start later than I had intended, and obliged the limits of stuff transported to be narrowed.

Grave of the Southern Party.

2. The weather throughout the outward journey, and especially the heavy gales in 83° S., stopped us.

3. The soft snow in lower reaches of glacier again reduced pace.

We fought these untoward events with a will and conquered, but it cut into our provision reserve.

Every detail of our food supplies, clothing and depôts made on the interior ice-sheet and over that long stretch of 700 miles to the Pole and back, worked out to perfection. The advance party would have returned to the glacier in fine form and with surplus of food, but for the astonishing failure of the man whom we had least expected to fail. Edgar Evans was thought the strongest man of the party.

The Beardmore Glacier is not difficult in fine weather, but on our return we did not get a single completely fine day; this with a sick companion enormously increased our anxieties.

As I have said elsewhere, we got into frightfully rough ice and Edgar Evans received a concussion of the brain – he died a natural death, but left us a shaken party with the season unduly advanced.

But all the facts above enumerated were as nothing to the surprise which awaited us on the Barrier. I maintain that our arrangements for returning were quite adequate, and that no one in the world would have expected the temperatures and surfaces which we encountered at this time of the year. On the summit in lat. 85° 86° we had -20°, -30°. On the Barrier in lat. 82°, 10,000 feet lower, we had -30° in the day, -47° at night pretty regularly, with continuous head wind during our day marches. It is clear that these circumstances come on very suddenly, and our wreck is certainly due to this sudden advent of severe weather, which does not seem to have any satisfactory cause.

I do not think human beings ever came through such a month as we have come through, and we should have got through in spite of the weather but for the sickening of a second companion, Captain Oates, and a shortage of fuel in our depôts for which I cannot account, and finally, but for the storm which has fallen on us within 11 miles of the depôt at which we hoped to secure our final supplies.

Surely misfortune could scarcely have exceeded this last blow. We arrived within 11 miles of our old One Ton Camp with fuel for one last meal and food for two days. For four days we have been unable to leave the tent – the gale howling about us.

We are weak, writing is difficult, but for my own sake I do not regret this journey, which has shown that Englishmen can endure hardships, help one another, and meet death with as great a fortitude as ever in the past.

We took risks, we knew we took them; things have come out against us, and therefore we have no cause for complaint, but bow to the will of Providence, determined still to do our best to the last. But if we have been willing to give our lives to this enterprise, which is for the honour of our country, I appeal to our countrymen to see that those who depend on us are properly cared for.

Had we lived, I should have had a tale to tell of the hardihood, endurance, and courage of my companions which would have stirred the heart of every Englishman. These rough notes and our dead bodies must tell the tale, but surely, surely, a great rich country like ours will see that those who are dependent on us are properly provided for.

R. Scott.

Over their bodies a great cairn of ice was raised, surmounted by a cross, made from ski; and a sledge was stood on end in a smaller cairn, near-by, to be an additional mark.

A search was made for Captain Oates' body, but it was never found. 'The kindly snow had covered his body, giving it a fitting burial.' A cross was placed on the scene of the search, with the inscription:

HEREABOUTS DIED A VERY GALLANT GENTLEMAN, CAPTAIN
L. E. G. OATES, OF THE INNISKILLING DRAGOONS.

Later, at Hut Point, a cross was erected to the memory of Captain Scott, Dr Wilson, Captain Oates, Lieutenant Bowers, and Petty Officer Evans, on which this line from Tennyson's *Ulysses* was carved – than which no man had ever a nobler epitaph:

TO STRIVE, TO SEEK, TO FIND, AND NOT TO YIELD.

The End of the Expedition

I have told my story; and it only remains for me to add a few words about the end of the Expedition.

Taylor left for Australia on the same day that we landed in New Zealand; Day and Meares elected to return to England via Rio Janeiro; whilst Simpson and I went home by way of Sydney and the Suez Canal. Lieut. Evans stayed awhile in New Zealand to recover his health before proceeding home.

On arrival in London, I found a wholly groundless belief current that there had been a 'race' to the Pole. I, therefore, addressed a letter to *The Times*, which was published, and from which I quote the following extracts. At that time it was, of course, not known that a disaster had happened.

The popular idea that there has been a race to the South Pole is an error. Captain Scott has not been racing, nor has he been engaged in a mere 'dash to the Pole.' He is leading a great scientific expedition – perhaps the greatest ever sent out from any land – and the reaching of the South Pole was but one part of the extensive programme laid out. To race would have been to jeopardise the success of the main objects of the enterprise, and Captain Scott would not allow the presence of a rival in the field to move him from the course which he considered best and wisest.

Within four months of our departure from New Zealand he had lost nine ponies out of nineteen, nearly half the total transport on which he was relying. It would be impossible to overstate the seriousness of this loss. Had any more ponies succumbed, the main objects of the Expedition could not have been achieved, as success was entirely dependent on the transport animals. It was due to this misfortune that Captain Scott did not start on the Pole journey till November 1st, 1911. His original plans provided for leaving his base on October 1st; but October is a very cold and tempestuous month, and to have exposed the surviving transport animals to the additional hardships such weather entailed, would have involved too grave a risk. He, therefore, reluctantly postponed the start a month. That month perhaps lost for Scott the honour of being first at the South Pole. But for this delay it is conceivable that the rival explorers might even have met at the goal of their hopes.

Captain Scott will be heartiest of all in congratulating Amundsen on his splendid achievement. More than any other man can he appreciate what it means to press such an enterprise to success. He himself would have scorned October's hardships – for that is a word I have never heard him use – but he would not allow any unnecessary exposure of the animals (he was dependent on) to mar his chances of success. Failure to get to the Pole this year would have meant the ruin of all his next year's plans. He told me he was more interested in the work mapped out for the second season, and considered it of greater geographical importance than reaching the Pole.

The work of the Expedition in each scientific department has yielded results equalling, if not exceeding the most sanguine hopes. There is no branch of the enterprise that has not justified the final words of Captain Scott's despatch: 'I am staying in the Antarctic for another year in order to continue and complete my work.'

In October, 1912, Evans – who had been promoted to the rank of Commander – having recovered his health, left London for New Zealand, to join the *Terra Nova* for her third voyage to the Antarctic to bring the Expedition home.

In December, as I was much run down with the strain of my work in the South, I went to Switzerland for a few weeks' rest. In February, 1913, when at Wengen, I received a cablegram from the Central News, stating: 'Captain Scott and entire Polar Party perished whilst returning from the South Pole.'

Completely dazed by such terrible and wholly unexpected news, I could not believe it, and cabled for confirmation. A few hours later I received a further wire: 'Regret to state information is authentic. Entire Polar Party perished.'

This shocking news struck deep into the heart of every civilised nation. Then, as the details of the disaster and the dead Leader's story of the tragedy became known, the whole Empire mourned, whilst priding itself that these undaunted adventurers, who in death had found immortal fame, were British.

I returned to London immediately, and was present at the Memorial Service at St. Paul's Cathedral, where, later, a tablet was erected to the Memory of Captain Scott and his four comrades who had reached the Pole.

After the return of the Expedition, in July, 1913, King George presented each member of the Staff with a silver Polar medal, and each of the men with a bronze replica. Each of the Staff also received a silver medal from the Royal Geographical Society 'For Polar Exploration.' The honour of C.B. had previously been conferred upon Commander Evans, as official head of the survivors of the Expedition; all other naval officers received promotion, and Petty Officer Crean and mechanic Lashly were awarded the Albert medal for their gallantry in saving Commander Evans' life.

The public generously responded to the appeal to meet the obligations of the enterprise, and contributed £75,000 to a Fund raised for that purpose. Some thousands of pounds were added to this from the proceeds of the exhibition of the kinematograph films. With the Government pensions in addition, Captain Scott's dying hope – that 'a great rich country like ours will see that those who are dependent upon us are properly provided for' – was munificently realised; and an ample sum was allocated for the publication of the scientific results.

A statue of Captain Scott was presented by the Officers of the Fleet to London. This monument – which stands in Waterloo Place, and appropriately faces the statue of Sir John Franklin, who completed the discovery of the North West Passage – is not only one of London's latest and most virile works of art; but it is unique, in that it is the work of the great explorer's talented widow, Lady Scott.

In view of the tragic ending to the enterprise, I felt it more than ever incumbent upon me, as the holder of the lecturing rights, to conform to the wishes my late Chief had expressed to me, by carrying out my original plans. A beautiful and complete series of the photographs and films of the adventure, and of the Nature life of the South, was therefore arranged, and to these I lectured at a London Hall for ten months in 1914, until the outbreak of the great war ended what had been a highly successful beginning to a novel feature in the entertainment world.

In May, 1914, I had the honour to receive the Royal Command to show my kinematograph record, and tell the story of the Scott Expedition, at Buckingham Palace, before Their Majesties the King and Queen, the Royal Family, the King and Queen of Denmark, and several hundred guests. On that occasion, His Majesty King George expressed to me the hope that it might be possible for every British boy to see the pictures – as the story of the Scott Expedition could not be known too widely among the youth of the nation, for it would help to promote the spirit of adventure that had made the Empire.

In 1915, in response to an appeal from the Front, I gave sets of the films for the benefit of our soldiers in France, and they were shown to more than 100,000 officers and men of the British Army. The following is an extract from one of the letters received from the Rev. F. I. Anderson, Senior Chaplain to the Forces:

I cannot tell you what a tremendous delight your films are to thousands of our troops. The splendid story of Captain Scott is just the thing to cheer and encourage out here ... The thrilling story of Oates' self-sacrifice, to try and give his friends a chance of 'getting through,' is one that appeals so at the present time. The intensity of its appeal is realised by the subdued hush and quiet that pervades the massed audience of troops while it is being told. We all feel we have inherited from Oates and his comrades a legacy and heritage of inestimable value in seeing through our present work. We all thank you with very grateful hearts.

The kinematograph, properly applied, is the greatest educational contrivance ever conceived by the genius of man. In it the art of photography finds its highest mission. Believing, as I do, that the moving-picture is one of the most potent moral influences of the time, and that it is destined to play a wide and ever-increasing part in education in the future, I feel that the pictorial record of an adventure which 'cheered and encouraged' British soldiers in the greatest crisis in the history of the Empire can have none other than an uplifting effect on British boys. I believe it will have a good effect on boys and girls, and men and women too, the wide world over.

A high official in the Department of Education, Washington, U.S.A., wrote:

The pictures and story of this great example of courage, endurance, and perfect fidelity to high ideals are of great help in the development of the truly heroic in the rising generation. I wish every boy and young man in this city and throughout the country could see these pictures and hear their story. We need in the future all the Captain Scotts we can develop, and this story and these pictures will help to develop them.

Still more, in the future, shall we need all the Captain Scotts we can develop in England; and we shall need all the sinewy 'Uncle Bills' and hardy Birdies, and gallant gentlemen like 'Titus,' and strong men like Petty Officer Evans, too.

Twenty, fifty, a hundred, five hundred years hence, the story of the Immortal Five who perished after conquering the South Pole will inspire our youth just as it does to-day – ten years after.

It was my privilege to be the producer of the kinematograph record of that great adventure – which is now of priceless historical value – and it is my intention during my lifetime to arrange for its exhibition from time to time, to assist in perpetuating the story of my late Chief and comrades of glorious memory.

H. G. PONTING.

Epilogue

What is the motive for such perilous work as Polar Exploration, and, after all, whom does it benefit?

To this question, so often asked, perhaps no better reply can be made than to quote the words spoken by the Rt. Hon. A. J. Balfour, in 1916, when he unveiled the statue of Captain Scott, which was presented by Officers of the Navy to London. On that occasion the ex-First Lord of the Admiralty said:

It is no bad thing, when the British Fleet is supporting the whole of the Entente Powers in their efforts, that we should remember that Peace hath her victories no less renowned than War. What the Fleet has done for the safety of these shores, the greatness of this Empire and for Freedom throughout the world is common knowledge; but we are sometimes apt to forget how much it has done in the unwarlike, yet most dangerous work of exploration, of wresting from Nature her jealous secrets.

To wrest from Nature her jealous secrets was the motive for Captain Scott's journey to the South Pole – a kindred aspiration to that which urges the ever deeper researches of the scientist into the products of the earth, the elements and the mysteries of the universe. Scientist and explorer alike, their one great end in view is to benefit humanity by adding to our sum of knowledge. What greater aim in life than this?

We have been willing to give our lives to this enterprise, which is for the honour of our country.

Let these immortal words, written whilst Death stood at his elbow, be Captain Scott's answer to those who ask 'Whom does it benefit?'

Captain R. F. Scott, R.N., C.V.O.

Captain Robert Falcon Scott, though of Scots descent, was a Devonshire man. Born at Outlands, near Devonport, on June 6th, 1868, he inherited a love of salt water from the seafaring stock of which he sprang. At a very early age the sea was chosen by his parents for his profession. He began his education at Foster's Naval Preparatory School at Stubbington, near Fareham, in Hampshire. At the age of fourteen he entered the *Britannia* Training-ship, and served subsequently in various vessels of the Navy.

It was in 1899, whilst serving as First Lieutenant in H.M.S. *Majestic*, that Antarctic exploration first attracted his attention, through an accidental meeting with Sir Clements Markham, the Commodore of the Training Squadron, who informed him that a project for sending a Naval expedition to the Antarctic was under discussion by the Admiralty. Scott at once applied for the leadership of the enterprise, and in due course was appointed to command it.

This, the *Discovery* Expedition, 1901–4, resulted in most valuable contributions to our knowledge of the Antarctic Continent. It placed some hundred of miles of new coast line on the map, and the unknown South was penetrated to Lat. 82° 17' S., about five hundred miles from the South Pole, an advance of some three hundred miles on Sir James Ross's record.

On the return of the Expedition Commander Scott was promoted to a Captaincy in the Navy, and he was made a Commander of the Royal Victorian Order by King Edward VII.

In August, 1906, he returned to sea duty, and in 1908 he became Flag Captain of H.M.S. *Bulwark*. In September, 1908, he married Miss Kathleen Bruce, daughter of Canon Lloyd Bruce, at Hampton Court Chapel. In March, 1909, he went to the Admiralty as Naval Assistant to the Second Sea Lord, and in September the same year his only child, Peter Markham Scott, was born.

Ever since the *Discovery* Expedition, it had been the dearest hope of Scott's life to return to the Far South, to continue his scientific researches and complete the work of exploring the frozen continent. With this object in view, at the end of 1909 he therefore resigned his post at the Admiralty to prepare for his second voyage to the Antarctic – the successful attempt to reach the South Pole, on the return journey from which he and four comrades perished on the Great Ice Barrier.

Scott was a great reader and lover of good literature; and his books *The Voyage of the Discovery*, and *Scott's Last Expedition* – the diary of the great adventure to which he gave his life – have demonstrated his ability as a writer. There is probably nothing more soul-stirring in all our literature than the closing pages of Scott's Journal, and his 'Message to the Public,' which the great explorer wrote whilst death was staring full into his eyes. They should be taught in every school, and committed to memory by every British boy, for it should be the resolve of every true Englishman 'to meet the end with a similar spirit.'

A few days before leaving England for the Antarctic, Captain Scott said to a friend, 'I cannot imagine a finer death than that of a man who, having attained the object which he sought, dies rejoicing in his achievement.'

The story of how the Leader of the Expedition attained his ideal is now a proud heritage of his race.

Doctor E. A. Wilson

Dr Edward Adrian Wilson, the Chief of the Scientific Staff of the Expedition, was the son of Dr Edward Wilson of Westall, Cheltenham, and was born there in 1872. He was educated at Cheltenham College, and took his degree at Cambridge. A medical man by profession, he was also a well-known naturalist, and one of the most eminent Polar zoologists of his day. He had been a member of the *Discovery* Expedition under Captain Scott; and for several years previous to joining the present enterprise was engaged on the Grouse Commission, investigating the disease which was rapidly devastating the game on our moors. The trouble was traced to a parasite in the heather, and methods were suggested for exterminating it which were put to the test with happy results.

Dr Wilson's contributions to the literature of zoology and ornithology were many, varied and of great value. His death was an irreparable loss to science, for his knowledge of Antarctic fauna, gained by intimate study of the creatures that he so dearly loved, in their native haunts, was probably greater than that of anyone else of his time. He was an artist of much ability, and did fine work in recording in colour the scenes amidst which he and his fellow explorers lived in the South. Cool and courageous, nothing could dismay him, and even the Leader's love of Polar exploration was no greater than that of his Chief of the Scientific Staff. His never-ceasing energy was conspicuous for the valuable uses to which he applied it; and the amiability of his disposition was second only to his learning and the quality of his logic.

'Uncle Bill' now sleeps for ever amid the snows of the Great White South, with the same kindly smile upon his features that his comrades knew so well in life – and loved him for it.

At the last, Captain Scott wrote of him: 'He died, as he lived, a brave, true man – the best of comrades and staunchest of friends.'

Captain L. E. G. Oates

Captain Lawrence Edward Grace Oates was in charge of the Siberian ponies. He was born on March 17th, 1880, at Gestingthorpe Hall, near Halstead, Essex. Both his father and uncle had done much travelling in wild parts of the earth, and Oates therefore inherited to the full the spirit of adventure.

He was educated at Eton, and, joining the 6th 'Inniskilling' Dragoons in 1900, fought with his regiment in the South African War. In the following year he was in charge of a patrol in an attack on the Boers in a river-bed. His patrol made a gallant fight, and as each man finished his ammunition, Lieutenant Oates, as he then was, ordered him to crawl away, until, at the end of four hours' fighting, he was left alone. Twice during the engagement the Boer commander sent a white flag demanding the surrender of the force, but each time Oates sent back the reply: 'We are here to fight, not to surrender.' Eventually the Boers retired, but with one of the last shots fired Oates was wounded in the thigh, the bone being broken. For his bravery he was mentioned in despatches, and he became known to his comrades by the soubriquet: 'No Surrender Oates.'

Captain Oates was granted leave of absence from his regiment to join the Expedition, and was deputed by Captain Scott to take charge of the ponies because of his skill with horses and his experience as a cavalry officer, especially in India, and on the Tibetan Expedition.

Oates was tall, broad shouldered and athletic; full of wit, humour, and ready repartee, and was one of the kindliest and most modest and unassuming of men. A soldier by profession and a soldier at heart, he died, as he hoped to die, in the service of his country, and the whole of his life was summarised in the words which Scott wrote of the manner of his death: 'It was the act of a brave man and an English gentleman.'

Lieut. H. R. Bowers.

Lieut. Henry Robertson Bowers – who learnt his sailorcraft on the Training-ship *Worcester*, and served for several years in the Indian Ocean and on the Irrawaddy, in the Royal Indian Marine – was the Commissariat Officer of the Expedition. He was chosen by Captain Scott for the Polar Party because of his never-flagging energy, strength and efficiency; and for the stamina, ability and resource which he had displayed in the unparalleled mid-winter journey to Cape Crozier during the present enterprise.

Bowers' humour and never-failing high spirits were a great asset to all his comrades, especially during the months of the Polar winter, when long continued darkness might have been expected to cast gloom over our little band. His cheery nature and pleasant railleries went far to foster the remarkable spirit of camaraderie which prevailed.

There are numerous high tributes in Scott's Journal to his hardihood, and to his eagerness to help others; and it was of Bowers that the Leader wrote: 'I believe he is the hardiest traveller that ever undertook a Polar journey, as well as the most undaunted ... His untiring energy and astonishing physique enable him to work under conditions which are absolutely paralysing to others. Never was such a sturdy, active, undefeatable little man.'

At the last, Captain Scott wrote: 'As the troubles have thickened his dauntless spirit ever shone brighter, and he has remained cheerful, unselfish, self-reliant, splendidly hopeful and indomitable to the end, believing in God's mercy.'

Petty Officer E. Evans

Petty Officer Edgar Evans, the 'strong man' of the Polar Party, was a big, broad, sinewy Welshman – a native of Rhossilly, near Swansea. He was in charge of the sledging equipment. He had taken part in the Discovery Expedition of 1901–4, during which adventure he earned Captain Scott's highest praise for his presence of mind and resource in the face of difficulties and danger. It was because of the reliance that he knew he could place in the strength and ability of this fine specimen of the 'handy-man' of the British Navy, that the Leader's selection fell on Evans as one of the chosen four to accompany him to the Pole. He knew that Petty Officer Evans would ever be ready at a moment's notice to repair any damage to sledging gear, and that his previous Polar experience would be of the utmost value in times of peril.

When estimating, as we so often did during the long winter months, each other's chances of taking part in the journey to the Pole, none ever doubted that 'Taff' Evans would be one of the elect.

In life, Petty Officer Evans realised his one ambition – to stand beside his beloved Chief at the South Pole. In death, the once mortal home of his indomitable soul lies deep in the eternal ice – his, the uttermost sepulchre on earth. H. G. P.

In Memoriam

Not for the fame that crowns a gallant deed
They fixed their fearless eyes on that far goal,
Steadfast of purpose, resolute at need
To give their lives for toll.

But in the service of their kind they fared,
To probe the secrets which the jealous Earth
Yields only as the prize of perils dared,
The wage of proven worth.

So on their record, writ for all to know –
The task achieved, the homeward way half won –
Though cold they lie beneath their pall of snow,
Shines the eternal sun.

O hearts of metal pure as finest gold!
O great ensample, where our sons may trace,
Too proud for tears, their birthright from of old,
Heirs of the Island Race!

Owen Seaman.

Notes

Chapter I

1   In 1918, the King conferred upon Mr Kinsey the honour of knighthood in recognition of his great services to Antarctic exploration.

Chapter II

1   Mr Cheetham, who already held the record for crossing the Antarctic Circle, again went to the Far South in 1914, with the Shackleton Expedition, as Bo'sun of the ill-fated *Endurance*, and was one of the party marooned on, and gallantly rescued by Sir Ernest from Elephant Island. This fine sailor lost his life in 1918, his trawler being torpedoed by a German submarine whilst mine-sweeping in the North Sea.

Chapter XII

1   In low zero temperatures mercury freezes; therefore spirit thermometers are used to record the degrees of frost.

Chapter XVI

1   Owing to the death of Dr Wilson his pictures could never be reproduced for sale, as he had intended. His widow, therefore, considered it better that they should be exhibited separately. The whole beautiful series of his water colours was shown at the Alpine Club, whilst my photographs were exhibited at the Fine Art Society's galleries, London.

The End of the Expedition

1   A *sastrugus* is a hard ridge of snow.

2   The Norwegian party reached the South Pole on December 14th, 1911. On December 30th they crossed 87° S. *Northward* bound. Scott's party crossed 87° S. *Southward* bound on December 31st. About that time, therefore, the rival explorers passed each other, some 100 miles apart. The courses of the two parties converged at the point where Scott found the black flag on January 16th.

Amundsen's party left the Pole on December 17th, with 16 dogs, temperature - 2° F. They arrived at their base on the Bay of Whales on January 25th, 1912, with 11 dogs, having experienced remarkably fine weather and comparative immunity from storms on both outward and homeward journeys. They covered the 770 miles in 39 days, an average of about 20 miles per day. Amundsen's route was shorter than Scott's by 60 to 80 miles each way.